SOCIAL PROTECTION FOR DEPENDENCY IN OLD AGE

Social Protection for Dependency in Old Age

A study of the fifteen EU Member States and Norway

JOZEF PACOLET
RIA BOUTEN
HILDE LANOYE
KATIA VERSIECK

Comparative Report commissioned by the European Commission and the Belgian Minister of Social Affairs

Ashgate

Aldershot • Burlington • Singapore • Sydney

Published by
Ashgate Publishing Limited
Gower House
Croft Road
Aldershot
Hampshire GU11 3HR
England

Ashgate Publishing Company
131 Main Street
Burlington, VT 05401-5600 USA

Ashgate website: http://www.ashgate.com

British Library Cataloguing in Publication Data
Social protection for dependency in old age : a study of
    the fifteen EU Member States and Norway
    1.Aged - European Union countries - Case studies 2.Aged -
    Services for - European Union countries - Case studies
    3.European Union countries - Social policy - Case studies
    I.Pacolet, Jozef
    362.6'094

Library of Congress Control Number: 00-134490

ISBN 0 7546 1266 X

Printed and bound in Great Britain, by Antony Rowe Ltd., Chippenham

Contents

v

List of Boxes, Figures and Scheme

List of Tables

Acknowledgements

This report is based on a comparative study on the social protection of the dependent elderly, commissioned by the Directorate-General V: Employment, Industrial Relations and Social Affairs, Commission of the European Communities and the Belgian Minister of Social Affairs.

The report updated a previous report on six Member States and enlarged it to the other Member States. Also one country of the EEA, Norway, was included in the comparison.

The aim of the project is to provide an overview of the social protection arrangements which are available in the EU Member States and Norway for dependent elderly people above normal retirement age and in need of long-term care. The comparative study is concentrated on the needs of dependent elderly persons, without ignoring the fact that ageing is not synonymous with dependency.

Nevertheless, the ageing of the population in the EU means that there are and will continue to be an increasing number of dependent elderly people with long-term care needs and these needs will have to be catered for. There are several ways in which the risks can be covered, and all new proposals within this context have to be compared with the present levels of social protection and the various forms that it assumes. We have opted for a holistic approach to the dependency risk in the present social protection system.

The aim of the study is not only to provide an overview of the present social protection arrangements for dependency in old age, but also to give some insight into present and future policies.

The project was coordinated by the following members of the central study team of the Higher Institute of Labour Studies at the Catholic University of Leuven: Jozef Pacolet, Ria Bouten, Hilde Lanoye and Katia Versieck.

The report was written by this central study team on the basis of country reports prepared by national experts:

Austria   Kai Leichsenring
Belgium   Jozef Pacolet, Hilde Lanoye, Ria Bouten
Denmark   Eigil Boll Hansen

Germany	Bernd Schulte
Greece	John Yfantopoulos, Theodore A. Georgakopoulos
Spain	Gregorio Rodriguez Cabrero
Finland	Marja Vaarama, Mikko Kautto
France	Marie-Eve Joël
Ireland	Eamon O'Shea
Italy	Francesco Belletti, Harmke Keen
Luxembourg	Nicole Kerschen
The Netherlands	Norma Schuijt-Lucassen, Kees Knipscheer
Portugal	Manuel de Almeida, J. Manuel Nazareth
Sweden	Lennarth Johansson
United Kingdom	John Bond, Debbie Buck
Norway	Svein Olav Daatland

We owe gratitude to the Commission of the European Communities and the Belgian Minister of Social Affairs for the research possibilities. Funding from the Higher Institute of Labour Studies also made this study feasible (the project 'Pensions and Pension Funds' financed by the Mecenate credit of the Christian Trade Union in Belgium).

We want to thank our colleagues from those nations for their careful and far-reaching contributions to this project. The information used in the comparative report and this synthesis is, to a large extent, based on their work (see list of prepared reports on last pages). The analysis and conclusions presented in this report, along with any possible misinterpretation or errors, remain the responsibility of the authors of the comparative study. At the closing of this project we were informed that our colleague from Portugal Manuel de Almeida died in May 1998. We commemorate him as a gentle person, dedicated to this research and social-economic policy field.

The national and the comparative reports have been commented on by a second group of national experts (see list in Annex) without, however, attributing to them any responsibility for the results.

All reports have been prepared by independent experts and should not be taken to represent the views of the European Commission or the Belgian Minister of Social Affairs. Here we want to take the opportunity to alert the reader to this comparative report, and comparative, synoptic tables. Each figure has in its country a specific definition, an institutional setting, a changing policy strategy, and probably also statistical problems behind it. Each figure can tell a complete story and this is sometimes illustrated in our comments. This report should be read in combination with its volume of annexes and also, most importantly, the national reports, which are the basis of most of this information.

Finally, we want to thank Ria Bouten, Hilde Lanoye and Katia Versieck for their contribution to the project at various stages and the huge amount of work that has been done. We owe also special thanks to the secretaries for their help in preparing this report.

Prof. dr. Jozef Pacolet
Head of Social and Economic Policy Sector
Higher Institute of Labour Studies, Catholic University of Leuven

Summary

1   A Completed Debate or an Emerging One?

The European Year of the Older Person in 1993 created a momentum of increased interest in the role of older citizens in the EU, and an awareness of the challenge that the ageing of the population creates for the existing systems of social protection. At the same time it created great expectations in the Member States that high standard systems of social protection for older people would be maintained or completed. Although it is inappropriate to assume older people to be dependent persons, and there is substantial progress in changing that relationship older people continue to face growing concern about their present and future income and expenditure on health care. This personal feeling of insecurity is reflected at macro-level in the overall concern of governments about pension schemes and health expenditure in the next decade. It has been very well documented in previous research (Walker, Alber, Guillemard et al., 1993) that older people feel comfortable about their personal surroundings, but uneasy about the political concern about their cause, and perhaps also about the ability of governments to cope with those problems. In particular, the increasing proportion of very dependent older persons concerned many groups. It is in this context that the European Commission and the Belgian government supported comparative research into the social protection of dependent older persons. While at first sight the European Union demonstrates a diversified and highly developed care mix and public support for dependency, a second look reveals aspects of under insurance or no insurance for the new risk of long-term care. This explains why the issue of long-term care is on the agenda in some countries. In several countries electorates were promised, as a response to this insecurity, that the cost of most long-term care would be covered by insurance in one way or another. Following the long debate on long-term care insurance in Germany the question has been whether other countries will follow the German example and establish a new pillar of social insurance. In some countries this route has been followed (Austria, Germany) and even very recently (decision of May 1998) in Luxembourg; in other countries the debate continues but is sometimes undecided (France,

Belgium). In other countries it is not so explicitly on the agenda. This can be for different reasons: in the Nordic countries because it exists already and policy makers are sometimes still considering reduction rather than expansion; in the Mediterranean countries because of other care models or because the budgetary constraints are too heavy. The comparative report gives an inventory of social protection in macroeconomic, institutional and micro-terms, and a description of the ongoing political debate for change.

2   Aim of the Comparative Report

The aim of this comparative study is to give a detailed overview of the social protection arrangements for dependent older people above retirement age and in need of long-term care in the EU. The study examines the coverage of the needs and dependency risks of older people in the welfare states of the European Union. A description of the current arrangements and an assessment of policy trends and perspectives is given. The focus is on the availability of, and the eligibility conditions for, access to the systems of social protection, taking into account the living conditions of dependent older people. The report concentrates on the social protection elements whilst also situating these within the complete set of provisions, including those which are private or informal in character.

Dependency can be caused by several factors and may imply a need for help or support in a number of ways. Dependency needs are broadly defined and refer both to aspects of income, housing, health and social care, and to integration and empowerment.

The adequacy of care for dependent older people is determined by the interaction of a comprehensive set of formal and informal provisions (in kind aid, income support, savings, informal support by main carer, etc.). To ask how many people have access to a given care system and to what extent the total amount of their needs is covered by these systems, is just one part of the picture. Adequacy will also depend on the amount of resources at their own disposal or available through their network of family or friends.

Provision and funding of protection may be the responsibility of different institutional levels and may account for a larger or smaller percentage of total spending. Formal social protection includes three main systems:
– income support – pension systems;
– health care – health insurance;
– (social) services for the elderly.

In addition to these formal systems, informal care and support facilities continue to be provided quite extensively and are becoming progressively integrated into the formal sphere. Within this formal and informal care framework, new risks or needs in other areas of care are calling for various kinds of protection. What are or will be the relative roles of the public, private and voluntary sectors in new provisions?

In this report basic emphasis has been placed on data collection and crosschecking of information by means of a multiple research strategy. Institutional aspects (facts and figures on the arrangements available), macro-information (macroeconomic spending, policy debate) and micro-aspects have been considered.

There is a considerable amount of evidence on the level and structure of pension provision for older people and on health care expenditure. This research attempts to draw a more comprehensive overall picture of those elements of social protection relevant to the needs of dependent older persons. These range from income, health, social care to support for the informal care and integration and empowerment.

Information is given on the care systems followed by additional information on the average profile of each service. The advantage of this approach is that it gives a complete institutional picture and a quantitative, macroeconomic overview of the social protection systems. The amount of detail available depends on the existing administrative information system, which is sometimes limited. This report summarises the available information and looks at it from a second approach starting from dependent older people themselves. This methodology assesses on a theoretical institutional basis what options are open for certain categories of the elderly population. It reveals how older people with a certain degree of dependency and a certain level of income experience significant differences in coverage of their care needs. The advantage is that it gives a clear view of the situation of similar groups of older people in different countries. This allows missing information on the cumulative effects of certain care systems, or the remaining blank spots, to be detected. At the same time it helps to characterise further the social protection systems in each country.

Information on the socioeconomic and political debate on the need for changes in the way social protection for older people is financed and organised provides a further insight into how provisions function and are perceived by older people and policy makers in the Member States.

3   Dependency

There is no homogeneous and operational definition of dependency. Mostly it is reduced to physical or mental aspects, but a social and economic dimension can be added to it and has for the purpose of this study been used to define the scope of the inventory of systems of social protection.

After retirement individuals usually become dependent on social protection for part or all of their income. In the more narrow definition of dependency referring to physical and mental aspects, it is inappropriate to identify older people as such with dependent persons. Many older persons are completely self-reliant and independent for several years after retirement. Furthermore, there are indications that the relation between age and dependency is changing for the better. The onset of dependency appears to be happening later in life than before.

Yet the ageing of the population will result in a significant increase in the number and proportion of the very old and hence by implication in the amount and share of dependent persons. In the 65+ group, currently between 3 and 5 per cent of people are severely dependent, whereas the partly dependent constitute up to 15 per cent of this part of the population. For persons 75+ the prognostics of highly dependent persons increases to 10 per cent, while the partially dependent make up 25 per cent. This amounts to a population of very dependent persons of, on average 3 per cent of the total population, or about nine million persons in Europe. On the basis of the national reports there are at least 7.6 million older persons who in some way or another are counted as dependent or receive some form of social protection, in cash or in kind because of dependency.

The pressure from growth in life expectancy and the number of dependent older persons, places a higher burden on the existing care systems than they were originally designed for. This has been the case in many countries, stimulating the debate on long-term care insurance. But the major impact of the greying of the population is to be found in the existing systems of social protection and concerns primarily pensions and health care expenditure. There is, however, no clear-cut relationship between the share of the population above 65 and the share of pension expenditure in relation to GDP (varying from 5 to 15 per cent of GDP). For the pension schemes for instance we concluded that there is no substantial shift away from pay-as-you-go systems. This is confirmed by the European Commission's 1997 report on Social Protection, which adds the observation that there is a new reinforcement of the relationship with previous income, so reinforcing the insurance character

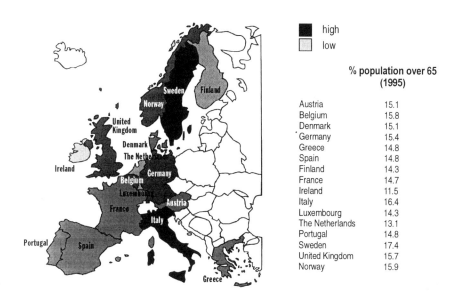

% population over 65 (1995)

Austria	15.1
Belgium	15.8
Denmark	15.1
Germany	15.4
Greece	14.8
Spain	14.8
Finland	14.3
France	14.7
Ireland	11.5
Italy	16.4
Luxembourg	14.3
The Netherlands	13.1
Portugal	14.8
Sweden	17.4
United Kingdom	15.7
Norway	15.9

Figure 1   The ageing of the European population

of the social insurance (European Commission, 1998).

The level of expenditure on health care is the second major category of social expenditure: it varies from 4 to 8 per cent of GDP, increasing with the level of national income. After years of cost containment and declining expenditure shares the cost of health care has been increasing in almost all Member States since the beginning of the 1990s. However, the most recent evidence in the above mentioned EU report on social protection, which includes an extra year of information (1995) and distinguishes two sub-periods 1990–93 and 1994–95, shows a decline in the latest period, after an initial increase.

Thirty to 50 per cent of this expenditure is directed towards the population of above 65 years of age. On top of this, in many countries, social expenditure on personal social services for the elderly amount to a budget between 0.19 and 2 per cent of GDP.

The picture from this overview is not entirely clear due to lack of information on many aspects, but there remains a picture of substantial differences in levels of expenditure and levels of social protection.

4   The Welfare Mix

The study makes an inventory of additional dependency-related income support such as support for housing costs and a growing list of support systems for housing accommodation and adaptation, residential and semi-residential services for older people and community care services. Many of these have been studied in greatest detail elsewhere (e.g. payment for care systems, social housing, etc.) but this is the first time that such a broad set of elements has been brought together. The comparative study concentrates on further describing these health and personal social services for the older people. A picture emerges of a growing and maturing mix of differently organised but mostly publicly financed care provision within a mainstream public discourse of budgetary austerity.

4.1   Variety

The study identifies eight systems of permanent residential and semi-residential services for the elderly, 17 temporary residential and semi-residential services and 22 community services. This variety illustrates the diversification that has taken place in this sector over the last two decades, and it was only possible within a context of a further expanding welfare state. After a period of quantitative expansion of the traditional systems of social protection, from the second half of the 1980s the sector entered a period of innovation and qualitative differentiation into new institutional arrangements within a framework of cost-containment. Since then (and this is also reflected in health expenditure) a quantitative expansion has occurred again. This expansion path need not necessarily be the same in all countries, and different countries certainly are not the same stage, but the impression remains that there exists a common European way, combined with national characteristics.

4.2   Availability

Although almost all countries refer to similar existing or emerging services, the absolute level and the relative importance of the mix of services vary significantly. Most of the countries remain oriented towards an institutional care system, with a high number of places available in several types of institutions per 100 older persons. In some countries these institutions remain traditional old age homes. In others a transformation of those homes into care intensive nursing homes or other types of sheltered housing has already taken place. The borderline between housing and services is fading. Several countries mention the unbundling of housing and care, but in reality more and more integrated and variable services emerge. The level of development of this form of institutional care is remarkably low in the Mediterranean countries.

Although much more diversified, the level of development of community care seems to be even lower. Many countries with a relatively high degree of institutional care show lower levels of availability of community care (measured as number of personnel in the main community care services per 100 aged 65+). This is for instance the case in Austria, Belgium and the Netherlands. On many countries, however, clear information is missing. The general picture is one of a topping-up of residential and community care instead of a clear substitution. Those already with good residential services, also have better community services.

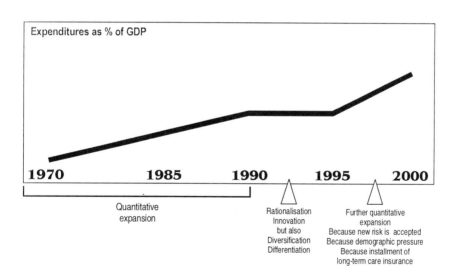

Figure 2   Stylised expansion path of the development of social protection for older people: a common European way?

Also to be noted, emerging both from this European comparison and from previous research on the state of the welfare state (Pacolet and Versieck, 1998) is that the choice between formal and informal care has led in the Nordic countries to a substantial level of job creation in those activities, jobs which add value and therefore contribute to economic growth. For the Mediterranean countries, this option still remains open.

This huge difference in services available could imply in some countries some form of underinsurance for certain categories of services or in general. Considering this, it becomes understandable that the debate started about the creation of long-term care insurance in some countries. It is however even more driven by the aspect of affordability.

4.3   *Affordability*

Besides availability, affordability is also an important element in describing the degree of social protection. The more cure-intensive services remain to a large extent publicly financed, as they are situated close to the health care system. Examples are nursing homes and especially district nursing that is completely publicly financed almost everywhere. The more care-intensive systems, or those services concentrated on housing and household aspects, tend to have a lower degree of public financing. But care and cure are also difficult to distinguish, which is probably why there remains a reasonable overall degree of public financing. There is some indication that the financing of services for older people is reasonably protected – where it is available, which is not always the case (quantitative rationing) – but in some cases the level of co-payment is already very high. Elements of underinsurance are emerging, calling perhaps for the creation of long-term care insurance.

5   Present Characteristics of the European Care System

It is more instructive to distinguish common characteristics in the social protection of older people in Europe than to highlight and typologise the differences between the Member States. There is convergence in a number of areas despite the fact that social protection is determined in the context of subsidiarity and has national historic roots. Sometimes the direction of new solutions springs from the existing national system, at others inspiration is down from solutions in other Member States, leading to convergence. For example, systems based on state provision may seek to involve the private

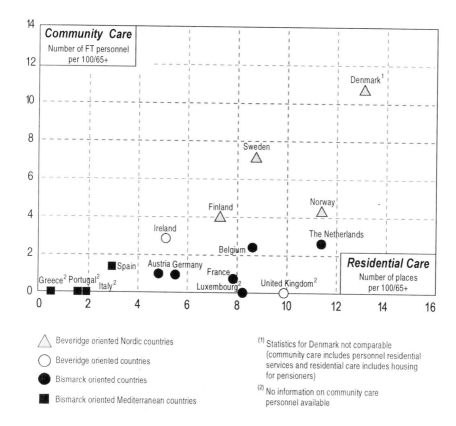

Figure 3   Development of (semi-) residential and community services for older people in Europe

sector, flat-rate systems may introduce elements of earnings-related pensions, etc. But convergence or similarity of systems does not mean equalisation of levels of protection. The case studies reveal how people with similar degrees of dependency and income enjoy different levels of social protection.

There is a trend to shift from service provision to cash support. In fact, apart from pensions, the provision of services is the major part of social protection for older people. Levels and types of formal services differ, but for almost all countries a long list of services is mentioned. Almost all Member States also mention payment for care or allowances in some way. Rent subsidies are also common.

The trend is towards substituting formal care with informal care, but in many countries there are limits to this substitution. Some reports mention that in hours terms, informal care is five times more important than formal care. Many countries have introduced some payment for care, sometimes as a benefit paid to the person being cared for, sometimes paid directly to the informal carer.

The quantitative expansion of basic provisions came to an end because of budgetary austerity. This is at odds with new demographic needs. A possible solution is diversification and differentiation within mature systems. For example care in a nursing home is less expensive than care in a hospital; provision of sheltered housing is less expensive than provision of care in nursing homes; community care may be less expensive than residential care, depending on how on views the issue of dependency; paid informal care is less expensive than paid formal care. There are however limits to the contribution of diversification to cost containment: sheltered houses need more services; there is a growing upward convergence between service flats, old age homes and nursing homes which eventually end up meeting the same needs for the same groups of older people. Quantitative expansion in certain areas arises: the need for long-term care insurance has become a common characteristic in many Member States.

Differences remain on the organisational aspects of social protection (Bismarck- or Beveridge-oriented welfare states, lower or higher degree of state provision) but the fundamental point is the total amount of formal services available. Although the focus of this comparative study is to provide a comprehensive overview of this availability, figures need to be handled carefully. Given that caveat, reported levels in residential care differ on a scale of between one and five for the higher and lower group and between one and three in the case of community care. The range for financial differences is even larger. The Nordic countries and the Mediterranean countries are situated at the upper and lower extremes of this range.

6   Debate for Change Towards Long-term Care Insurance

Despite the fact that the level of public financing of care for older people remains high and approaches figures for financing in health care (80 to 85 per cent of total cost in some services), there continues to be growing concern in many countries about public financing of those services, now and in the future. Despite the high level of social protection, there are in many countries indications of underinsurance. In France and Germany, there are lower levels of provision than could be expected according to the general standards of social protection. In several countries there is recourse to social assistance when older people cannot bear the total costs. In some Nordic countries, older people lose their pension when entering residential care and are left with only pocket money. In other countries contributions by older people themselves represent such a high proportion of average income that the net effect is to leave older people with only pocket money. In other countries recourse to the family is legally enforceable, or older people tend to live with their children's families. The high level of co-payments are another sign of underinsurance.

In some countries (Germany, perhaps also France and Austria) a low level of services is observed, while the opposite would be expected based on income, age structure and average level of social protection. This has been the subject of political debate in those countries. The issue of underinsurance has been under debate in Germany: too many people had to have recourse to assistance; there is a lack of services; a substantial increase of supply has occurred since the creation of the new insurance arrangements, confirming that there was underdevelopment before the changes; a substantial amount of 'new money' had to be raised (1.7 per cent of wages net on savings). In France the same issues have been raised: problems of underprovision and underfinancing, but also concern about the lack of 'new money' in the existing proposals. In Belgium, when the new needs have been identified and quantified, the need for 'new money' is more limited, illustrating that the existing systems already provided better insurance cover.

Where there is debate for change, it suggests deficiencies in the existing system of social protection, in that long-term care at home or in residential accommodation seems not to be covered completely. In Germany it was an explicit concern for policy makers that so many people had to have recourse to assistance when confronted with the cost of long-term care because of dependency. Dependency was considered as a normal risk of life, in the same way as deteriorating health. In several countries of the central region, there is sometimes a high level of payments by older people themselves for these long-term care services, sometimes with recourse to family resources (for instance Luxembourg, France, Belgium, Germany). Sometimes the older persons financial resources must be completely depleted before they can have recourse to social assistance. In the southern countries there are in general fewer residential at community services.

So, there is a clear problem of underinsurance (be it public or private) for the cost of long-term care. Too large a proportion of these costs has to be

Box 1   Long-term care: uninsured risk?

The problems:
- new risk: growing number of older persons (not necessarily growing dependency)
- higher costs: less informal care and upgrading of services, including demand for payment for care

Signs of uninsured risk:
- in some countries recourse to family remains
- in some countries recourse to assistance
- in some countries services remain underdeveloped
- formal care withdrawn when there is informal care
- in some countries high levels of payments from older persons themselves

covered by the current income or even by previous savings. An alternative form of financing these services via a long-term care insurance system has been discussed. This debate is summarised in the last part of the research. Among the questions addressed is whether long-term care for dependent older persons, at home or in institutions, is financed implicitly within the existing systems of health insurance and social insurance, or whether new and more explicit schemes of long-term care insurance are being planned and established. There is also an attempt to delineate how the debate is evolving in each country. The Member States with Beveridge-oriented systems of social protection seem to have long-term care integrated in existing health and personal social services, be it at a high or a more moderate level. The Member States with more Bismarck-oriented welfare states are experiencing, or have concluded, an often lengthy debate on the creation of an explicit social insurance scheme for long-term care. In the Netherlands an explicit insurance scheme for exceptional medical expenses has been in existence for several years. In Austria, Germany and Luxembourg the systems are more recent. In Belgium and France there is a long list of proposals and new initiatives, but a final system has yet to emerge. In 1998 a Royal Commission on Long-term Care was set up in the United Kingdom. Long-term care has characteristics of both health insurance (triggered to a large extent by medical reasons, organised by the same or similar providers) and old age (pensions) insurance. In the UK those systems have been organised differently within the social protection system: health insurance in the pay-as-you-go, state financed, universal National Health Services, and pensions increasingly through privately-organised, funded schemes. With both experiences and traditions in this country, the outcome of

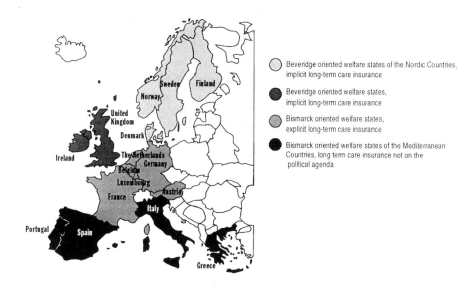

Beveridge oriented welfare states of the Nordic Countries, implicit long-term care insurance

Beveridge oriented welfare states, implicit long-term care insurance

Bismarck oriented welfare states, explicit long-term care insurance

Bismarck oriented welfare states of the Mediterranean Countries, long term care insurance not on the political agenda

Figure 4　Relation between type of social protection and type of long-term care insurance: some common features

the Royal Commission's work could help lead to a better understanding of the nature of long-term care insurance.

In the Mediterranean countries there has been less debate on the need for long-term care insurance, perhaps because there is an attachment to the family-based informal care model (care in the family, by the family) or because those countries were concentrating more on budgetary discipline. In the Nordic countries it is not on the agenda because the welfare states are highly developed, sometimes even subject to debate on downsizing.

Where they already exist, long-term care insurance systems are not limited only to older people; they cover all long-term care situations. They are oriented towards services as well as cash support for the recipient or the main carer, implying some form of support or payment for informal care. This broadening of the scope is in line with the observation that, in general, in many countries fairly wide definitions of costs to be covered are used (including cure, care, housing, hotel costs). This illustrates the difficulty of determining what should be publicly financed, and what privately, and the fading borderline between health care, social care, institutional care and community care, housing and living costs. The borderline between health and social services, between and within residential and community services, and between all kind of professional work tends to have disappeared. Perhaps in future the distinction between formal and informal care will also begin to lose its relevance, since informal carers will receive training and become more professional in their work and to some degree even be paid for their work. There is also no clear choice in favour of cash or in-kind support. Cash support (apparently allowing perhaps more consumer choice and empowerment) is in practice to a large extent oriented towards the financing of services. The mature welfare states seem to want to support both formal and informal care.

Only limited evidence has so far been found relating to widespread private involvement in long-term care insurance, at least as regards the insurance and financing aspect.

Box 2   How the risk of long-term care is covered

– sometimes implicit in the existing health and social care financing schemes – sometimes financed by retaining pension income – in the Bismarck-oriented systems with explicit insurance schemes – most of the time, of a pay-as-you-go (unfunded) nature – situated in health insurance or close to it – with wide definitions of costs – most through public provision – enlarging its coverage to payment for care

7   Conclusions

Concern about the social protection of dependent older persons and growing interest in the organisation of long-term care insurance are probably based on the observation that this risk is underinsured. The report puts forward several indicators on this. The report also describes the diversity, availability and affordability for large groups of the population of the benefits and services for the older people developed in the welfare state. Where the risk is insured, the political debate on the new risks of care for dependent older persons is still evolving along classical lines relating to social protection systems that have historically proved their viability. New systems of long-term care insurance seem to cover, currently, more than seven million European citizens. The principles according to which those systems continue to be developed are:

- in many countries long-term care is included in social expenditure or, more precisely, health insurance, organised in the same way as the rest of social protection in those countries;
- especially in the Bismarck-oriented system, there is some willingness, but not an absolute commitment, to define a new pillar for long-term care;
- wide definitions of the risk to be covered are maintained, since there is an increasingly unclear borderline between social services and health care;
- prioritising in-kind provision, or at least not rendering it unaffordable (for example, Germany has double the amount of resources available for in-kind help compared with cash help);
- including housing costs in the covered risk very often, but to a varying degree;
- enlarging the welfare state by (supplementary) systems of payment for care or support for the main carer, representing a shift to more support for informal care and to cash support;
- resistance to including it in social assistance systems, or to placing too much emphasis on income testing; retaining a preference for social security schemes. There is less willingness to require recourse to the family for help with financial costs, depletion of personal resources, and recovery of costs from inheritance;
- almost no presence of funded systems. Most of the solutions are pay-as-you-go, publicly-financed (or social security) systems. Some countries have chosen funded pension systems, but the 'funded' solution is almost absent from the practical European debate on long-term care;
- after a period of rationalisation in health care expenditure there is a renewed expansionary trend in expenditure, while services for older people continue to grow in variety and availability. This appears not to be at odds with the requirements of budgetary discipline;
- although the cost of long-term care is huge for older people who have to pay for it themselves, long-term care insurance, when existing, seems to be affordable at macro-level.

Whilst this conclusion is generally positive, it should not be forgotten that there are problems of under-protection, deteriorating quality, uncovered needs, or social protection falling behind the rest of the economy. Long-term care insurance can help prevent this. Although based on current facts and figures at this moment in time, this conclusion could change as illustrated above, and close monitoring of these phenomena is needed.

8   Need for Basic Data Collection

This comparative European report has been drawn up on the basis of reports by national experts on policy towards older people or on social protection. On several occasions no information could be obtained on certain aspects, leaving many comparative overviews with blank spots. This problem applies not only to expenditure data, but also to information on aspects of the care systems. Continued efforts to complete the facts and figures and to harmonise definitions, would greatly improve this situation. It would therefore be helpful for the authorities concerned to commit themselves to collecting uni-dimensional data on output, financing and clients of social and health services (for older people among others).

Introduction

1 Scope of the Project and Research Procedure

The aim of the project is to give an overview of the social protection arrangements which are available in the EU Member States and Norway for dependent elderly people above normal retirement age and in need of long-term care. The comparative study is concentrated on those needs of dependent older persons, without ignoring the fact that ageing is not synonymous with dependency.

Nevertheless, the ageing of the population in the EU means that there are and will continue to be an increasing number of dependent elderly people with long-term care needs and these needs will have to be catered for. There are several ways in which the risks can be covered, and all new proposals in this context have to be compared with the present levels of social protection and the various forms that it takes. We have opted for a holistic approach to the dependency risk in the present social protection system.

The aim of the research is not only to give an overview of the present social protection arrangements for dependency in old age, but also to give some insight into present and future policies.

This report contains results which partially combine elements from existing international surveys on social protection and information from the national experts set down in the country reports.

The present report contains:
1 a macroeconomic and budgetary overview of social protection in the different countries;
2 an overview of the existing institutional provisions;
3 an assessment of the way in which countries differ in their treatment of similar categories of dependent elderly people and of the way methods change within individual countries from one type of case to another;
4 an overview of present policy discussions in the countries regarding steps which are to be taken in this field of social protection for dependency in old age, as it is culminating in a debate on long-term care insurance.

This multiple research approach naturally provides different points of view, but was also applied as a crosscheck of information and to understand each national situation in more depth.

By confining the discussion to social protection, the picture will be incomplete for countries (or case studies) where private protection is preferred. However, we acknowledge that the 'privatisation' is of a gradual nature. Examples of the private-oriented movement include the increasing number of personal charges, private insurance plans and private care consumption and organisation.

In the same context, social expenditures for housing, fiscal expenditures, and tax and social contribution exemptions can influence substantially the level of protection, the level of public spending and the situation of the elderly themselves. It was also not possible to cover these elements completely in the comparative report.

It is often very difficult to distinguish social protection from total protection for elderly persons. Various components of private protection will inevitably crop up during the discussion, but they are too numerous to mention them all.

The impact of the ageing of the population on social protection will be felt in the level and scope of the health and social services, as well as in the expenditures for and financing of the pension schemes. These are objective needs. However, the expenditures for them are also determined by the stage of economic development (the possibilities) and the political discourse about them (the choices). These choices are partly influenced by economic arguments. Most European countries expect the ageing of the population and especially the increase of the very old to occur in the next two decades, though certain elements of increased pressure are already being observed at the present time.

2   Research Methodology

2.1   *International Overview*

The research will focus on the availability of and the eligibility conditions for access to the systems of social protection, taking into account the living conditions of the dependent elderly. No attention will be paid to the organisational aspects. We will concentrate on the social protection elements, situated however within the complete set of provisions of private character.[1]

Several approaches are possible for obtaining an overview of the social protection provided for the dependent elderly. Dependency can result from various factors and it implies a need for help or support in a number of ways.

Care for the elderly is determined by a comprehensive set of formal and informal aspects (in-kind aid, income support, wealth, informal support by main carer, etc.). Care provision and funding may be the responsibility of different institutional levels and it may account for a larger or smaller percentage of total spending. Formal social protection includes three main systems:
- income support – pension systems;
- health care – health insurance;
- (social) services for the elderly.

In addition to these formal systems, informal care and support facilities continue to be provided quite extensively and are becoming progressively integrated into the formal sphere. Within this formal and informal care framework, new risks or needs in other areas of care are calling for various kinds of protection.

This is illustrated in the matrix in Figure 1.3 (see chapter 1, section 3) regarding the financing structure of care for the elderly. This matrix needs to be extended with information on eligibility for the several systems and with the actual results of the available choices: how many people have access to a given care system and to what extent is the total amount of their needs covered by these systems?[2]

Normally, studies start from the coverage of certain care systems and then additional information is given on the average profile of each service. The disadvantage of this approach is that a picture cannot be derived of how, for certain categories of patients in some countries, caring systems can be cumulated or topped up or what higher levels of social protection mean, nor of the risk of cumulation of costs for society or for the patient, while in other situations, blank spots remain. The advantage of this approach is that it gives a complete institutional picture and a quantitative, even macroeconomic, overview of the social protection systems. The amount of detail available depends on the existent administrative information system. The results can be presented in the matrix (Figure 1.3), completed by a list of provisions available for the dependent elderly. This report summarises the available information.

2.2 *Typology of the Elderly Population*

An alternative methodology starts from a sample of the older population, sketching their socioeconomic situation, and especially their dependency situation and the care systems available to them. The problem is that these surveys are not always available, so they need to be specially organised and may not be representative enough, particularly for health and dependency questions. When the information is available, then average situations can be described according to certain criteria, such as age, family situation, income, etc., and even statistical instruments can be used (e.g. factor analysis) to identify certain representative profiles.

Since these typologies based on identical surveys imply an extensive gathering of data and institutional analysis, this research method will not be used.

2.3   Case Studies

A third methodology assesses on a theoretical institutional basis what options are open for certain categories of the elderly population. The advantage is that it gives a clear view of the situation of similar groups of elderly persons in different countries. The problem, however, is how representative the categories are, as well as the different solutions that are open to them. For the theoretical availability of certain systems, it is probably reliable, but there remains a problem of quantifiable representativeness.

This methodology is sometimes used in the case of relatively simple situations as, for example, a specific group of handicapped persons and a limited number of (often also specific) elements of social protection. What is typical for the circumstances of the elderly people, however, is the great variety of health, social, economic and care situations. The number of case studies can therefore be multiplied to an almost unlimited extent, raising questions about the representativeness of these cases.

This methodology is very convenient, however, for comparing how people in similar objective situations are treated in the social protection systems of the different countries. Therefore in chapter 4 of the report we use the methodology based on examples.

Notes

1   For the moment in many countries, the long-term care of the elderly is not completely covered by the national systems of social security, partly because much of the in-kind support was regarded to be a regional or local responsibility. We have partial evidence that regional disparity is increasing, so that the regional factor is becoming an important discriminating factor.

2   See, for instance, data used in health care relating to how many persons are protected by health insurance, and what share this is of the total cost (see OECD health data).

1 Definition of Dependency and the Need for Social Protection

1 Definition of Dependency

Dependency can be defined in terms of four dimensions. It can be expressed in *physical* terms and, as such, can be measured by means of scales (e.g. Katz Index). Such a scale can be expanded to contain *mental* aspects. In addition to these two dimensions, there is the *social* dimension and, finally, the *economic* dimension.

In the case of physical dependency, care services – supplied by professionals or nonprofessionals – will have to be focused upon. In the case of social dependency, a support network will have to be established, and in the case of economic dependency, income support will be necessary.

• **Limited definition of dependency**

° Functional criteria			° Clinical criteria	
Mobility	Self-care	Household activities	Incontinence	Mental

• **Wide definition of dependency**

Physical (more like limited definition)	Mental and emotional	Economic and surroundings	Social and integration (cultural)
Crisis		Transitory	Permanent

———————————————— **Satisfying needs** ————————————————

Figure 1.1   Definition of dependency

Source: based on Wilkin and Thompson, 1987.

Because the focus of the study is on dependent people in need of long-term care, special reference should be made to the physical and mental dimension

21

of this dependency. These, as well as other dimensions of dependency come back in the case studies. The social dimensions (living alone or having the support of a network) and the economic dimensions seem to have substantial operational meaning in these case studies: eligibility criteria are sometimes related to aspects of living condition and income.

For a clear description of who is 'to a large extent disabled or physically dependent', the Katz Index of ADL containing six personal activities is used. It is supplemented with four instrumental activities because attention should also be given to activities experienced by older persons living in the community, such as housekeeping, transportation and shopping. Definitions of the four instrumental activities (I-ADL) and six personal activities (P-ADL) can be found in Table 1.1. In executing one of the 10 activities, an older person can be either 'independent' (meaning that no third person is involved in the activity) or 'dependent'. A cumulative scale has been constructed on the basis of these 10 activities. Research on the basis of this scale (Sonn and Åsberg, 1991) showed that people were either independent or dependent on I-ADL or dependent on both I-ADL and P-ADL; nobody was dependent on P-ADL and independent of I-ADL. In defining our case studies, only elderly persons dependent on I-ADL and P-ADL are retained. This means that of the grades I+P-ADL as described in Table 1.2, all elderly persons of grade five and above are included in the study. Comparisons have also been made with one of the six dimensions in the WHO handicap classification scale, the dimension of physical independence, which is based on the actual performance of the persons and not on their capability. Physical independence/dependence continuum is broken down into eight different levels:

0 = fully independent;
1 = aided independence;
2 = adapted independence;
3 = situational dependence;
4 = long-interval (>24 h.) dependence;
5 = short-interval (every 10 h.) dependence;
6 = critical-interval dependence;
7 = special care dependence;
8 = intensive-care dependence.

Categories 4–8 are considered as being equivalent to the categories of elderly people retained for our research.

Table 1.1   Definitions of I-ADL and P-ADL

Definitions of four instrumental activities and six personal activities included in Katz Index of ADL and of independent, partly dependent and dependent.

Shopping	Gets to the store, manages stairs or other obstacles, takes out groceries, pays for them and carries them home.
Independent	Performs the activity when necessary.
Partly dependent	Performs the activity but together with another person.
Dependent	Does not perform the activity or needs assistance with some part of the activity.

Cleaning	Performs housing-cleaning, vacuum-cleaning, washing floors.
Independent	Performs the activity when necessary.
Partly dependent	Gets assistance in taking the carpets outdoors or assistance very seldom.
Dependent	Does not perform the activity or gets assistance with some part of the activity regularly.

Transportation	Gets to the stop for public transportation, gets on and goes by bus, tram or train.
Independent	Performs the activity when needed.
Partly dependent	Performs the activity but together with another person.
Dependent	Does not perform the activity.

Cooking	Gets to the kitchen, prepares the food, manages the stove.
Independent	Performs the activity when needed.
Partly dependent	Does not prepare dinner food, or only heats up prepared food.
Dependent	Does not perform the activity.

Bathing	Means sponge bath, tub bath, or shower.
Independent	Receives no assistance (gets in and out of tub by self if tub is usual means of bathing).
Partly dependent	Receives assistance in bathing only one part of the body (such as back or a leg).
Dependent	Receives assistance in bathing more than one part of the body (or does not bathe self).

Dressing	Means getting all needed clothing from closets and drawers and getting dressed, includes using fasteners, and putting on a brace, if worn.
Independent	Gets clothes and gets completely dressed without assistance.
Partly dependent	Gets clothes and gets dressed without assistance except for help with tying shoes.
Dependent	Receives assistance in getting clothes or in getting dressed, or stays partly or completely undressed.

Table 1.1 cont'd

Toileting	Means going to the 'toilet room' for bowel and urine elimination, cleaning self after elimination and arranging clothes.
Independent	Goes to the 'toilet room', cleans self and arranges clothes without assistance.
Partly dependent	Receives assistance in going to the 'toilet room' or in cleaning self or in arranging clothes after elimination, or in using the night bedpan or commode.
Dependent	Does not go to the 'toilet room' for elimination.
Transfer	Means moving in and out of bed and in and out of chair.
Independent	Moves in and out of bed and in and out of chair without assistance (may use support object such as a cane or walker).
Partly dependent	Moves in and out of bed or chair with assistance.
Dependent	Does not get out of bed.
Continence	Means the function of controlling elimination from the bladder and bowel.
Independent	Controls urination and bowel movement completely by self.
Partly dependent	Has occasional 'accidents'.
Dependent	Supervision helps keep urine or bowel control, or catheter is used, or is incontinent.
Feeding	Means the basic process of getting food from plate or equivalent into the mouth.
Independent	Feeds self without assistance.
Partly dependent	Feeds self except for getting assistance in cutting meat or buttering bread.
Dependent	Receives assistance in feeding or is fed partly or completely trough tubes or with intravenous fluids.

Notes

Partly dependent is assessed as:
i) dependent in cooking, shopping and transportation and as independent in cleaning;
ii) dependent in toileting, transfer, and continence and as independent in bathing, dressing, and feeding.

Source: Sonn and Åsberg, 1991, pp. 193–202.

Table 1.2   Cumulative scale on the basis of I-ADL and P-ADL

Katz ADL grade	Grades I + P-ADL	Definitions
B	5	Dependent in all I-ADL and one more activity
C	6	Dependent in I-ADL, bathing and one more activity
D	7	Dependent in I-ADL, bathing, dressing and one more activity
E	8	Dependent in I-ADL, bathing, dressing, going to the toilet and one more activity
F/G	9	Dependent in all activities
Others	Others	Dependent in two or more activities but not classifiable as above

If the item of continence is included, the definitions of the last two steps will be as follows;

F	9	Dependent in I-ADL, bathing, dressing, going to the toilet, transfer and one more activity
G	10	Dependent in all activities

Source: Sonn and Åsberg, 1991, pp. 193–202.

2   Risks

There are various risks dependent people can be confronted with, and the ways in which they can insure themselves against these risks are equally various. They need income support and various forms of professional and nonprofessional care. The following scheme summarises this well. The means to cover these needs for care are as diverse as the needs themselves. Normally, the social security system covers the income and health care risks and different levels are responsible for other forms of care. Sometimes the costs have to be borne individually or by private insurance. Finally, a lot of care is still provided by the family.

The systems that have been developed in the past, however, are no longer able – or prepared – to bear some risks. Surely this opinion has grown out of the realisation that the greying of the society will multiply the needs for resources in the future. Proposals have thus been made to let the elderly bear more of the burden, and ideas concerning new care systems which will assure this care, publicly or privately, have been developed.

To inform ourselves on how care for the elderly is insured nowadays, the next matrix should be filled in. The matrix is constructed in ascending order (private to public), illustrating the idea of subsidiarity that inevitably accompanies the organisation of care.

We have clearly opted for a broad definition of dependency. We can be sure of some of these aspects that they are guaranteed and will be guaranteed in the future. Income support in the form of pensions will be provided on an index-linked level. The health care system as it now exists will not be called into question. The degree to which the risks are covered, however, differs greatly from country to country.

3   Some Theoretical Concepts Relating to the Organisation of the Care

Care of the elderly concerns to a great extent the acquisition of personal help. These needs of the elderly are usually considered to be vital – as a kind of 'merit want'. Nobody should be excluded from it. The provision can be made either by assistance in kind (services provided) or in cash. The latter means income support and redistribution policies so that the elderly can buy the services on the market. Advocates of assistance in kind argue that the state or service providers can better assess the needs of the client, while advocates of assistance in cash stress consumer sovereignty. Further, we will show that there need not be an opposition between these two. An extreme position, finally, could be that of no intervention by the state. There is a substitution between aid in cash and in kind. When there are more services available at a low price, then there is less need for income support, and vice versa. So when looking at services for the elderly, we must not forget the income policy with regard to the elderly (when comparing countries and looking into the future).

Aid in kind includes a complete set of organisational models of what can more and less be called intervention by the government in the financing or organisation of services. This picture should be further completed by the distinction between the formal and the informal sector, since income support and services in kind could be provided both by the formal sector (the state or the market) and by the informal sector (individual responsibility, self help, family help and social networks).

Figure 1.3 gives a summary of these different organisational forms, together with the financing methods.[1]

Services can be financed by personal resources, charity,[2] private insurance,[3] or by public subsidy. The public subsidy can be complete or partial. It mostly goes to the formal professional services. These can be provided by

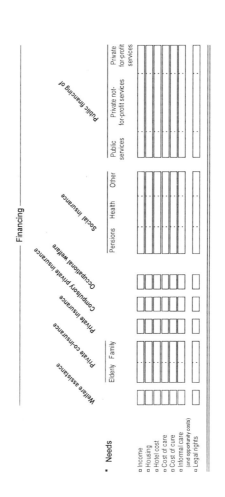

Figure 1.2   Financing several components of care for the elderly

Organisation \ Financing	Informal sector	Formal sector — Private	Formal sector — Public
in cash / Informal care	Self help mutual help (altruism and charity)	Insurance and savings (pays-as-you-go or funded)	Transfers (social security, minimum income)
in kind / Informal care	Self help (help by social network)	Paid voluntary work	Supported by the government
Formal professional care — Private — For-profit (commercial)	Sometimes even commercial organisers of charity market	Commercial firms or firms on a private market	For-profit organisations on a subsidised market
Private — Not-for-profit	Private not-for-profit sponsored by charity	Own contributions	Subsidised private non-profit
Public		Own contributions	Completely public financing

Figure 1.3   Matrix of financing and organising care of the elderly

private for-profit or non-profit organisations, or by public firms. In rare cases, the informal sector is financed (for instance a fee for the main carer or paid volunteers).

4 Macro-assessment of the Risk of Old Age Dependency in Theory

There is limited information available on the risk of old age dependency; it relates basically to four factors:
- the increasing number of older persons;
- the increasing life expectancy;
- the increasing degree of dependency;
- the increasing need for several types of care.
This is summarised in the scheme illustrated in Figure 1.4.

5 Macro-assessment of the Risk of Old Age Dependency in Practice

Based on a certain combination of macro-figures and micro-information of dependency, we give some indication of this overall risk, defined as the share of the population whose long-term care needs have to be covered. This overall risk is determined by the number of older persons, their life expectancy and the degree of disability or dependency.

5.1 Age Structure of the Population

The number of older persons overwhelmingly determines the macro-risk related to the cost of old age and dependency. The proportion of people above 65 will increase in the EU between now and 2020 from 15 to 20 per cent of the total population. Figure 1.5 and Table 1.3 give more detailed information: most of the EU Member States currently have a population aged above 65 of between 11 per cent (Ireland) and 17 per cent (Sweden) of the total population. Generally the average proportion is around 15 per cent. In the year 2020 it will be between 18 per cent and 23 per cent. This ageing of the population will be the result of the increasing life expectancy of the population (which between 1980 and 1995 was 0.5-5 years, see Figure 1.8). Ireland will remain the youngest country.

The proportion of the 75+ now amounts to 6 per cent. It will increase to 9 per cent by 2020.

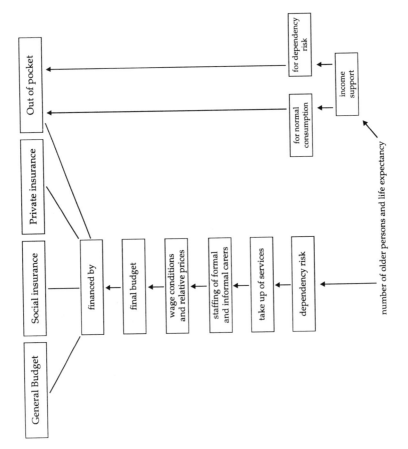

Figure 1.4   Macro-assessment of the risk of old age dependency

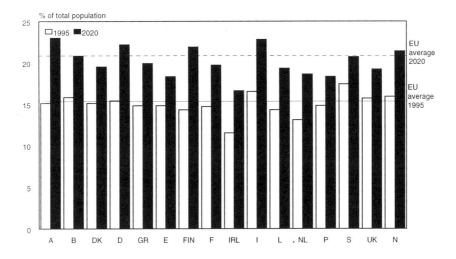

Figure 1.5 Percentage elderly persons (65+) in total population, present situation and forecast for 2020

5.2 Life Expectancy

All Western countries are facing a similar pattern: a lower fertility rate and a higher life expectancy. This makes the problem of the ageing society more pronounced: a (relatively and absolutely) smaller number of younger people will have to carry the burden of the larger proportion of the elderly. The following two figures present the life expectancy of persons at age 65 and at age 80. In all countries life expectancy of women at age 65 (80) is higher than that of men of age 65 (80).

The evolution of the expectation of life at birth during the years 1980–95 can be found in the Figure 1.8. In all countries life expectancy has been growing during the last 15 years.

5.3 Dependency

'Dependency' is multidimensional and can be defined in physical, mental (or emotional), economic and social terms. On a micro-level, dependency can be defined by using various scaling techniques or assessment procedures, (for instance those needed to define dementia). In the country reports some partial evidence is given relating to these aspects. It is remarkable that no standardised

Table 1.3   Demographic structure, present situation and forecast for 2020

		Total population (x 1,000)		65+ (% of total population)		75+ (% of total population)	
A	1995	8,053		15.1		6.4	
	2020	8,369		23.0		9.4	
B	1995	10,131		15.8		6.1	
	2020	10,382	(UN)	20.8		9.1	
DK	1996	5,251		15.1		7.0	(1994)
	2020	5,113	(UN)	19.5		8.2	
D	1995	81,539		15.4		6.3	
	2020	77,936	(UN)	22.2		10.6	
GR	1993	10,368		14.8		6.3	
	2020	10,080	(UN)	19.9		9.2	
E	1994	38,662		14.8		6.0	
	2020	38,348	(UN)	18.3		7.9	
FIN	1995	5,117		14.3		5.9	
	2020	5,393	(UN)	21.9		8.7	
F	1994	58,038		14.7		6.1	
	2020	60,021		19.7		9.4	
IRL	1994	3,571		11.5		4.8	
	2020	3,876	(UN)	16.6		6.1	
I	1995	57,269		16.4		6.5	
	2020	53,649	(UN)	22.8		10.7	
L	1991	385		14.3		7.1	
	2020	439	(UN)	19.3		8.2	
NL	1994	15,382		13.1		5.5	
	2020	16,286	(UN)	18.6		7.4	
P	1995	9,927		14.8		5.6	
	2020	9,955		18.3		6.3	
S	1994	8,816		17.4		8.1	
	2020	9,466		20.7		9.7	
UK	1994	57,808		15.7		7.0	
	2020	61,130		19.2		8.5	
N	1996	4,370		15.9		7.5	
	2020	4,670	(UN)	21.4	(2030)	10.5	(2030)

Note: (UN) = forecast from the United Nations.

Source: OECD Health Data 1996; NIS, Bevolkingsstatistieken; Alber and Guillemard, 1993; Walker, Alber and Guillemard, 1993; Eurostat, 1996; country reports.

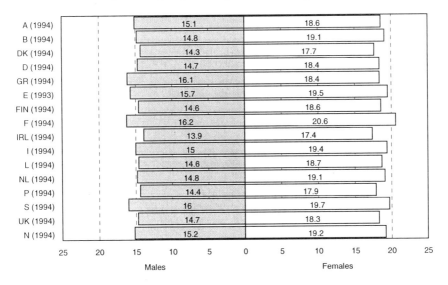

Figure 1.6   Life expectancy at 65, in years

Source: Eurostat, 1996.

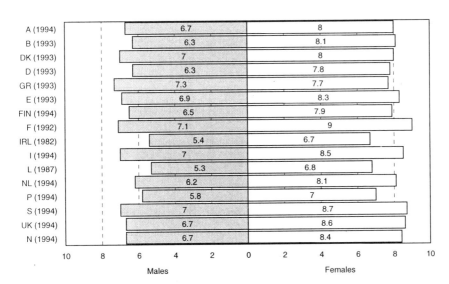

Figure 1.7   Life expectancy at 80, in years

Source: OECD Health Data 1996.

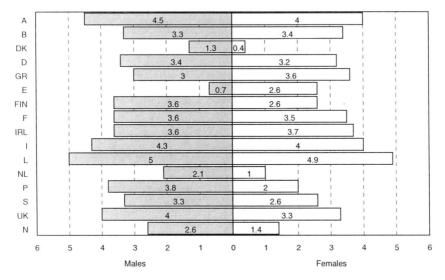

**Figure 1.8   Expectation of life at birth 1980–95, increase of the
number of years**

Source: Eurostat, 1996.

definitions and figures have been available until now, and hence each country
and service provider, and even each researcher investigating services for the
elderly, defines dependency in a different way. In Table 1.4 sometimes either
definitions applied in existing regulations or definitions illustrating the real
take-up of certain services or benefits are presented. Most studies limit
themselves to considering degrees of disability or degrees of dependency in
certain categories of activities. In future, not only for the purposes of
international comparison but also to be able to estimate care needs, there will
be some need for the harmonisation of these definitions and of the data-
gathering process.

Generalising and aggregating to a macro-level the findings of Figure 1.5
and Table 1.4, we can conclude that the old-age risk is now linked with ±15
per cent of the population, ±20 per cent of whom will be dependent on PADL
(Personal Activities of Daily Living) and IADL (Instrumental Activities of
Daily Living) after the age of 65. Approximately 5 per cent of the 65-plusers
are expected to be severely dependent on PADL ('median figure').

The ageing and the double ageing of the population will imply a significant
increase in dependent persons. The pressure of this increasing dependency

and increasing life expectancy places a higher fiscal burden on the existing systems than they were originally designed to bear. This has been discovered in many countries and has led to the debate on long-term care insurance. The European Year of the Elderly in 1993 brought this phenomenon to public attention in many countries. This growing public awareness could transform a 'fact of life' into a source of political pressure.

The proportion of dependent persons in the population varies significantly with age. Of the 65-plusers there are between 3 and 5 per cent severely dependent persons, and up to 15 per cent are partially dependent. If we consider persons 75 and older, the number of highly dependent persons increases to 10 per cent, and the partially dependent goes up to 25 per cent. The largest degrees of dependency are noticed particularly in the age groups 75+ and 80+. This leaves us with a population of highly dependent persons of on average 3 per cent of the total population, or about nine million persons in Europe. On the basis of the national reports, we identified in the Member States at least 7.6 million persons who are dependent or who in some way or another are receiving an allowance because of dependency (see also Tables 1.4 and 1.5). However, we must be very careful when drawing conclusions from these figures, because they are only estimates. Moreover, the definition of 'dependency' differs from country to country.

Therefore it is inappropriate to identify the elderly with dependent persons. The elderly are, to an increasing extent, healthy and even wealthy citizens, who are seeking empowerment and high-standard living conditions. However, this is not the total picture. Older persons are often confronted with an early exit from the labour market, which implies at least one form of exclusion. The elderly are especially confronted by increased concern about their present and future income and health expenditure. This personal feeling of insecurity is present on a macro-level, in the overall concern of governments about the future of the pension schemes and health expenditure in the next decade, exacerbated by the pressure of the ageing population. Previous research by A. Walker (Walker, Alber and Guillemard, 1993) has documented that the elderly feel comfortable about their personal surroundings, but uneasy about the political concern for their cause, illustrating that individual morale and collective morale do not necessarily coexist. For some, this concern about economic insecurity has already become a reality, and for others it has never been anything else. In many countries, older persons are in a deprived situation and are confronted with high care expenditure. However, most of the time their needs are covered and protected by well developed welfare state systems. A description of the present situation regarding the social protection of dependent older persons provides us with an opportunity (because the starting point is dependency, and therefore people in need of care) to show the map of the welfare state for this target group. Even more, the way we take care of the frailest elderly best illustrates the level of social quality and dignity of the care systems and the welfare state in general. Dependency can be enlarged from narrow to broader definitions so that we can illustrate how the complete welfare state responds to these dependency risks and needs.

Notes

1   A comparable structural arrangement of the welfare organisation can be found in Grindheim and Selle, 1990, p. 64.
2   This type of private solution is not always a guarantee of cost-efficiency: some commercially organised charity actions show extremely high costs and, considering the usual tax subsidy, they do not raise much extra money.
3   Here, too, inefficiency is possible. Most current Medicare supplemental insurers in the USA spend 40 per cent of the premiums on marketing, administrative expenses and profits (Rivlin and Wiener, 1988, p. 213). The organised health care system in the USA, which is to a large extent private, takes a higher proportion of GNP for a lower degree of protection of the population.

Table 1.4   Degree of dependency of the elderly

Country	Definition of dependency	Number of dependent elderly	% dependent elderly
A	The assessment of dependency is based on the number of hours a person needs care. All people with disabilities and/or chronic illness, who are in need of at least 50 hours of attendance and care per month, are entitled to an attendance allowance.	±250,000 pensioners received an attendance allowance in 1996.	±21% of 65+.
B	A person is considered to be physically dependent if he is at least dependent in bathing, dressing, transfer and/or toileting.	57,150 persons in homes (1996). 30,793 elderly persons in the community (1992).	3.5% of 65+. 2% of 65+.
DK	Elderly persons are considered to be dependent if they are dependent as regards performance of the four instrumental activities: cooking, shopping, cleaning and transportation. Furthermore they are dependent on assistance as regards carrying out at least one of the following six personal activities: eating, dressing, bathing, toileting, continence and walking.		10% of 70+ is dependent on help to PADL (1989).
D	Persons in need of long-term care are persons who in the field of personal hygiene, alimentation or mobility need help at least once a day for at least two activities, and who require help with household affairs several times a week.	Persons in need of long-term care aged 60–80: 650,000; >80 years: 600,000 (1995).	5.6% of age group 60–80; 18% of 80+.
GR			
E	Fully disabled means having very serious difficulties in performing personal care, domestic activities and external relations (shopping, visits to relatives, …) and needing permanent care of relatives or social services for at least 8 hours per day.	± 35,650 elderly over 65 years are severely incapacitated.	5% of 65+.
FIN	There is no universal definition of dependency, but various need indicators are implemented. Often they are based on the ADL and IADL indexes.	290,000[1] (1990). 370,000[2] (1990).	3.6%[1] of 65+. 4.6%[2] of 65+.
F	Fully disabled means that the persons are either bound to bed or chair,[1] or else not bound to bed or chair but in need of help for toileting and dressing.[2]	66,000 old people living at home are functionally disabled (1988).	17% of 65+.
IRL	Functionally disabled means requiring assistance with mobility and personal care, as well as having medical and psychological problems.	2,024,770 older persons: not self-sufficient in at least one activity (1994).	22% of 65+.
I	Persons not self-sufficient to perform the Activities of Daily Living in part or completely.	901,943 are not self-sufficient in at least three activities (1994). total disability: 184,070 older persons (1994).	9.8% of 65+. 2% of 65+.

Table 1.4 cont'd

Country	Definition of dependency	Number of dependent elderly	% dependent elderly

L	Fully disabled means according to the Luxembourg legislation 'dependent in one or more physical or mental functions to that extent that the help or constant care of a third person is needed'. Three levels of dependency can be distinguished:
	   level 1: needing help different times a week;
	   level 2: needing help once a day;
	   level 3: needing help on a permanent basis.
		Older persons living at home:
		level 1: 1,200;
		level 2: 1,242;
		level 3: 389 (1995).
		Older persons living in an institution:
		level 1: 932;
		level 2: 1,553;
		level 3: 1,123.
			2.1% of 65+.
			2.2% of 65+.
			0.7% of 65+.
			
			1.6% of 65+.
			2.7% of 65+.
			2% of 65+.

NL	The definition of dependency is based on a combined index of impairment of ADL and IADL activities, reduced to a division into four categories: 1 little or no impairment: no ADL problems and IADL activities can be performed almost completely alone (help for at most one activity is needed); 2 moderate impairment: independent in conformity with the ADL-index and help needed for at most two housekeeping activities; 3 severe impairment: dependency on one or two ADL activities and simultaneously difficulty with many housekeeping activities; 4 very severe impairment: difficulties with many ADL activities and any of the housekeeping activities can no longer be performed.	697,450 older persons report problems in performing at least 1 ADL-activity; 1,754,180 older persons report problems in performing IADL-activities.	34.3% of 65+. 86.2% of 65+.
P	Fully disabled means 'being in need of permanent help'.		
S	B-category = dependent in all I-ADL and one more activity; C-category = dependent in all I-ADL, bathing and one more activity; D-category = dependent in all I-ADL, bathing, dressing and one more activity; E-category = dependent in all I-ADL, bathing, dressing, going to the toilet and one more activity; F-category = dependent in all I-ADL, bathing, dressing, going to the toilet, transfer and one more activity; G-category = dependent in all activities; Others = dependent in two or more activities but not classifiable as above.		65+ in nursing homes: A: 5%; B, C, D: 9%; E, F: 58%; G: 25%; Others: 3%. 65+ in the community: B: 11.3%; E: 2.4%.

Table 1.4 cont'd

Country	Definition of dependency	Number of dependent elderly	% dependent elderly
UK	People defined as short-interval dependent may have needs such as bathing and washing which need to be met at specific times of the day and at least once a day. People who are critical-interval dependent have needs which are unpredictable such as assistance with toileting and they usually require 24 hour supervision	1,320,000 elderly are short- or critical-interval 'dependent'.	15% of 65+
N	Fully disabled persons = persons with long-term and rather severe dependency in instrumental and/or personal activities of daily living	All residents in institutional care are severely dependent.	6–7% of 67+ 20–25% of the 65+ living at home: dependent upon help for shopping and cleaning; 2–4%: help for dressing and to move around indoors (1995)*

Note

* Only the latter criteria (dressing and moving indoors) imply a dependency level fairly close to a 'need for institutional care'.

Source: definitions and figures mentioned in the national reports.

Table 1.5   Summary table on ageing and dependency

	A	B	DK	D	GR	E	FIN	F
Ageing								
Total population (x 1,000) (1996)	8,106	10,159	5,237	81,922	10,490	39,674	5,126	58,333
Population over 65 (x 1,000) (1996)	1,187	1,618	791	12,528	1,717	6,080	729	8,998
% population over 65 (1996)	15.9	15.1	15.3	16.4	15.3	14.2	15.4	
% population over 65 living alone (1995)	20.9 (55–74) 53.1 (75+)	50 (1996)	29.2 (55+) (1991)	25 (1988)	19 (1989)		30.3 (1982)	
Total population (x 1,000) (2020)	8,369	10,382	5,113	77,936	10,080	38,348	5,393	60,021
% population over 65 (2020)	20.8	19.5	22.2	19.9	18.3	21.9	19.7	
Dependency								
65+, fully dependent Number		87,943		650,000 (60–80)			35,650	660,000
%		5.5		5.6 (60–80)			5	8.2
65+, partly dependent Number	250,000							
%	21							
70+, fully dependent Number			36,000	600,000 (80+)				
%			10	18 (80+)				
70+, partly dependent Number								
%								

Table 1.5 cont'd

	IR	I	L	NL	P	S	UK	N
Ageing								
Total population (x 1,000) (1996)	3,554	57,226	412	15,575	9,808	8,819	58,144	4,348
Population over 65 (x 1,000) (1996)	401	9,371	57	2,063	1,469	1,512	9,177	683
% population over 65 (1996)	11.3	16.4	13.8	13.2	15.0	17.1	15.8	15.7
% population over 65 living alone (1995)	24 (1991); 10.3 (men 60+); 31.4 (women 60+)	39.8 (1994)	30.7 (1985)	17.9 (1986)		38 (1991)	23 (men) 49 (women)	
Total population (x 1,000) (2020)	3,876	53,649	439	16,286	9,955	9,466	61,130	4,670
% population over 65 (2020)	16.6	22.8	19.3	18.6	18.3	20.7	19.2	21.4 (2030)
Dependency								
65+, fully dependent — Number		184,070	1,512					41,690
65+, fully dependent — %		2	2.7					6
65+, partly dependent — Number	17 (of the elderly at home)	2,926,713	4,927	697,450			1,320,000	
65+, partly dependent — %		31.8	7.2	34.3			15	
70+, fully dependent — Number								
70+, fully dependent — %								
70+, partly dependent — Number								
70+, partly dependent — %								

Source: Nijkamp, Pacolet, Spinnewyn et al., 1991, p. 131; country reports.

2 Some Macro-observations Regarding Social Protection of Dependent Older Persons

How are the needs of the (dependent) elderly met? A broad definition of needs has been used in this study. Income, housing, health, social services, rights of participation and legal rights to maintain privacy, autonomy and empowerment are included. Dependency refers not only to functional or clinical criteria, but also includes physical, mental, economic and sociocultural aspects relating to the elderly, ill or handicapped persons. The needs derived from this complete set have to be met by social protection systems. These systems have until now exhibited a high level and largely differentiated mix of care for the elderly.

Actual utilisation, the supply of services, the quality of care and the cost of supplying this care determine the financial risk related to the actual care expenditures. This risk depends on the likelihood of care being required, the length of care and the intensity with which it is used. Detailed (actuarial) studies are not readily available. The actual level of services being supplied reflects only the needs which are now being recognised and satisfied. It does not inform us as to the unmet needs.

A detailed micro-analysis of social protection for the elderly gives a long list of initiatives, regulations and institutions, engaging in some way or another the public authorities in public money or imposing at least some legal obligations on society or individuals. The research approach explicitly uses a very large definition to broaden the scope of the protection elements. In the institutional overview a distinction is made between income support and the provision of services.

Before we enter into detail, in the next chapter, on those services for the elderly, we give in this chapter an overview of the other institutions of social protection, especially related with income protection and health care. This gives a macro-overview of the general level of social protection. At the same time it is described in macroeconomic terms.

1 Income Protection

1.1 Poverty

On average, 14.3 per cent of the households of the 12 relevant European countries in 1988 lived below the poverty line. In most countries, poverty is larger among retired households than among younger households. There is a relatively low poverty ratio of retired households in Belgium and Denmark compared with the European Union as a whole. Also, in Luxembourg and the Netherlands, the percentage of poor households is lower than in the EU as a whole. In contrast, the consumption expenditure of one retired household in four in Spain, Italy and the United Kingdom is equivalent to or below the poverty threshold. We even find a proportion of one retired household to three in Greece and Portugal. The rates calculated for Germany, France and Ireland are situated in between these two groups.

Table 2.1   Poverty rates of households, 1988

	All households	Households of which the head is retired	Single persons aged 65 or over
B	6.1	4.0	2.7
DK	3.6	4.0	2.4
D	10.8	13.7	14.6
GR	20.6	30.4	33.1
E	16.7	23.2	25.8
F	14.0	16.7	22.6
IRL	16.9	15.6	23.2
I	20.6	26.8	28.7
L	8.8	9.3	6.1
NL	4.3	6.6	7.4
P	25.2	42.5	47.2
UK	14.6	21.7	23.7

Source: Eurostat, 1996, p. 213.

1.2 Pensions

1.2.1 The basic and supplementary pension schemes Figure 2.1 presents the public expenditure on pensions for 13 EU Member States, as a percentage of social security expenditure.

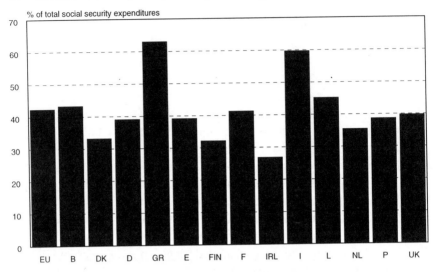

% of total social security expenditures

**Figure 2.1   Pension expenditures as a percentage of total social
security expenditures, EU, 1995**

Source: De Ryck, 1997, p. 566.

In all EU Member States, pension expenditure accounts for the lion's
share of social security expenditure. Nonetheless, significant differences exist
between Member States: in Greece and Italy, the share for pensions is
approximately twice as high as in the Netherlands, Finland, Denmark and
Ireland.

Table 2.2 aims to give an estimation of the evolution of pension
expenditures in ECU per older person and of the level of pensions as a
percentage of GDP. The national reports are the source for the information
provided in this table.

Using the following figures and tables, an attempt is made to acquire a
better understanding of the factors determining pension expenditure.

Ageing of the population Firstly, the EU countries and Norway are compared
on the basis of their position regarding ageing (proportion of those over 65)
and the scope of expenditure for first and second tier pensions (as a percentage
of GDP). In this figure a larger definition of pension expenditures is used
than in Table 2.2, where for most countries only reference was made to the
statutory pension schemes.

The share of persons above 65 varies from 11.5 per cent (Ireland) to 17.4
per cent (Sweden). For basic and supplementary pensions, spending varies

Table 2.2   Pension expenditures (old age + survivor pensions) as a percentage of GDP and in ECU per older person

	Pension as a percentage of GDP				Pension expenditures in ECU per older person				
	1987	1992	1994	1995	1987	1992	1993	1994	1995
A	16.4	15.4	15.3	15.5	11,557	14,472		15,376	16,281
B	9.2	8.9	9.10		8,655	10,367	10,772	11,227	
DK[11]	4.04			5.22				6,384	9,913
DK[12]	7.6			10.02	8,542				
D	11.35				8,707				
GR	6.5 (1975)	10.7 (1990)							
E	9.83[5]	10.9[5]	11.0[5]	11.10[5]	2,971[6]	4,598[6]		5,238[6]	5,425[6]
FIN		8	7.9			9,531		9,502	
F	12.06		12.2		9,067		10,952		
IRL	3.80	3.21	2.97	2.74	4,081	4,886	5,065	5,296	5,430
I		15.4 (1993)[8]	16.0[8]	15.7[8]					
L									15,276[2]; 8,149[3]; 10,968[4]
NL	9.59				7,101			8,784	
P		5.9[1]	6.1[1]	7.2[1]	860[10]	1,810[10]	1,883[10]	1,981[10]	2,082[10]
S			8.7	8.0				10,062	10,062
UK	9.61				2,746[7]	3,888[7]	4,064[7]	3,776[7]	3,852[7]
N	6.5	7.1	6.3	6.2	6,531[9]	8,764[9]		9,578[9]	10,054[9] (estimation)

Notes

1   Retirement, invalidity and survivor pensions.
2   For men.
3   For women.
4   Survivor pensions.
5   Public pensions: social security, no contributory pensions and civil servant pensions.
6   Average pension of contributory pension system of social security.
7   Only state retirement and earnings-related pensions.
8   Includes a severance pay.
9   Includes state expenditures to state occupational pensions and some other state pensions.
10 Only the general regime.
11 Public old age pension (*Folkepension*) for people aged 67+ (the increase from 1987 to 1995 is mainly due to the fact that as from 1994 old age pension has been paid out as a taxable gross amount. Before the amount was lower, but no tax was paid out of basic pension).
12 Includes also civil servants' pension, grants from approved pension funds and certain life insurance companies, statutory occupational pension and early retirement pension.

Source: Pacolet, Versieck and Bouten, 1994; country reports.

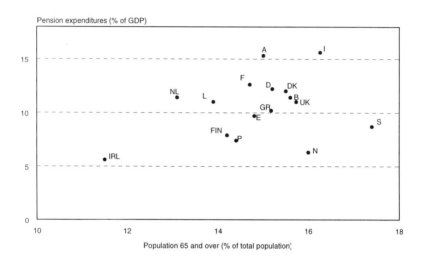

Pension expenditures (% of GDP)

Population 65 and over (% of total population)

Figure 2.2   Pension expenditures (basic + compulsory occupational + voluntary occupational) as a percentage of GDP and percentage of population aged 65 and over, 1994

Source: Eurostat, 1996.

from 5.6 per cent of GDP in Ireland to more than 15 per cent in Austria and Italy. Figure 2.2 demonstrates the positive link between the degree of ageing of the population and the proportion of pension expenditure as a percentage of GDP. In other words, countries with a relatively older population also spend more, generally speaking, on pensions. Ireland, for example (relatively younger population and relatively lower pension expenditure), can be compared with Denmark (relatively older population and relatively higher pension expenditure). Nonetheless, it is equally clear that such a link has to be placed within a broad margin of institutional choices concerning the level and structure of protection. The organisation of the pension scheme, replacement ratios, the overall level of social protection and the preference for in cash or in kind support can all influence the picture. In addition, problems of definition are always present. For instance, in 1994 the number of those over 65 in Portugal and France was identical, while the difference in relative expenditure is considerable. On the other hand, the Netherlands and Belgium have very similar pension expenditures, although they differ in terms of relative ageing. The same is true for Luxembourg and Belgium.

It is clear from the above that the degree of ageing is only one factor which explains the proportion of pension expenditure. Other factors are related to the overall level of social protection and to the characteristics of the pension systems. Thus, the method of calculation is also important – whether or not the pension is linked to former wages, which replacement rate is used and whether funded alternatives exist. In addition, the retirement age and the extent to which people of a pensionable age are allowed to continue to be gainfully employed obviously play a role too, as do schemes for early retirement.

Average pension benefit Figure 2.3 gives some indication of the differences between pension systems, with the average benefit (basic and supplementary pension benefit) as a percentage of GDP per capita as an indicator. However, it should be noted that this indicator does not point exclusively to differences between pension systems but also, for example, to the previous and present wage profile. Thus, the aforementioned difference between Portugal and France, for almost the same degree of ageing, can be attributed at least partially to the difference in the average pension. The difference quoted between Luxembourg and Belgium cannot be explained by differences in the average pension compared to GDP per capita.

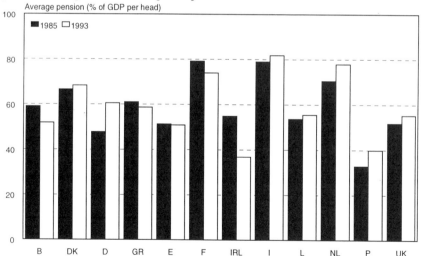

Figure 2.3   Average pension as a percentage of GDP per head, 1985 and 1993

Source: own calculations on Eurostat, 1996; OECD Health Data, 1997.

Method of calculating the basic pension Denmark, Ireland, Sweden, the Netherlands, Norway and the United Kingdom give all their inhabitants a universal but rather low flat-rate, basic (indexed) pension, financed using the pay-as-you-go system (Beveridge system). In the United Kingdom, this amount can still be accumulated with an earnings-related pension.

In Austria, Finland, Luxembourg, Belgium, Germany, France, Greece, Italy, Portugal and Spain, substantial state-funded, earnings-related pensions are awarded (Bismarck system). Generally speaking, these benefits are relatively high. This is also the reason why the second tier system is less well-developed in this latter group than in the first group (France and Greece are two of the exceptions to this rule).

In all EU countries, the statutory pension system is financed by pay-as-you-go. This contrasts with Japan and the USA, for example, where the statutory pension is also partially funded.

In Denmark, France and Portugal, some changes have recently been made to the statutory pension. In both cases, this involves measures to reduce pension expenditure. Until recently, the basic pension in Denmark was a flat-rate benefit, independent of income and assets. Now, it is reduced if the earnings from work exceed a certain amount. Until 1 January 1994, the pension in France was based on earnings from work in the best 10 years. However, since 1994 the best 25 years have been taken as a basis. Before 1993 the pension of employees in Portugal was based on the five best years of earnings out of 10; now it is based on the average of earnings of the 10 best years out of the last 15 years. Before 1993 the pension of civil servants was based on the last salary; now it is based on the average of earnings of the last two years.

Existence of funded alternatives In recent years, supplementary pension systems have been developed, partly as a way of alleviating the difficulties of financing state pensions. In the Netherlands and the United Kingdom, supplementary pensions already account for a substantial proportion of total pension benefits (see Figure 2.4).

Different countries have in the past opted for different systems: some concentrate on the legal pension (Belgium, Germany, Spain, Italy, Luxembourg and Portugal), others on the substantially funded pension (the Netherlands and the United Kingdom), and still others on a system in between the two (Denmark, Ireland and also, remarkably, France). It can also be observed from this picture that those choices have not changed substantially over the last 15 years. The relative importance of 'second pillars' remains stable, at least in the payout of the pension system. In future this can/will change because there

Table 2.3   Statutory pension scheme, 1996

Type of benefit

A   Linked to average earnings during working life (employees: 180 months of highest contributions).

B   Linked to average earnings during working life (employees and self-employed).
Linked to average earnings of last five years (civil servants).

DK   Basic pension has until lately been a flat rate benefit independent of income and wealth, but now the basic pension is dependent on income from personal work (if working income exceeds a certain amount, basic pension is reduced) + means-tested supplementary pension (ATP).

D   Linked to average earnings during working life.

GR   Linked to final salary.

E   Linked to average earnings during working life.

FIN   Earnings-related employment pension and guaranteed minimum pension (national pension).

F   Linked to average earnings of best 25 years (instead of best 10 years: before 1 January 1994).

IRL   Flat-rate.

I   Linked to average earnings of last five years.

L   Linked to average earnings during working life.

NL   Flat-rate.

P   Flat-rate for non-contributors; earnings-related for contributors General Regime: based on the average of earnings of the 10 best years out of the last 15 years. Regime of Civil Servants: based on the average of earnings of the last two years.

S   Flat-rate basic pension + earnings-related supplementary pension (universal).

UK   For all residents: flat-rate (higher for married than single) + for workers: linked to average earnings during working life – opting out of the earnings-related pension permitted by company plans and by individuals.

N   Flat-rate basic pension + earnings-related supplementary pension (universal).

Sources: Neyt, 1995; Turner and Watanabe, 1995; Besseling and Zeeuw, 1993; country reports.

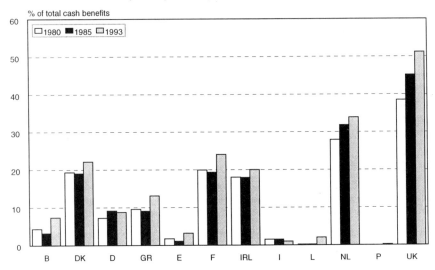

Figure 2.4   Compulsory and voluntary supplementary pensions as a percentage of total pension benefits

Source: Eurostat, 1996.

is some change in the number of persons contributing to 'second-pillar' pension schemes. The legal pension system remains the major part of social protection, although second and 'third pillar' solutions occur and are growing.

The first and second pillars are two elements of the same pension income. No simple answer can be given to the question as to whether they are linked to one another by shared objectives or whether they develop independently of one another. After all, the answer is not the same for all European countries. For example, in France it could be said that shared objectives influence the development of the first and second pillars: after all, the objective there was that the first and second pillars together should achieve a gross replacement rate of 75 per cent. On the other hand, in Germany no consistent public policy exists with respect to the first and second pillars together. The second pillar is entirely voluntary.

One of the most important policy objectives of a compulsory system of supplementary pensions is to provide access to a supplementary pension for as large a group of citizens as possible. The figures above reveal that this has largely been achieved (in Denmark, France, Greece, the Netherlands, Sweden and the United Kingdom). In the Netherlands and the United Kingdom, the fact that everyone had to be able to receive a supplementary pension – not

Table 2.4 Supplementary schemes

	Supplementary pensions	Number of persons covered	Coverage (% of labour force)	Type of plan	Type of benefit	Financing	Taxation
A 1993	Voluntary occupational	186,082	6.3%	Defined benefit	Predominantly lump sum pensions	Predominantly book reserves	Contributions deductible
B 1995	Voluntary occupational	800,000	33.0%	Defined benefit and defined contribution	Annuities/lump sum	Funded	Contributions deductible, benefits taxed
DK 1995	ATP (compulsory)	2,254,872	80.5%	Defined benefit	Annuities	Funded	Contributions deductible, pension assets taxed, benefits taxed
	Occupational (compulsory)	1,499,000	51.5%	Defined contribution	Annuities/lump sum	Funded	Benefits taxed
	Civil servants' pension (compulsory)	230,000	7.9%	No contribution, benefits dependent on final salary	Annuities	Pay-as-you-go	
D 1992	Voluntary occupational	14,000,000	46.7%	Defined benefit	Lump-sum pensions or annuities, linked to average salary	Predominantly book reserves	Employer contributions deductible, benefits partially taxed depending on financing method
GR 1991	Compulsory occupational, statutory or by collective agreement	3,360,186 (TEAM/OGA)	85.3%				
E 1992	Voluntary occupational	225,000	1.5%				
FIN 1995	Employer-related voluntary schemes	300,000	15.0%	Defined benefits, linked to final salary	Annuities	Partly funded, book reserve, insured	Employer and employee contributions deductible, benefits liable for income tax
F 1994	Compulsory occupational, statutory or by collective agreement	17,988,000 (ARCCO/AGIRC)	74.5%	Defined benefit	Annuities	Pay-as-you-go	Employer and employee contributions deductible. Benefits liable for income tax
IRL 1995	Voluntary occupational	548,800	46% for all of those at work in 1995 (±67% in 1996)	Defined benefit and defined contribution	Lump sum pensions or annuities, linked to average salary	Pay-as-you-go/ predominantly funded	Benefits liable for income tax

Table 2.4 cont'd

	Supplementary pensions	Number of persons covered	Coverage (% of labour force)	Type of plan	Type of benefit	Financing	Taxation
I 1994	Voluntary occupational	1,500,000	5%; mainly only for executives	Defined benefit	Annuities	Insured, pay-as-you-go, or book reserve	Benefits liable for income tax
L 1995	Optional for the enterprise, but compulsory for the employees if enterprise takes the initiative	34,509 in 459 enterprises (404 private enterprises and 55 enterprises in the public sector)	35% of the employees of the private sector	Defined benefit (defined contribution in preparation)	Annuities or lump sum	Funded	Employer contributions deductible. Employee contributions: book reserve: deductible; group insurance or external pension plan: non-deductible. Benefits: liable for income tax
NL 1994	Partly compulsory occupational, statutory or by collective agreement (*bedrijfstak*). Partly voluntary	3,000,000	±85%	Defined benefit; defined contribution / Linked to final salary	Annuities	Book reserves	Benefits liable for income tax, contributions deductible
P 1994	occupational Compulsory occupational, statutory or by collective agreement Voluntary occupational	226,690	less than 5% of white-collar workers (estimation)	Defined benefit and defined contributions	Annuities or a percentage increase of regular pensions	Pay-as-you-go	Contributions deductible from poll taxes and benefits taxed as income
S 1995	Compulsory	1,289,000	83.5%	Defined benefit	Annuities	Pay-as-you-go	Employer contributions deductible; pension income taxed
UK 1994	statutory Compulsory statutory (SERPS)	22,700,000	79.4%	Predominantly defined benefit	Lump-sum pensions or annuities (linked to final salary)	Funded	Employer and employee contributions deductible. Benefits liable for income tax, except lump-sum payments up to a ceiling
N 1996	Voluntary occupational Occupational (collective) pensions: a) public (state – municipal); b) private sector	a) Compulsory – nearly 100% b) 40% covered	Nearly 100% in public sector about 40% in private sector	Defined benefit	Annuities	Pay-as-you-go	Employer contributions deductible; pension income taxed

Sources: Neyt, 1995; Turner and Watanabe, 1995, pp. 12–15; Besseling and Zeeuw, 1993, p. 8; country reports.

Table 2.5   Proportion of people covered by supplementary pensions by age

		20–24	25–29	30–34	35–39	40–44	45–49	50–54	55–59	60–64	65+ (% receiving benefits)
A	1993										6.6%
B											
DK¹	1993	19%	36%	41%	46%	45%	42%	32%	30%	17%	30%
D											
GR											
E											
FIN	1995		1%		2%		4%		5%		5%
F											
IRL		n.a.	n.a.	n.a.	n.a.	n.a.	n.a.	n.a.	n.a.	n.a.	n.a.
I											
L											
NL	1994										79% of 65+ households
P											
S	1995										83.5%
UK											
N											52% (67+)²

Notes

1   The figures refer to occupational pension schemes based on general agreements.
2   The figure refers to occupational pension schemes, and not to the national supplementary pension (statutory pension scheme).

Source: country reports.

just the higher earners, executives and employees of larger companies – and the concern not to restrict labour mobility were clearly explicit objectives in making the supplementary pensions compulsory.

Where supplementary pension schemes are voluntary and do not have to be compulsorily organised, the middle and higher earnings brackets of the workforce in particular appear to be covered. The likelihood of not being eligible for a supplementary pension is higher for low-paid employees, for part-time employees, for women and for employees in smaller companies. However, this assertion may not be generalised for all EU countries which do not have a compulsory second pillar, since the coverage provided by the supplementary pensions in one country are much higher than in another country. Thus, voluntarily organised supplementary pensions reach a relatively high proportion of the workforce in Germany, Ireland, the Netherlands and the United Kingdom. For example, in Germany in 1992, 46.7 per cent of employees in the private sector were covered by supplementary pensions. However, coverage of full-time employees was considerably higher (51.6 per cent) than that for part-time employees (19.9 per cent) (European Commission DGV for Employment, Industrial Relations and Social Affairs (hereafter EC DGV), 1994, p. 60). Male employees were also more likely to be eligible (55.9 per cent) than female employees (33.1 per cent). The smaller the company, the lower the chance that a supplementary pension plan is organised and the smaller the percentage of employees benefiting from a supplementary pension plan.

In Ireland, two-thirds of the workforce are already covered by supplementary pension plans. Those employees not covered come primarily from the following categories: employees in smaller companies, employees in agriculture and fishing, part-time and temporary employees and employees who choose not to participate in a pension plan – at least if membership is not compulsory.

Where employees in the Netherlands are not members of a supplementary pension plan, this is either because the employer did not want to finance a plan or because the employees were married women or part-time workers and were excluded from the pension plan. Employers who do not provide a supplementary pension plan usually come from one of the following categories: small businesses with fewer then 10 employees aged 25 or over; employers providing mainly part-time work; employers who are not bound by any collective labour agreement or who do not belong to an employers' organisation; and employers in the services sector.

Supplementary pensions in the United Kingdom are considerably more prevalent in the public sector than in the private sector (72.4 per cent, compared to 38.9 per cent of employees) (EC DGV, 1994, p. 62). Here, too, the size of the business, together with the sex of the employees and the occurrence of part-time work are very important factors in determining the coverage.

Estimates for Belgium calculate that 800,000 employees are covered by a supplementary pension plan: ±70 per cent of them are white-collar workers; 30 per cent blue-collar workers. This corresponds to 52 per cent and 15 per cent respectively of the total in each group. The majority of these 800,000 are covered by collective insurance. The largest group would seem to belong to the higher income brackets of the population (EC DGV, 1994, p. 63).

The high coverage by state pensions in Italy, Spain and Portugal (see further) are the main reason why supplementary pensions are not widespread.

In the short term, it is fairly unlikely that coverage by optionally provided supplementary pensions will increase significantly. After all, the level of unemployment remains considerable and new, additional jobs are often created in sectors where supplementary pensions are less common. Secondly, it is fairly unlikely that the authorities will be in a position in the near future to increase the fiscal advantages which are necessary for expansion of the second pillar. Rather, the reverse is noticeable (e.g. in Belgium and Italy).

In the Netherlands, Finland and the United Kingdom, company pensions are linked chiefly to the final salary. As a result of future financing problems and the fact that the labour market is being distorted by 'defined benefit' plans, Denmark is increasingly switching to 'defined contribution' plans (Besseling and Zeeuw, 1993, p. 7). In general, however, fixed benefits linked to the average salary still appear to be the most frequently used.

In some countries, pay-as-you-go is used as a financing technique, for example, for the supplementary pensions for civil servants in the United Kingdom and Denmark, in Ireland, Portugal, Italy, Sweden and France.

Germany is, next to the Netherlands and Austria, one of the few countries where company pensions are predominantly financed from book reserves. This means that the pension reserves are not separated from the normal operating capital. For companies, this means a substantial source of self-financing and does not necessarily lead to more investment for the capital market.

Denmark, the Netherlands and the United Kingdom operate pension funds which are separate from the companies.

The development and importance of supplementary pensions is clearly not the same in all the countries of the European Union. Their contribution to social protection and their impact on the labour and capital markets differs considerably from country to country. A large amount of capital has been accumulated in the United Kingdom, the Netherlands and Ireland. In the rest of the European Union this is not as considerable, but nor is it negligible at national level.

The financial impact of the supplementary pensions can be measured using the quantity of assets at a given point in time. This yardstick gives an indication of the amount of resources present for fulfilling future obligations and of the investment potential held by the pension fund managers.

In some countries, the reserves are already reaching the extent of gross national product (GNP). The question is whether they are also actually used for the long-term investments useful for economic growth.

Table 2.6   Assets as a percentage of GNP, EU, 1991

	Pension funds	Group insurance	Total
Austria (1993)			0.05
Belgium	4	11	15
Denmark	25	27	52
(West-)Germany *	16	22	38
France	1	18	19
Greece	5	2	7
Ireland	39	32	71
Italy	1	1	2
The Netherlands	86	39	125
Portugal	6	2	8
Spain	2	4	6
United Kingdom	63	32	95

*   Including book reserves

Source: Neyt, 1995.

Replacement rates In the Table 2.7 net replacement rates of first and second tier pensions are shown. The replacement rate is an indicator of the level of social protection offered by pensions. In the table below ratios are calculated in net terms (after deduction of compulsory social contributions and taxes). The following assumptions are made:
– the pension is for a married man entitled to a basic or first tier pension together with any compulsory supplementary pension;
– a full labour market career corresponds with 35-45 years of employment;
– the replacement rates concern the people on average earnings.

Table 2.7   Net replacement rates of first and second tier pensions

Replacement rate (35–45 years of employment, gross salary as 100% proportion of the average)

	1989	1995
A		Employees: ±75% (max.: 2,055 ECU); civil servants: 80% of last income (no upper limit)
B	88%	Employees: 63% (1993)
DK	74%	86% (with occupational pension and without rent subsidies); 62% (without occupational pension and rent subsidies)
D	69%	
GR	114%	
E	97%	
FIN		60% (actual (not theoretically calculated) replacement rate for a single pension recipient in 1993)
F	83%	80% (1993)
IRL	64%	
I	92%	
L	76%	70 to 100% (private sector)
NL	82%	77%
P	98%	minimum 30–maximum 80%
S	70%	
UK	64%	57%
N		54% (basic + national supplementary pension)

Sources: Walker, Alber and Guillemard, 1993, p. 31; Bouchet, De Doncker and Timmermans, 1997, p. 554; country reports.

To be able to draw some comparisons between average and high earnings groups, the following table on replacement rates for employees earning twice an average wage is added. The figures in the table below refer to the earnings for 1989 and the pensions on 1 January 1990. The ratios relate to married male employees. Normally speaking, only the first pillar is considered. Countries with compulsory national second tier systems are the exceptions to this rule.

In many countries, the newly retired receive a very high proportion of their earnings before retirement, particularly if the comparison is made on a net basis. This confirms the general impression that higher earners receive relatively less from the state (see Table 2.10) and that taxation is generally lower for pensioners than for those who are working.

Table 2.8   Replacement rates for employees earning twice the average wage in manufacturing

	Full career		20 years' cover	
	Gross rate (%)	Net rate (%)	Gross rate (%)	Net rate (%)
B	43	62	24	38
D	29	46	29	46
DK	39	55	18	24
GR	78	89	45	59
E	90	97	63	71
F	31	40	17	21
IRL	24	35	24	.35
I	69	79	39	49
L	54	65	30	39
NL	24	37	24	37
P	79	103	45	59
UK	17	24	8	11

Source: Social Europe, 1994, p. 12.

The southern countries generally belong to the countries which have a high replacement rate. These countries are definitely more cash oriented in the social protection. The countries where the first pillar (including compulsory national supplementary pension) does not replace such a significant share of the earnings before retirement – not even on a net basis – are mostly also the countries where second tier systems are highly developed.

Despite the fact that the replacement rate forms a good yardstick for measuring the level of protection of pensioners, care must be taken in interpreting it. First and foremost, many pensioners have not completed a full career of 35–40 years (women and people who have been unemployed, have undertaken longer training or have retired early). Secondly, the replacement rates are also often overestimated because the earnings from previous years of work are not always revalued for calculating the pension: inflation and wage trends are not always taken into account when calculating the benefit. In a number of southern countries, the pension is indeed calculated on much lower average earnings from work than in the rest of the European Union (e.g. in Spain, Portugal and Italy). Thirdly, replacement rates only reflect the situation at the time of retirement. The pension is, after all, not necessarily always adjusted to the development in welfare throughout the period of retirement.

Since 1989, trends in replacement rates have been negative. We can illustrate this using various examples.

As in Germany, the Italians have begun to realise that maintaining the present pension system will cause problems in the future. Until recently, the pension level in Italy amounted to 80 per cent of the average wage. This has since fallen to 70 per cent. At the same time, the statutory retirement age will rise from 60 for men and 55 for women to 65 and 60 respectively. Moreover, the Italian pension legislation of 1992–93 envisages a new calculation of the pension for employees who have just become covered, which means that a further fall in the replacement rate can be expected in the future.

In Greece, the increase in retirement age (gradual increase to the age of 65) and the reduction in pensions since 1993 will lead to lower replacement rates.

Law no. 329 of 25 September 1993 will also lead to a fall in replacement rates in Portugal. This law envisages various changes to the calculation of the pension, including the gradual increase in retirement age for women from 62 to 65, raising the minimum number of contribution years from 10 to 15, calculating the pension on the basis of the average wage in the best 10 years out of the last 15, rather than the best five years out of the last 10.

Retirement age and early retirement schemes Europe does not have such a thing as a 'standard' retirement age or a generally accepted pension system. Official retirement ages vary between 57 and 67. Some countries still differentiate between men and women (Greece, Belgium, Austria, Italy, Portugal and the United Kingdom). Some countries, such as Belgium, Portugal, Italy, the United Kingdom and Austria, are in the process of doing away with this sex discrimination. The intention in Belgium is that both sexes will retire at the age of 65 by the year 2009. In Portugal, until 1 January 1994 the statutory retirement age for women was 62 years. The law De329/93 (25 September 1993) established the same retirement age for both men and women. As a consequence women see their age of retirement progressively increased by six months a year until 1999. At that time both genders will retire at the same age. In Italy a definitive retirement age of 65 (men) and 60 (women) must be reached in the beginning of January 2000. In the United Kingdom pensionable age for women will be increased from 60 to 65 between 2010 and 2020. An increase in the retirement age will also be introduced in Austria, but over a slightly longer period than in Belgium, Italy or Portugal. The gradual alignment of old age pensions will take place between 2024 and 2033. The gradual alignment of the early retirement systems (men can currently retire early at

60 and women at 55) will take place between 2019 and 2028.

Table 2.9 shows that the actual retirement age is lower in all European countries than the statutory retirement age. An average of one in four 60–64 year-olds is still working. The numerous mechanisms for early retirement, the schemes for the long-term unemployed and the disability systems are the chief reasons why the actual retirement age is an average of four years lower than the official age. Many of these early retirement mechanisms were set up at the beginning of the 1980s to bring down the surplus on the labour market. For example, Belgium, Denmark, France, Germany, Spain and the United Kingdom operate part-time retirement systems. With the exception of Belgium and Denmark, the part-time function thus released must be filled by an unemployed person.

Early retirement is sometimes possible in Belgium, France, Italy and Luxembourg if redundancies are necessary in certain sectors. This scheme also exists in Germany, but the intention is gradually to scrap it by the year 2001. The minimum ages for eligibility for this special form of early retirement are lower than for normal early retirement, as this exists in Belgium, Denmark, Germany, Italy, Luxembourg and the Netherlands. In Italy and Germany (where early retirement can be taken from 63 for men and 60 for women), the person must have been active on the labour market for a minimum of 35 years. In the Netherlands (early retirement from 61), this minimum is 10 years. At the moment, there is a discussion going on in Italy about the abolition of the early retirement scheme.

In France, the retirement age of 60 is not a compulsory age limit. The right to a pension exists from that age, but if one continues working for longer, the pension will be higher. If someone has not yet reached the maximum pension by the age of 65, an additional 10 per cent is awarded for each additional year worked. In Germany too, an extra 6 per cent is awarded from the age of 65. In Greece, an extra 3.6 per cent is awarded per year worked over the statutory retirement age, in Spain 2 per cent and in the United Kingdom 7.5 per cent (for a maximum of five years). In Luxembourg, a bonus is also awarded to people who work beyond their 65th birthday. However, this bonus is only awarded for a maximum of three years.

By contrast, people in some countries are punished if they want to retire earlier than the statutory retirement age. In Greece, it is possible for men to retire from their sixtieth birthday onwards and for women from their fifty-fifth birthday, but in order to do so they have to forfeit 6 per cent per year. Retirement is possible in Spain from the age of 62, but this involves a loss of pension amounting to 8 per cent per year.

Table 2.9   Retirement age

| | Statutory retirement age, 1996 | | Actual retirement age, 1990 |
	Men	Women	
A	65 (old age pension)	60 (old age pension)	57.9 for men; 56.6 for women
	60 (early retirement)	55 (early retirement)	(exc. civil servants) (1995)
B	65	60	59.3
DK	67	67	62.7
D	65	65	61
GR	65	60	63
E	65	65	62.3
FIN	65	65	59 (estimation)
F	60	60	59.6
IRL	66	66	63.7
I	62	57	61.2
L	65	65	60.1
NL	65	65	60.4
P	65	63	63.9
S	65 (old age pension)	65 (old age pension)	58 (1993/1994)
	60 (early retirement)	60 (early retirement)	
UK	65	60	62.5
N	67	67	61–64 (estimation)

The actual retirement age is calculated as follows:

$$\frac{(P_{55\text{-}59}\text{-}P_{50\text{-}54})*55+(P_{60\text{-}64}\text{-}P_{55\text{-}59})*60+(P_{65\text{-}69}\text{-}P_{60\text{-}64})*65+(P_{70+}\text{-}P_{65\text{-}69})*70+P_{70+}*72}{P_{50\text{-}54}}$$

with P_i equal to the activity rate of the age category i.

Sources: Besseling and Zeeuw, 1993, p. 12; country reports.

The heterogeneity among (early) retirement schemes in Europe is one of the causes – in addition to other factors such as the social security system and socioeconomic factors – of the differences in levels of activity between European countries and of the differences between the actual and the statutory retirement age. Of 50–54 year-olds, approximately 70 per cent are still working; among the 60–64 age group, this is down to 1 in 4. In the Benelux countries and France, this is only 1 in 6.

In Portugal, the United Kingdom, Ireland and Greece, high levels of activity are recorded for 60–64 year-olds. It is not improbable that this is related to the narrow possibilities for early retirement in these four countries.

The average actual retirement age is four years below that which is legally stipulated in most European countries. This inevitably affects the pensions bill.

Belgium scores the lowest in the EU for both men and women. However, caution must be exercised in the mutual country comparison: after all, whether work is full- or part-time is not taken into account when calculating levels of activity.

1.2.2 Third pillar Little if any statistical information can be found at European level about the third pillar. Given the relatively high combined level of benefits from the first and second pillars, this third pillar may be expected to be less well-developed in most European countries.

1.2.3 Income structure of retired households The first pillar is currently the most important source of income for pensioners. Supplementary pensions are clearly more prevalent in countries where the state pension is relatively low.

1.3   Other Elements of Income Support: Cash Benefits and Allowances

Since the focus of the study was on the protection of the dependent elderly, this macro-overview of the income support is completed with certain micro-information on additional cash benefits and allowances related to dependency. That income support for the elderly is not limited to the pension system is also illustrated by the detailed analysis of individual case studies (see chapter 4).

In many countries, income support is accompanied by a rent subsidy system for lower income groups. Rent control could be an alternative: in Portugal a remarkable example is given how this can benefit older persons. Rent subsidies are highly developed in Denmark, the Netherlands and the UK. In some countries there is a highly developed system of social housing, whereas in others home-ownership is encouraged. This also has a positive effect on welfare in old age: house ownership is pension saving (even in a real asset) *avant la lettre*.

In certain countries, additional benefits are provided to older people (and others) with a high degree of dependency. This extra income support is based on the need to offset the additional costs people incur because of their dependency. In some cases, it is specifically intended to be a payment for the main carer. Among other initiatives in this field that are already in operation in some Member States, new initiatives are taken in some countries in the context of long-term care insurance (see below). This increases the theoretical

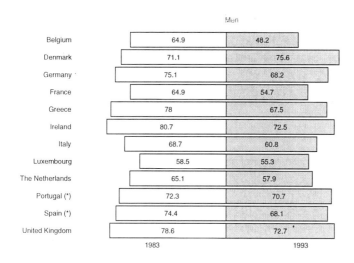

Figure 2.5   Activity rates (%) of men aged 50 and over, 1983 and 1993

Source: S.N., Werken wanneer je ouder bent dan 55, June–July 1996, p. 15.

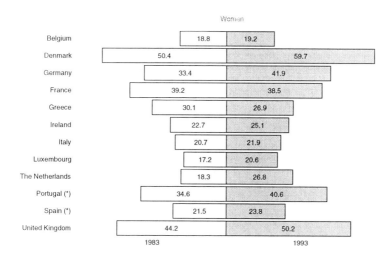

Figure 2.6   Activity rates (%) of women aged 50 and over, EU, 1983 and 1993

Source: S.N., Werken wanneer je ouder bent dan 55, June–July 1996, p. 15.

Table 2.10 The third pillar

	Third pillar	No. of persons covered	Type of plan	Type of benefit	Financing	Taxation
A	Private (voluntary)	*	Defined benefit	Predominantly once-in-lifetime payments	Premiums, capital	Contributions deductible
B	Private (voluntary)					
DK (1995)	Private (voluntary)	1,000,000	Individual	Lump sum/ annuities	Funded	Contributions deductible, pension assets taxed, benefits taxed
D						
GR						
E						
FIN		Not significant				
F						
IRL	Personal pension plans					
I						
L						
NL	Private (voluntary)		Individual	Lump sum/ annuities		Contributions deductible, benefits taxed
P (1995)	Private (voluntary)	112,931	Individual	Lump sum/ annuities	Funded	Contributions deductible from income taxes till 2,099 ECU a year. However, pensions are taxed as income.
S	Personal (private-voluntary) pension plans	200,000 (estimated)	Individual	Lump sum/ annuities	Funded	Contributions deductible, pension assets taxed, benefits taxed
UK						
N (1996)	Private (personal) insurance		Individual	Lump sum/ annuities	Funded	Contributions deductible provided they follow public regulations; benefits taxed

*   In 54% of households with at least one employed person (1.3 million households), at least one person has a life insurance.

Source: country reports.

Table 2.11   Income structure of the retired households (in percentage of total income)

		Salaries, wages[1]	Public pensions, social security and other transfers[2]	Occupational/ private pensions	Savings, investment property	Other
		%	%	%	%	%
A						
B						
DK	1989	6	57	10	12	15
	1993	7	54	22	17	0
	1994	4.2	66.4	19.3	8.4	1.7
D	1989	20	71		9	0
GR						
E	1995	2.8	91.8	1.5	2.4	1.5
FIN	1994	6	76	2	16	
F	1984	6.1	81.5		12.4	0
IRL	1995	5	55	23	3	14
I		0.2	97		1	1
L		5.8	92.8	0	1	0.4
NL	1989	13	52	23	11	0
	1994	17	45	26	12	0
P	1994	24	49	0	5	22
S	1990		76			
UK	1993	6	53	25	16	0
N	1993	3	64	16	15	2

Notes

1   Includes income from self-employment and profits.
2   Includes early retirement allowances.

Sources: Walker, Alber and Guillemard, 1993; country reports.

Table 2.12 Overview of in-cash benefits (payments for care)

	Name	Recipients	Number of beneficiaries	Amount	Conditionalities
A	Pflegegeld	– The dependent person – If staying in old age/nursing home: provider receives 80% of amount – Attendance allowance is frozen if staying in a general hospital for more than 4 weeks	± 250,000 60+	Paid in 7 levels: range between 160–1,600 ECU/month	– Non-means-tested – In need of care for more than 50 hours/month
B	Hulp van derden (Allowance for help from a third person within the framework of an occupational disease or industrial accident)	– The dependent person		13,216 ECU per year (1994)	– Active or has been active as an employee – Needing help from a third person – Having an occupational disease /being disabled – Non-means-tested
	Tegemoetkoming voor hulp aan bejaarden (Allowance for help for older persons) Integratietegemoetkoming	– Older persons who have become disabled before the age of retirement	3% of the elderly in 1992	Max. 2,800 to 4,008 ECU per year (1996)	– Above age of 65+ – Dependency-related – Means-tested
DK					
D	Pflegeleistung in Geld (Aid for persons in need of assistance) Leistung bei schwerer Pflegebedürftigkeit der Gesetzlichen Krankenversicherung Pflegeld (Pflegeversicherung)				– Income-related and means-tested – Income-related and means-tested
GR				Between 200 and 600 ECU/month	– Dependency-related

Table 2.12 cont'd

	Name	Recipients	Number of beneficiaries	Amount	Conditionalities
E	Ayuda tercera persona (Allowance for help for older or handicapped people)				
F	Omaishoidon tuki (home care allowance)	– Payable for carers caring at home		445 ECU/month	– Dependency-related – Dependent person lives at home
	Eläkkeensaajan hoitotuki (pensioner's care allowance)	– Payable to recipients of disability or old age pension, whose functional capacity has diminished due to an illness or injury		Paid in 3 categories	– Dependency-related – Not paid if staying in institutions
F	Allocation compensatrice		124,400 60+ (=60% of beneficiaries) (1992)	Between 311 and 622 ECU/month	– Income-related – Dependency-related
	Allocation pour majoration de tierce personne				
IRL	Carer's allowance	– Designated for carers who live in the same household as the dependent older person		82.5 ECU/week	– Means-tested
I	Payment for care				– Local standards
L	Allocation de soins (AS)	In theory only for persons who keep an elderly dependent person at home, paid to the carer		381 ECU/month (1999: 508 ECU/month)	– Means-tested (income <2.780 ECU/month) – Dependency-related
	Allocation pour personnes gravement handicapées (APGH)	Is accorded to the handicapped person, irrespective of the place where the old person is staying		381 ECU/month (1999: 508 ECU/month)	– Dependency related
	Prestation en espèces (assurance-dépendance) (from 1 January 1999; for people only receiving AS or APGH they have the choice)	Paid to the dependent person but 'ear-marked' to pay for informal or formal help		Maximum 800 ECU/month	– Dependency-related

Table 2.12 cont'd

	Name	Recipients	Number of beneficiaries	Amount	Conditionalities
NL					
P	Payment for care Payment for care	Subsidises the help of a third person Pension supplement for a cohabiting informal carer		51 ECU (1995) 23 ECU (1995)	
S	Care salary – cash – Attendance allowance – Carers allowance – employment	An attendance allowance (not taxed) is paid to the dependent in order to be used as reimbursement for care given by the spouse, the daughter or whatever person actually responsible for the caring. A carer's allowance is the term used for those situations where a family member is employed by the municipality to care for a next of kin. In these cases the payment goes to the carer and is seen as any other remuneration for salaried work (tax-wise, social protection, ...)		Attendance allowance: 141–588 ECU/month	– Dependency-related
UK	Attendance allowance	– Dependent person		Payable at two rates: 39.7 or 59.4 ECU/week	– Non-means-tested – Dependency-related – Not paid if staying for more than 4 weeks in institution
	Severe disability premium	– Dependent person eligible for the attendance allowance		44.6 ECU per week	– Dependency-related – Being eligible for the attendance allowance
	Invalid care allowance	– Payable to people who care for someone who is in receipt of attendance allowance			– Means-tested (carer is not gainfully employed) – Carer is under pensionable age at the time of the first claim – Dependency-related

Table 2.12 cont'd

Name		Recipients	Number of beneficiaries	Amount	Conditionalities
UK (cont'd)	Carer's premium	– For those receiving invalid care allowance, although the person receiving the care will lose any entitlement to a severe disability premium		15.9 ECU per week	Income support (means-tested)
	Regulated Social Fund	– One-off payments for those in receipt of income support			– Additional criteria
	Community Care Grants				– Income support (means-tested)
N	Omsorgslön	– Care salary for relatives	Not earmarked for the elderly, but quite a few of the 'users' are older persons		
	Assistance allowances (to compensate for high expenditures for sickness)		Few apply (±1%)		– Means-tested – Dependency-related

discussion as to whether the further use of (in-cash) benefits should be preferred to the further financing of services. Sometimes mixed forms appear, such as the voucher systems (a cheque for certain services). Related to these forms of additional allowances is the idea of providing substantial support for the informal carer (payment for care, social insurance rights for the main carer) or only in a symbolic way. Another debate concerns the relative advantages of social protection in the form of cash, for instance by means of giving a budget to the dependent person or to a budget-holder.

For some countries we have indications of the relative importance of these categories of income support.

1.4   Summary of the Income Protection Elements

See Table 2.13.

2   Health Expenditures and Services for the Elderly: Macro-information

Apart from the fact that the health care expenditures are only partly related to older persons, the information in the following table gives a first impression of the level and structure of the health expenditures. The highest expenditures related to GDP are found in France, Austria and Germany. The lowest expenditures are found in Greece, Luxembourg, Denmark and the United Kingdom.

Figure 2.7 presents the national income for 1985, 1990 and 1994. The middle income countries among EU-Member States (Greece, Portugal, Spain and Ireland) are now catching up with the rest of Europe. To make the figure more readable, the origin does not start at 0. This influences the picture. The graphic representation using two sub-periods illustrates possible changes of regime.

Studies by the OECD have shown that the higher the (per capita) GDP, the higher the expenditure on health care.[1] For the 27 OECD countries, it has been found that each 10 per cent difference in per capita GDP is associated with a 14 per cent difference in per capita health spending (Schieber and Poullier, 1989). In Figure 2.7, the share of GDP spent on health care is also shown. Most EU Member States spend similar proportions of their national income on health, but the Scandinavian countries and Bismarck-oriented welfare states such as Germany, France and Belgium also have a higher expenditure.

Table 2.13 Income and cash benefits

Type	A	B	DK	D	GR	E
1 Income						
1.1 *Legal pension* General old age pension	Gesetzliche Pensions-versicherung (ASVG/GSVG) (1.840.047 recipients; 1995) Normale Alterspension (912,048 recipients; 1995) Witwer-/Witwenpensionen (479,094 recipients; 1995)	Rustpensioen Overlevingspensioen	Folkepension (88,620 DKK (1995))	Statutory Pension (Gesetzliche Pensionsversicherung)	+ (old age pension)	Pensión Contributiva
Personal allowance			Personlige tillaeg	Subsistence aid		
1.2 *Occupational welfare* Pension funds	Betriebspension (78,676 recipients; 1995)	Pensioenfondsen	ATP (up to 13,600 DKK (1995)) Occupational pension Civil servants' pension	Betriebliche Vorsorge Large variety of schemes		+
Group insurance		Groepsverzekering		Group insurance		
1.3 *Guaranteed minimum income for elderly*	Ausgleichszulage (273,153 recipients; 1995)	Gewaarborgd minimum inkomen voor bejaarden			+ (public assistance pension)	Pensión no Contributiva Pensión asistencial
2 Private life insurance Individual retirement account	Private Lebensversicherung	Private levensverzekering Pensioensparen (Pension savings)	Private pension	Private Vorsorge		+
3 Other in-cash benefits Payment for care	Pflegegeld (± 250,000 recipients (60+); 1995) Sozialhilfe	Hulp van derden (bij beroepsziekten en arbeidsongevallen); Tegemoetkoming voor hulp aan bejaarden; Integratietegemoet-koming		Pflegeleistung in Geld Leistung bei schwerer Pflegebedürftigkeit der Gesetzlichen Krankenversicherung		Ayuda tercera persona

Table 2.13 cont'd

Type	A	B	DK	D	GR	E
3 Other in-cash benefits (cont'd)						
Housing subsidy		Huursubsidies Zakgeld	Boligydelse	+		
'Pocket money'		+				
4 Fiscal expenditures				+		Desgravación fiscal

Type	FIN	F	IR	I	L
1 Income					
1.1 Legal pension General old age pension	kansaneläke (national pension) työeläke (employment pension)	Pension de Retraite	Old age contributory pension/retirement pension; Early retirement or baby-pensions	Pensione minima Pensione da lavoro o di riversibilita	Assurance-pension
Personal allowance					
1.2 Occupational welfare Pension funds Group insurance			Occupational pension schemes	Occupational pension schemes	Régimes complémentaires volontaires (externe et interne)
1.3 Guaranteed minimum income for elderly	viimesijainen toimeentulotuki	Minimum vieillesse	Income support/ noncontributory old age pension	Pensione sociale	Revenu minimum garanti
2 Private life insurance	henkivakuutus	Assurance-vie et PEP		Assicurazioni privati	
Individual retirement account	eläkesäästäminen		Personal pension schemes		
3 Other in-cash benefits (cont'd) Payment for care	omaishoidon tuki eläkkeensaajan hoitotuki	Allocation compensatrice (1992: 124,400 personnes 60+ = 60% des bénéficiaires) Allocation pour majoration de tierce personne	Carer's allowance	Assegno di accompagnamento	Allocation de soins Allocation pour personnes gravement handicapées

Table 2.13 cont'd

Type	FIN	F	IRL	I	L
3 Other in-cash benefits (cont'd)					
Housing subsidy	eläkkeensaajan asumistuki	Aide au logement (Allocation logement à caractère familial, allocation de logement sociale et aide personnalisée au logement)	Fuel allowance	Payment for housing problems	
'Pocket money'	'Pocket money'		Pocket money	Pocket money	Argent de poche en institutions pour personnes âgées
4 Fiscal expenditures		Abattements et réductions fiscaux (3,5 billion ECU, rapport Schopflin, 1991)			Abattements

Type	NL	P	S	UK	N
1 Income					
1.1 Legal pension					
General old age pension	General Old Age Pension Act (AOW)	Pensao de Reforma Pensao de Invalidez Pensao de Sobrevivência	Old age pension – basic (flat rate) – supplementary (earnings-related)	State retirement pension Widow's pension	Old age pension – basic (flat rate) – supplementary (earnings-related)
Personal allowance	Additional private pension				
1.2 Occupational welfare					
Pension funds	Numerous private funds for – Pension funds for industrial branches (n = 72) – Enterprise pension funds – Civil servants pension fund – Military pension fund – Railway pension fund – Pension fund of professionals	Pension funds	Occupational pensions – state employees – local government – private sector	Occupational pensions Private pensions	Occupational pensions for state employees, local government employees and for private sector
Group insurance	Group insurance	Group insurance			

Table 2.13 cont'd

Type	NL	P	S	UK	N
1.3 Guaranteed minimum income for elderly	Guaranteed standard minimum income	Pensao Social de Reforma Pensao Social de Invalidez Pensao Social de Sobrevivência			Income support
2 Private life insurance Individual retirement account	Lijfrentepolissen	+	Private pension insurance	Numerous private schemes in existence	Individual (private) pension insurance
3 Other in-cash benefits Payment for care		+	Care salary – cash (Attendance allowance, carer's allowance) – employment Housing allowance	Attendance Allowance	Omsorgslönn (Care salary for relatives)/Assistance allowances (to compensate for high expenditures for care/sickness) Housing allowance
Housing subsidy	Individuele huursubsidie (IHS)	Rent subsidy Substantial rent control for the elderly		Housing benefit/Council tax benefit/Regulated Social Fund. Cold Weather Payments and Community Care Grants	
'Pocket money' **4 Fiscal expenditures**		+ IRS			

Table 2.14 Health care expenditures and health care consumption, coverage of population and cost sharing

| | Health expenditures | | | | Social protection, ambulatory care consumption | | | | Social protection, inpatient care consumption | | | | Social protection, pharmaceutical consumption | | | |
| | Total expend. (%GDP) | | Public expend. (%GDP) | | Coverage[1] | | Cost sharing[2] | | Coverage[1] | | Cost sharing[2] | | Coverage[1] | | Cost sharing[2] | |
	1991	1995	1991	1995	1991	1995	1991	1995	1991	1995	1991	1995	1991	1995	1991	1995
A	8.5	9.6	5.6	6.2 (1994)	99	99	80	80	99	99	90	90	99	99	50	49
B	8	8	7.1	7	94	94	78	75	99	99	95	92	94	94	52	50
DK	6.5	6.5	5.5	5.4 (1994)	100	100	78	78	100	100	100	100	100	100	45	45
D	9	9.6	6.6	7	92.2	92.2	90	90	92.2	92.2	98	98	92.2	92.2	50	48
GR	4.3	5.2 (1994)	3.3	3.5 (1993)	100	100	85	85	100	100	95	95	100	100	75	74
E	7.1	7.6	5.6	6	99	99.3			99	99.3	82	82	99	99.3	77	75
FIN	9.1	8.2	7.4	6.2 (1994)	100	100	91	90	100	100	82	82	100	100	46	45
F	9.1	9.9	6.8	7.8	98	98	59.5	57	99.5	99.5	91.9	92	98	98	57	54
IRL	7	7.9 (1994)	5.4	6 (1994)	37	36.2	100	100	100	100	95	95	40	40	62	61
I	8.4	7.7	6.6	5.4	100	100	73	73	100	100	85	85	100	100	66	65
L	6.2	5.8 (1994)	6	6.2 (1993)	100	100	88	88	100	100	90	90	100	100	84	84
NL	8.6	8.8	6.4	6.8	72.2	73.3	66.1	65.1	72.7	73.7	80.8	82	61.3	100	66.7	90.2
P	7.1	7.6 (1994)	3.9	4.3 (1994)	100	100	100	100	100	100	100	100	100	100	67	65
S	8.4	7.7	7.5	7.4	100	100	80.3	73.8	100	100	99.7	98	100	100	71.7	69.8
UK	6.5	6.9	5.4	5.8 (1994)	100	100	88	88	100	100	99	99	100	100	91	90
N	7.2	7.3 (1994)	6.8	6.9 (1994)	100	100			100	100	100	100	100	100	60	58

Notes

1 Coverage rate: percentage of population entitled to the benefits of a public scheme (for countries without a census of the covered population, this is an estimate based on an institutional description of the various schemes in force)

2 Cost sharing: estimate of the average or typical share of medical bills or pharmaceutical consumption paid for by a public scheme. Both the nomenclature of medical services and the list of medicines include several hundreds entries; the weighted value of the users' co-payment for services delivered by a public system and of the reimbursements made is not available in most countries. The rates shown are crude estimates.

Source: OECD Health Data 1996.

Table 2.15   Total health expenditures, value per capita

	Total health expenditures, value per capita, current prices (ECU), 1994	% health expenditures for older people	Health expenditures in ECU per older person
A	2,037	±50% (1991 and 1995): very rough estimate	±1,000 (1991); ±1,300 (1994): very rough estimate
B	1,570	31.3 (1987)	2,531 (1987)
DK	1,613	32.5 (1987); 44 (1994) (60+)	2,772 (1993); 2,595 (1994) (60+)
D	2,026		
GR	387		
E	758	40	1,920
FIN	1,446	37.9 (1990)	65-74: 2,567 (1990) 75+: 5,034 (1990)
F	1,898	40.4 (for the 60+) (1989)	2,687 (for the 60+) (1989) 3,068 (for the 80+) (1991)
IRL	976	30 (1993) (estimated)	1,946 (1993) (estimated)
I	1,244		
L	1,729		
NL	1,634	± 40 (1987)	
P	568		
S	1,572	45 (1995)	
UK	964	47 (1987)	2,802 (1992–94)
N	1,787	45 (1994) (estimated)	

Sources: OECD Health Data 1996; country reports.

Ireland has an unexpectedly high level of expenditure (it is poorer and younger). In the other Member States, the younger or poorer countries (Greece for instance) have a lower expenditure. Over the years, all countries have experienced growing percentages of total health care spending per capita. Luxembourg, Ireland and Sweden did have a lower percentage in 1994 compared to 1985. However, we must also bear in mind that definitions of 'health care spending' may have changed between 1985 and 1994.

Relating to the question of 'Has there been a change in regime in the health expenditures?', Figure 2.7 is very illustrative. The arrows show the evolution of income per capita and total health care expenditures in 1985. The breaking point is 1990 and the end point is 1994. Ireland and Sweden are the only countries that cut their public health care spending between 1985 and 1990. Since 1990, Ireland has again expanded its expenditure on health care. Although the cost containment ideology is present in most of the health insurance schemes, expenditure on health care continued to increase in most countries, although with some convergence trend (the richer countries grew more slowly than the poorer, which were attempting to catch up with the more wealthy countries). One point of reference for those health care expenditures at the highest extreme of the spectrum is the high level of expenditures in the USA. This system can be characterised by a decade already of debate on cost containment, the introduction of HMOs, managed care and similar strategies to realise such cost containments. This was unable to prevent the expenditures in the USA from being the highest of the OECD-countries, having increased the most in recent decade (increase from 10.7 per cent to 14.2 per cent of GDP from 1985 to 1995). The European expenditures remain lower and deliver better protection than the US system.

To conclude this paragraph about health expenditures, the Figure 2.8 gives detailed information about the level and structure of the health expenditures in 16 European countries. The total expenditures, represented as the share of GDP spent on health care, are divided into public and private expenditures.

3 Summary of the Macro-characteristics of the Social Protection Systems

Table 2.16 aims to give a summary overview for each country of the main characteristics of social protection. These characteristics are only given as context variables, as there exists already a huge number of studies on pension and health care systems and on the general evolution of social expenditures (for older persons).

The level of social protection in the countries under consideration is reflected in the volume of public expenditure on this sector as a percentage of GDP. Expenditures on social protection are divided into three main categories: expenditures on pensions, public health care expenditures for the total population and for older people, and social expenditures for the elderly. In addition to relative figures on these expenditures, the amounts spent per year in ECU can also be found in Table 2.16. We see in the table that the bulk of public expenditure is earmarked for pensions and health care. In some countries, this expenditure is as high as 20 per cent of GDP. The major social expenditures related to dependency are situated in the health insurance.

The distinction between in-kind and in-cash aid may provide us with another angle from which to examine the welfare state. The Netherlands and – to a lesser degree – Belgium, Germany and France have more cash-oriented welfare systems. The UK and Ireland are more services-oriented. This

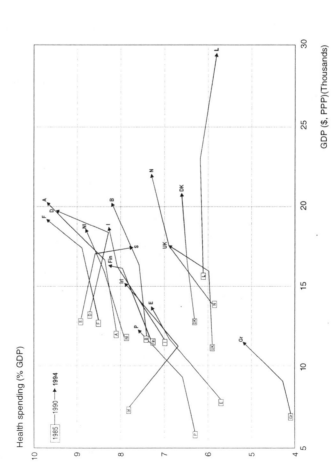

Figure 2.7   Relationship between health expenditure (as % of GDP) and GDP (in $, PPP) per capita for the OECD countries, 1985–1990–1994

Source: OECD Health Data, 1996.

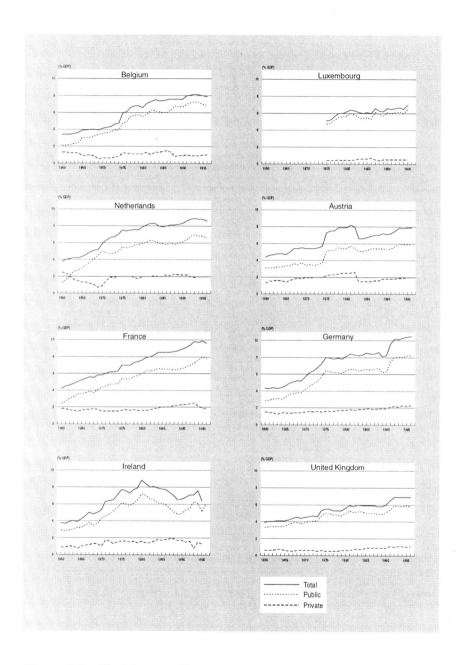

Figure 2.8   Health expenditure as a percentage of GDP, 1960–96
Source: OECD Health Data.

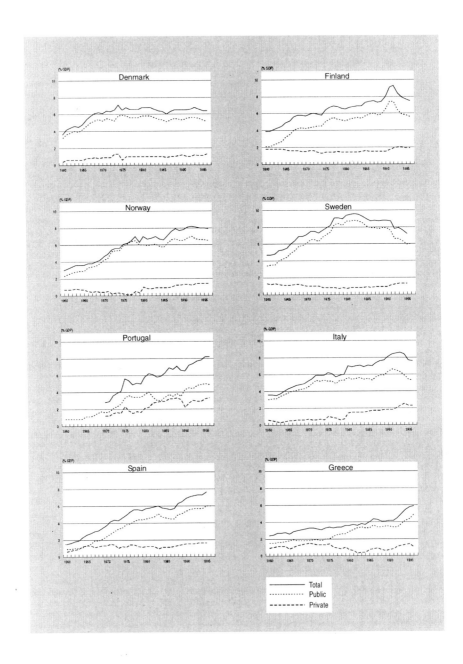

Figure 2.8   cont'd

distinction in systems, which is illustrated in the detailed analysis of the social protection systems, can influence the direction taken by new proposals.

Information on pensions is extended to the 'second pillar': What proportion of the population is covered by the 'second pillar', and what amount of assets does this 'second pillar' represent? Finally, we have tried to give a typology of the pension system in each country. This extra macro-information on pensions is only meant to maintain the complete scope of the social protection system for the (dependent) elderly.

Note

1   This does not mean that income (per capita GDP) is the only factor that influences per capita health care spending. The country's health care funding system is another very important factor.

Table 2.16   Macro-characteristics of social protection in old age, 1995

	A	B	DK	D	GR	E
GDP, value per capita (1994, ECU)	20,979	19,168	24,620	21,385	7,476	10,384
Ageing						
% population over 65	15.1	15.8	15.1 (1996)	15.4	14.8 (1993)	14.8 (1994)
Pensions						
Retirement age	65/60	65/60	67/67	65/65	65/60	65/65
Orientation of pension system	Bismarck Large Public	Bismarck Large Public	Beveridge Basic Public	Bismarck Large Public	Bismarck Large Public	Bismarck Large Public
Total pension benefits (old age + survivor) as % of GDP	15.5	9.10 (1994)	10.02 (including early retirement and supplementary schemes)	12.2 (1994) (including supplementary schemes)	10.2 (1994) (including supplementary schemes)	11.10
Pension per older person (in ECU)	16,281	11,227 (1994)	9,913 (public old age pension)	8,707 (1987)	5,169 (1994) (including supplementary schemes)	5,425
Net replacement ratio	75% (employees)	63% (1993)	86% (incl. occupational pensions)	69% (1989)	114% (1989)	98% (1989)
Assets of second pillar: % of GDP	0.05 (1993)	21.2	52 (1991)	23.4	7 (1991)	6 (1991)
Coverage of second pillar (% of labour force)	6.3 (1993)	31 (private sector, 1996)	51.5 (compulsory occupational) 7.9 (civil servants)	46	5	15
Health						
Public health expenditures as a % of GDP	5.9	7	5.3	8.2	4.4	6
% of public health expenditures for population over 65	±50	31.3 (1987)	44 (1994) (60+)			40
Public health expenditures for population over 65 as % of GDP	2.9	2 (1987)	2.4 (1994) (60+)			2.6
Social expenditures for population over 65 in million ECU		318[1] (1993)	2,309 (60+) (1993)	4.963 (1990)		

Table 2.16 cont'd

	A	B	DK	D	GR	E	FIN	F	IRL	I	L
Social expenditures for population over 65 as % of GDP		0.19[1] (1993)	2.0 (60+) (1993)	0.40 (1990)							
Orientation of care system	Bismarck Cash oriented	Bismarck Limited cash oriented / Service oriented	Beveridge / Service oriented	Bismarck More cash oriented / Limited service oriented	Bismarck Cash oriented	Bismarck Cash oriented					
	Universal	Universal Limited means-tested	Universal	Universal Relatively underdeveloped	Universal	Universal					
GDP, value per capita (1994, ECU)							17,446	19,493	12,351	14,907	30,011
Ageing — % population over 65							14.3	14.7 (1994)	11.5 (1994)	16.4	14.3 (1991)
Pensions — Retirement age							65/65	60/60	66/66	62/57	65/65
Orientation of pension system							Bismarck Large Public	Bismarck Large Public	Beveridge Basic Public	Bismarck Large Public	Bismarck Large Public
Total pension benefits (old age + survivor) as a % of GDP							7.9 (1994)	12.2 (1994)	2.74	15.7	11 (1994) (including supplementary schemes)
Pension per older person (in ECU)							9,502 (1994)	10,952 (1993)	5,430	14,333 (1994) (including supplementary schemes)	15,276 (for men); 8,149 (for women)
Net replacement ratio							60% (1993)	80% (1993)	64% (1989)	92% (1989)	70 to 100% (private sector)
Assets of second pillar: % of GDP								28.7	71 (1991)	2 (1991)	

Table 2.16 cont'd

	FIN	F	IRL	I	L
Coverage of second pillar (% of labour force)	15	90	46	5	35 (private sector)
Health					
Public health expenditures as a % of GDP	5.8 (1990)	8	5.1	5.4	6.5
% of public health expenditures for population over 65	37.9 (1990)	40.4 (1989) (60+)	30 (1993)		
Public health expenditures for population over 65 as % of GDP	2.4 (1990)	2.6 (1989) (60+)	1.9 (1993)		
Social expenditures for population over 65 in million ECU	973	1,364 (1989)			
Social expenditures for population over 65 as % of GDP	1.03	0.15 (1989)			
Orientation of care system	Beveridge Universal Income-related	Bismarck More cash oriented Service oriented Universal Underdeveloped	Beveridge Service oriented Universal Income-related and means-tested	Bismarck Cash oriented Universal	Bismarck More cash oriented Service oriented Universal Limited means-tested

	NL	P	S	UK	N
GDP, value per capita (1994, ECU)	18,487	7,456	20,326	13,984	24,493
Ageing					
% population over 65	13.1 (1994)	14.8	17.4 (1994)	15.7 (1994)	15.9 (1996)
Pensions					
Retirement age	65/65	65/65	65/65	65/60	67/67
Orientation of pension system	Beveridge Basic Public	Bismarck Large Public	Beveridge Basic Public	Beveridge Basic Public	Beveridge Basic Public

Table 2.16 cont'd

	NL	P	S	UK	N
Total pension benefits (old age + survivor) as a % of GDP	11.4 (1994) (including supplementary schemes)	7.2	8	10.4 (1993) (including supplementary schemes)	6.2
Pension per older person (1987, in ECU)	8,784 (1994)	2,082	10,062	3,852	10,054 (including state occupational pensions)
Net replacement rate of first and second tier pensions	77%	Maximum 80%	70% (1989)	57%	54% (incl. national supplementary pension)
Assets of second pillar: % of GDP	141.5	8 (1991)		145.9	
Coverage of second pillar (% of labour force)	85 (1994)	<5% of white collar workers	83.5	48	Nearly 100% (public) About 40% (private)
Health					
Public health expenditures as a % of GDP	6.8	5	5.9	5.9	6.6
% of public health expenditures for population over 65	40 (1987)		45	47 (1987)	45 (1994)
Public health expenditures for population over 65 as % of GDP	2.4 (1987)		2.7	2.3 (1987)	2.9 (1994)
Social expenditures for population over 65 in million ECU	3,725 (1991)[2]			1,946[3] (1987–88)	
Social expenditures for population over 65 as % of GDP	1.52 (1991)			0.3	
Orientation of care system	Bismarck More cash oriented Universal Means-tested and income-related	Bismarck Cash oriented Universal	Beveridge Service oriented Universal Income-related	Beveridge Service oriented Universal Means-tested and income-related	Beveridge Universal Income-related

Table 2.16 cont'd

Notes

1   Only Flanders.
2   Includes old age homes and home help services.
3   Includes residential care, day care and home care.

Sources: country reports; OECD Health Data, 1997; Bouten and Pacolet, 1998; European Commission, 1997.

3 The Variety, Scope and Coverage of Health and Social Services for the Elderly: the Welfare Pluralism

In this chapter we deal with the scope and variety of the care mix for the elderly. This constitutes the social quality of our welfare state. But quantity goes before quality. The first aspect even considered in studies on quality of services is the availability of services, the number of places and the number of caring personnel, etc. The second aspect should be affordability, the cost for the elderly. However, it is impossible to go into detail, and it is even impossible to characterise the 50 services or institutions in each Member State as being more oriented in this or that direction. For instance, is the welfare state in the Mediterranean countries more oriented to informal care than other countries when in some central or Nordic welfare states several schemes of payment for the informal care are present? The intention of the following discussion is to synthesise the information collected from the national reports and to allow the facts and figures to reveal the welfare pluralism of the European Union.

It is remarkable that the innovation and emergence of new systems has occurred particularly in the field of care for the elderly. This will probably evolve in the direction of private solutions. The question is how to maintain the level of provision and how to fill in certain remaining gaps.

1 Variety

For the services we were able to define, based on the systems present in each country, eight categories of permanent residential and semi-residential services, 17 temporary residential and semi-residential services, and no less than 22 community services. This illustrates the fact that the latter sector is the most diversified and has been the subject of the greatest amount of innovation during the last decade. However, social protection also includes more intangible aspects such as charters of rights for the elderly, the right of representation, the right of appeal, protection against fraud and misuse, the right of self-determination of care, and the right of determination of care by the family and advisory bodies. Informal care, which is the most important in quantity (four to five times as important as formal care in number of hours) and of course in quality, is also becoming more and more formalised, a fact which leads to certain implications, such as the obligation to help, payment for care, and the care contract or care plans.

The maturity of the welfare state is not only illustrated by the level of social expenditure but also by its diversity.

One problem which occurs immediately is the gathering of comparable data. Although this report is already a third exercise in collecting comparative data on services for the elderly and we tried insofar as possible to harmonise definitions, categories and characteristics, the problem remains the lack of data. This should be one of the first conclusions of this report: the commitment to collect unidimensional data on output, financing and clients of social and health services (for the elderly and others).

The following tables indicate whether or not a certain 'service' exists in the countries under consideration – in some cases with a long tradition, and in other cases as a new, emerging and innovative service. A special remark has to be added to Table 3.1, and to all the graphs and tables collecting figures on residential and semi-residential services. We added several forms of housing (e.g. sheltered housing) to the group residential and semi-residential services, although in several countries (e.g. the Nordic countries) (sheltered) housing was a system created in a strategy of de-institutionalisation. The underlying motivation for the inclusion is that this housing includes some care or permanence, and for that reason becomes institutional.

2   Availability

We have categorised a selected list of services for the elderly: permanent and temporary residential and semi-residential services, and community services. The figures are not complete, although for several countries it is already the third similar exercise (Nijkamp, Pacolet and Spinnewyn, 1991; Pacolet, Versieck and Bouten, 1994; Pacolet, Bouten, Lanoye and Versieck, 1999). In Figures 3.8 and 3.9 we compare some of the earlier results with the recent

Table 3.1   Availability of permanent residential and semi-residential services for the elderly

Type	A	B	DK	D	GR	E	FIN	F	IRL	I	L	NL	P	S	UK	N
1 Nursing homes	+	+	+	+		+	+	+	+	e	+	+	+	+	+	+
2 Psychiatric nursing homes	+	+	+	+		+	+	+	+		+	+	+	+	+	+
3 Housing for the disabled	+	+	e		+		+					e		+		+
4 Old age homes	+	+		+	+	+	+	+	+	+	+	+	+	+	+	+
5 Multilevel homes for the elderly		+	+	+						+			e	+	+	
6 Sheltered housing	e	+	+			+	+	+	+	+	+	+	e		+	+
7 Service flats	e	+				+	+	+	+	+	+	+	+	e	+	+
8 Innovative services	e	e					+	e			e	e	e	e	+	+

+   service exists

e   service is emerging

Table 3.2   Availability of temporary residential and semi-residential services for the elderly

Type	A	B	DK	D	GR	E	FIN	F	IRL	I	L	NL	P	S	UK	N
1 General hospitals	+	+	+		+		+		+	+		+	+	+	+	+
2 Geriatric units in general hospitals	+	+	+	+			+		+	+		+		+	+	+
3 Long stay wards in general hospitals		+				+	+		+	+						
4 Medium stay wards in general hospitals								+	+							
5 Psychiatric wards in general hospitals	+	+	+				+	+	+	+		+			+	
6 Geriatric hospitals	+	+		+		+	+	+	+	+				+	+	+
7 Psychiatric hospitals	+	+	+			+	+		+	+		+		+	+	
8 Psycho-geriatric wards in mental hospitals		+					+		+		+	+			+	
9 Rehabilitation homes	+	+				+	+		+	+		+				
10 Short-term nursing homes		+	+	+		+	+	+	+	+	+	+		+	+	
11 Short stay in old age homes	e	+		+		+	+	+	+	+	+	+	+	+	+	+
12 Geriatric day hospital	e	+		+		+	+	+	+	+	+	+		+	+	+
13 Day care	e	+	+	e		+	+	+	+	+	+	e	+	+	+	
14 Nightly care in old age homes		+	+			+	+		+			e	e	+	+	
15 Social centres for the elderly	e	+	+	+	+	+	+	+				+	+	+	+	+
16 Innovative services	e						+	e					e	e	e	
17 Preventive services							+								+	

+   service exists

e   service is emerging

Table 3.3   Availability of community services for the elderly

Type		A	B	DK	D	GR	E	FIN	F	IRL	I	L	NL	P	S	UK	N
1	District nursing	+	+	+	+	+	+	+	+	+	+	+	+	+		+	+
2	Paramedical care	+	+	+		+		+	+	+	+		+	+	+	+	+
3	Mental health services	+	+				+	+		+	+		+		+	+	+
4	Health advisory services and health education	+	+		+	+	+	+	+	+	+		+			+	+
5	Social work	+	+	+		+	+	+	+	+	+		+	+	+	+	+
6	Home help services	+	+	+	+	+	+	+	+	+	+	+	+	+	+	+	+
7	Cleaning services	+	+	+			+	+	e	+	+		+		+	+	
8	Odd job services	+	+	+				+	e	+	+		+		+		+
9	Domestic help	+	+			+	+	+	e	+	+	+	+	+	+	+	
10	Meal distribution	+	+	+	+	+		+	e	+	+	+	+	+	+	+	+
11	Foyer restaurant		+	+	+		+	+	e	+	+	+	+	+	+	+	+
12	Transport services	+	e	+			+	+	e	+	+	+	+	+	+	+	+
13	Care of terminally ill relatives		e	+			+	+	e	+	+				+	+	+
14	Family placement		e		+		e	+	e	+	+			+		+	
15	Sitting/respite services	+	e	+			+	+	e	+	+	+	+		+	+	+
16	Housing for pensioners	+	+	+			e	+	e	+	+	+	+	+	+	+	+
17	Home improvements	+	+	+		+	e	+	+	+	+	+	+		+	+	+
18	Tele-alarm and tele-communication services	+	+	+	+		e	+	+	+	+	+	+		+	+	+
19	Aids, facilities: technical aids; telephone; purchase of wheelchair	+	+	+			+	+	e			+	+		+	+	+
20	Social benefits and other initiatives	+	+				+	+								+	+
21	Other innovative services		e		e		e	+	e		e		+	+	+	+	
22	Preventive services or activities			+	+		e	+								+	+

+   service exists

e   service is emerging

information. We display here in the first place quantitative figures because they are what really matter: they illustrate the availability of services. We then focus on some aspects. There are countries with well developed services, such as the high levels of permanent residential and semi-residential services in Denmark, the Netherlands, Norway and the UK. Some countries have better organised housing for the elderly or housing for pensioners, such as the UK and the Netherlands (see also Figure 3.10).

Medium levels of places can be found in Austria, Belgium, Germany, Finland, France, Ireland, Luxembourg and Sweden. The third group is the Mediterranean countries where care by the family is culturally favoured, but at the same time determined by lower public spending for those facilities. Residential facilities are still rather scarce in countries like Greece, Spain, Italy and Portugal, i.e. in countries where many families are involved in the care for the elderly.

On top of this some countries with an already high level of permanent residential and semi-residential places developed temporary residential services (especially the UK, Austria, Finland and the Netherlands) (see Figure 3.5).

To quote some of the extremes: the number of available beds in nursing homes differs from 1.22 places per 100 persons of 65+ in Belgium to 4.7 in Norway. Some countries continue to rely on traditional old-age homes (see figure 3.3). The numbers of living units in old-age homes may differ from none in Denmark to 6.48 places per 100 65-plusers in Belgium. In previous years, some other countries, such as the Netherlands, were much more oriented towards institutional care, and so in one decade the relative position of a country can shift. However, changes are slow and not always in the expected direction: the number of residential units in the Netherlands remains high, even after years of stimulating de-institutionalisation. In Belgium, the number of residential units increased substantially, even during a period of increasing support for the idea of community care. Most situations remain unchanged, however, or they change because other categories are included in the overview.

Another extreme of the care continuum is community care. The intensity of community care is defined by number of personnel per 100 65-plusers. The highest intensity is found in the Scandinavian countries. The personnel in district nursing varies in terms of the number of personnel per 100 elderly from almost none in Sweden to 1.5 home nurses per 100 persons in France above 65 years of age. The number of personnel for home help and house cleaning varies from around one person per 100 65-plusers to more than seven in Sweden, but in many other countries it ranges from 1.5 to 2 per 100 elderly persons above age 65. The fact that for some countries only one category of personnel is used illustrates again the fading borderline between the two forms, i.e. the despecialisation or integration in the sector (see Figure 3.6). In Sweden all the community care personnel are qualified as home help. In France, home help is called 'social work', but by this is meant personnel from the social sector (as opposed to the health sector). In Denmark, all the personnel are categorised under 'social' (work), regrouping all the other categories but also including persons working in residential services. Hence the figure over-estimates the community care in that country. It illustrates that the borderline between residential and community care has disappeared since the services are provided by the same (local) 'operator'.

In Figures 3.1 to 3.9 we give some information on the quantitative availability and the actual utilisation of a selected list of services (see figures also in Table 3.4).

A wide variety of services for the elderly and a growing 'market' of care provisions for older persons may be observed in the 16 countries.

Some Member States continue to have more places in residential care than community care. This is the case in Belgium, France, Luxembourg, the Netherlands and Norway.

Permanent residential and semi-residential services are generally available in all the countries. It should be noted that in some countries the large number of 'integrated (independent) housing accommodations and care facilities', which are of a permanent but mostly semi-residential character, are coming more and more to replace the purely residential services. This innovation is in different stages of development in the different countries. In Denmark, for instance, it has been important since 1988. In Belgium (Flanders) a special programme was launched in 1991 and again in 1995. It is an important issue in the most recent report in the Netherlands on policy relating to the elderly. In France there are a significant number of experiments under way in this sector. This type of service has been developed in Norway in recent years and service flats are a rather innovative housing opportunity for the elderly in Austria.

The integration of all kinds of residential services in one grouped setting also seems to growing in importance. It is explicitly mentioned in the 'multilevel homes' (*Mehrgliedrige Einrichtungen*) category in Germany, but the trend towards this type can also be observed elsewhere.

The opposite trend can be observed in the degree of medicalisation of services. The purely medical services are coming more and more to be classified as temporary services, although in some countries significant groups of services are still available on a long-term basis.

We have classified the spaces in general hospitals under 'temporary provisions'. In the traditional permanent residential services for the elderly there is a reverse evolution taking place in comparison with the health sector. The places are becoming more medicalised, or at least the need to move in that direction is being observed. This can be caused by three elements: first, the ageing of the population implies an ageing of the residents in these services; secondly, the tendency to stay longer at home means that there is an acceleration of the dependency of the residents in the services because the elderly are older and more dependent when they leave their home to enter an institution; finally, there is a flow of dependent elderly persons from health services to old-age services.

The overview of the temporary residential and semi-residential services relates primarily to the short-term provisions in general hospitals, psychiatric hospitals and geriatric institutions. Innovations in all these institutions include the provision of day and night care and, in many countries, the temporary relief of the informal carer. Although these tables do not give a dynamic picture of the care supply, they do illustrate the emerging importance of certain systems just by virtue of the fact that they are mentioned more often.

The list of community services can be even longer because it is here that the most innovations have emerged. This reflects the recent attention being given to home care, which is not only a political priority, but is also attracting the attention of numerous service providers and associations. However, not all these initiatives are equally representative. The basic services are present in the 16 countries. The new services include odd job services in particular, several aspects of transport and telecommunication, family placement and sitting services, a number of social benefits and initiatives to improve the quality of life of the elderly and to promote their integration into society.

Table 3.4 contains the data on which the above graphs are based. The reasons why the level of services differ from country to country may be due to different factors: difference in intensity of care, difference of quality, different eligibility criteria, regional differences, etc. We have partial evidence that regional disparity is increasing, so that the regional factor is becoming an important discriminating factor in the provision of in kind (in cash) support.

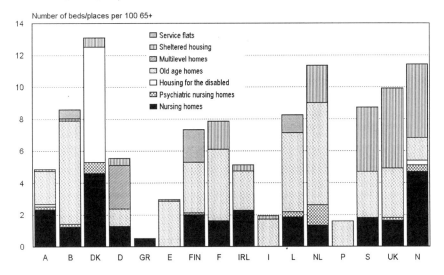

Note: This graph is based on the figures in Table 3.4, therefore remarks accompanying this table should be kept in mind when interpreting this graph. The number of places in sheltered housing in Ireland is underestimated: data are from 1986. Since then significant building has occurred in voluntary housing.

Figure 3.1 Availability of a selected list of permanent residential and semi-residential services for the elderly

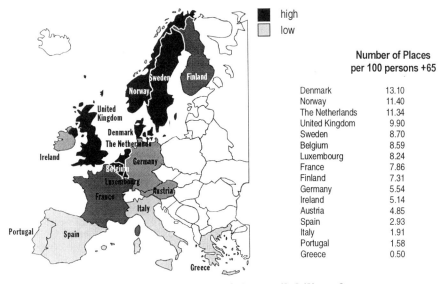

| high | | |
| low | | |

Number of Places per 100 persons +65	
Denmark	13.10
Norway	11.40
The Netherlands	11.34
United Kingdom	9.90
Sweden	8.70
Belgium	8.59
Luxembourg	8.24
France	7.86
Finland	7.31
Germany	5.54
Ireland	5.14
Austria	4.85
Spain	2.93
Italy	1.91
Portugal	1.58
Greece	0.50

Figure 3.2 Geographical overview of the availability of permanent residential and semi-residential services for the elderly

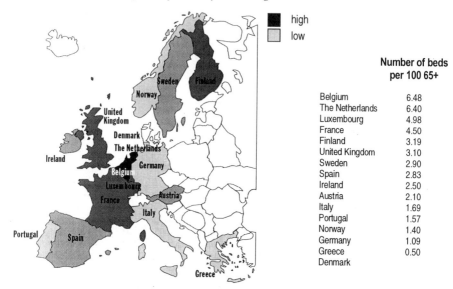

	Number of beds per 100 65+
Belgium	6.48
The Netherlands	6.40
Luxembourg	4.98
France	4.50
Finland	3.19
United Kingdom	3.10
Sweden	2.90
Spain	2.83
Ireland	2.50
Austria	2.10
Italy	1.69
Portugal	1.57
Norway	1.40
Germany	1.09
Greece	0.50
Denmark	

Figure 3.3   Geographical overview of the number of places in old-age homes (per 100 65+)

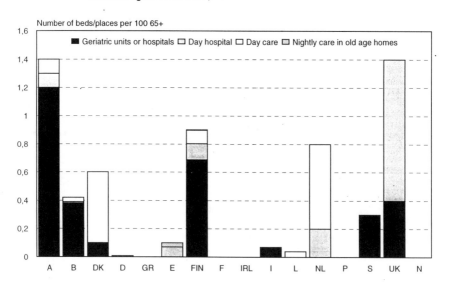

Note: This graph is based on the figures in Table 3.4, therefore remarks accompanying this table should be kept in mind when interpreting this graph.

Figure 3.4   Availability of a selected list of temporary services for the elderly

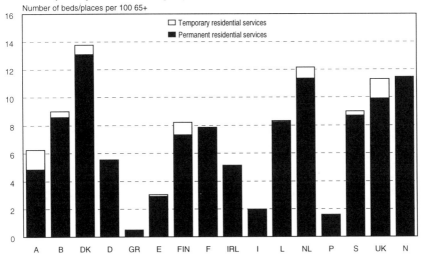

Note: This graph is based on the figures in Table 3.4, therefore remarks accompanying this table should be kept in mind when interpreting this graph. Number of places in sheltered housing in Ireland is underestimated: data are from 1986. Since then significant building has occurred in voluntary housing.

Figure 3.5   Availability of permanent and temporary services for the elderly

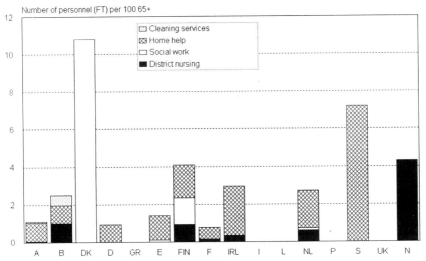

Note: This graph is based on the figures in Table 3.4, therefore remarks accompanying this table should be kept in mind when interpreting this graph.

Figure 3.6   Availability of a selected list of community services for the elderly

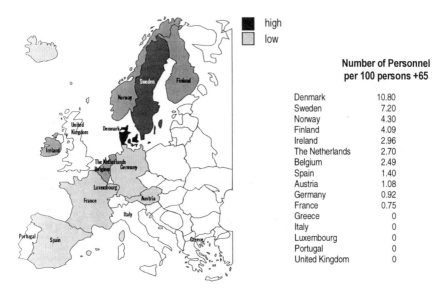

| high |
| low |

Number of Personnel per 100 persons +65

Denmark	10.80
Sweden	7.20
Norway	4.30
Finland	4.09
Ireland	2.96
The Netherlands	2.70
Belgium	2.49
Spain	1.40
Austria	1.08
Germany	0.92
France	0.75
Greece	0
Italy	0
Luxembourg	0
Portugal	0
United Kingdom	0

Figure 3.7   Geographical overview of the availability of a selected list of community services for the elderly

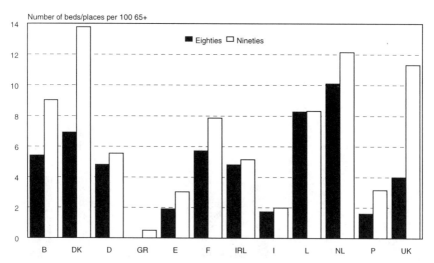

Note: This graph is based on the figures in Table 3.4, therefore remarks accompanying this table should be kept in mind when interpreting this graph.

Figure 3.8   Availability of institutional services for the elderly, 1982–97

Sources: see Figure 3.1 and Winters, 1991, p. 131.

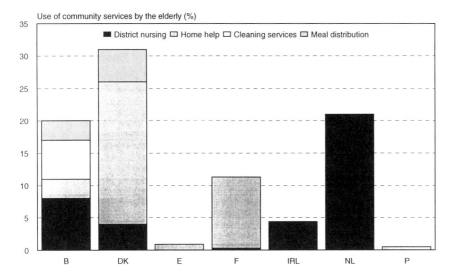

Note: This graph is based on the figures in Table 3.4, therefore remarks accompanying this table should be kept in mind when interpreting this graph.

Figure 3.9   Availability of community services for the elderly, 1989

Source: Spinnewyn, 1991, p. 99.

3   Affordability

The other element of relevance in addition to availability is affordability: this is determined by the level of public financing, which in turn determines the level of payments made by the users of the services. It is interesting to observe how those services are financed. Theoretically, it is to be expected that the more cure-intensive services will be publicly financed and the more care-intensive services will require more co-insurance. The cure-intensive services are similar to or identical with health services, and obtain as a 'merit good' more public financing. In the more care-intensive personal social services this is not the case in many countries. This is the case for most old-age homes, which are mostly financed by the elderly, although some countries provide high levels of public financing. In all the countries, this public financing is higher for the nursing homes, which are able to provide medical care. The future, however, will bring convergence again between these two systems (old-age homes and nursing homes), since the profiles for the persons entering

Table 3.4   Availability and relative importance of a selected list of services for the elderly

	Measure	A (1992)	B (1994)	DK (1995)	D (1992)	GR (1988)	E (1995)	FIN (1995)	F (1996)
Permanent									
Residential services									
1 Nursing homes	Number of beds per 100 65+	2.3	1.22	4.6	1.26		+	2	1.6
2 Psychiatric nursing homes	Number of places per 100 65+	0.2	0.18	0.7 (1994)	–	+	–	0.11	–
3 Housing for the disabled	Number of places per 100 65+	0.15	Very small	1.8 (staffed) 5.4 (unstaffed)[2]	–	–	–	+[20]	–
4 Old age homes	Number of beds per 100 65+	2.1	6.48 (1997)	–	1.09	0.51[19] (1990s)	2.83 (including nursing homes)	3.19	4.5 (1994)
Semi-residential services									
1 Multilevel homes	Number of places per 100 65+	–	+	–	2.74	–	0.1	–	–
2 Sheltered housing	Number of places per 100 65+	<0.1	0.15	0.6	0.44	–	+	+	1.76 (1994)
3 Service flats	Number of housing units per 100 65+	Very small	0.56 (Fl., 1996)	–	–	–	+	2.01	+
Temporary									
Residential services									
1 Geriatric units or hospitals	Number of beds per 100 65+	1.2 (units for internal medicine)	0.38	0.1 (1994)	+		+	0.687 (number of patients per 100 65+)	+
Semi-residential services									
1 Day hospital	Number of places per 100 65+	<0.1	0.01 (Fl., 1989)	–	+	–	0.07	0.117 (estimate, 1992)	+
2 Day care	Number of places per 100 65+	<0.1	0.03 (Fl., 1996)[16]	0.5	0.008	–	+	0.095 (in old age homes)	+
3 Nightly care in old age homes	Number of places per 100 65+	–	+	+	–	–	0.03	0.003	–
4 Social centres for the elderly	Number of persons served per 100 65+	–	+	13.2	0.937	+	0.05	1.3 (1993)	+
	Number of centres per 100 65+		0.01 (Fl., 1995)	0.07				0.0055 (1993)	
Community services									
1 District nursing	Number of personnel (FT) per 100 65+	0.04 (Vienna, 1993)	1.00 (1991)[1]	+	+	+	+	0.932[6]	0.154
2 Social work	Number of personnel (FT) per 100 65+	+	+	10.8[3]	–	+	0.1	1.397[7]	+

Table 3.4 cont'd

	Measure	A (1992)	B (1994)	DK (1995)	D (1992)	GR (1988)	E (1995)	FIN (1995)	F (1996)
3	Home help	Number of personnel (FT) per 100 65+	1.0 (Vienna, 1993)	0.95 (1990)[1]	+	0.48 (1996)[21] 0.92 (1997)[21]	+	1.3	1.763 (all personnel) +[17]	0.6
4	Cleaning services	Number of personnel (FT) per 100 65+	0.04 (Vienna, 1993)	0.54 (Fl., 1991)	+	–	–	+		+
5	Meals-on-wheels	Number of meals per 100 65+	2.4 per day (Vienna, 1993)(Fl. + Wal., 1991)	510.16	+	+	+	+	10.011 (estimate, 1992)	+
6	Family placement	Number of persons served per 100 65+	–	+	+	+	–	+	0.012	+
7	Housing for pensioners	Number of houses per 100 65+	0.04 (1993)	1.96 (Fl., 1993)		–	–	0.03	0.15	
8	Alarm systems	Number of persons connected per 100 65+	0.2	+	+	+	–	1	2.075 (1991)	+

Table 3.4 cont'd

	Measure	IRL (1991)	I (1991)	L (1995)	NL (1994)	P (1987)	S (1995)	UK (1994)	N (1995)
Permanent									
Residential services									
1 Nursing homes	Number of beds per 100 65+	2.25		1.84	1.3	+	1.8 (estimation)	1.6	4.7
2 Psychiatric nursing homes	Number of places per 100 65+	+		0.31	1.3	+		0.2	0.4 (estimate)
3 Housing for the disabled	Number of places per 100 65+	–		–	+	–	17	–	0.3
4 Old age homes	Number of beds per 100 65+	2.5	1.69	4.98	6.4	1.57 (1986)[15]	2.9 (est.)	3.1	1.4
Semi-residential services									
1 Multilevel homes	Number of places per 100 65+	–	small number	–	–	+	4.0 (estimation)	8	–
2 Sheltered housing	Number of places per 100 65+	0.39 (1986)	0.22	–	2.34 (1990)	+		5.0	4.6[4]
3 Service flats	Number of housing units per 100 65+	–	small number	1.11	+	0.01		–	Short-term stay + day care is provided within the frame of nursing homes (±10–15% of beds are used for short-term stay)
Temporary									
Residential services									
1 Geriatric units or hospitals	Number of beds per 100 65+	+	0.07 (1994)	–	+	–	0.3	0.4	
Semi-residential services									
1 Day hospital	Number of places per 100 65+	+	+	–	0.2	–	+	1.0 (est.)[9]	
2 Day care	Number of places per 100 65+	+	+	0.04	0.6	–	+	5.0 (10)	
3 Nightly care in old age homes	Number of places per 100 65+	+	–	–	+	–	+	–	
4 Social centres for the elderly	Number of persons served per 100 65+	+	+	+	+	1.58	+	2.0	15.0–20.0
	Number of centres per 100 65+	+	+	0.04	+	+	+	+	0.05
Community services									
1 District nursing	Number of personnel (FT) per 100 65+	0.34	+	+	0.6	+	0.0016	18.0 (11)	4.3 (5)
2 Social work	Number of personnel (FT) per 100 65+	+	+	–	0.1	+	+	+	+
3 Home help	Number of personnel (FT) per 100 65+	2.6[18]	+	+	2	+	7.2	5.3 (12)	4.3 (5)
4 Cleaning services	Number of personnel (FT) per 100 65+	+	+	–	–	+	+	7.0 (13)	+
5 Meals-on-wheels	Number of meals per 100 65+	2.96	–	+	+	+	+	5.1 (14)	+

Table 3.4 cont'd

The Variety, Scope and Coverage of Health and Social Services for the Elderly 103

	Measure	IRL (1991)	I (1991)	L (1995)	NL (1994)	P (1987)	S (1995)	UK (1994)	N (1995)
6	Family placement	Number of persons served per 100 65+	0.03 (1986)	–	–	–	+	–	+	–
7	Housing for pensioners	Number of houses per 100 65+	+	–	0.3	10.4 (1993)	–	+	5.0	(4)
8	Alarm systems	Number of persons connected per 100 65+ .	+	+	+	+	–	3.5 (1992)	+	+

Notes

+ service exists, but no quantitative information.

– service is not available in this country.

1 Estimation; in absolute terms.

2 Housing for pensioners included in housing for the disabled.

3 Services for elderly people in total, including residential services.

4 Housing for pensioners included in sheltered housing.

5 Figure refers to home help and district nursing.

6 0.270 of which are in home nursing (1992).

7 There are no 'earmarked' social workers for the elderly; the figure refers to all social workers and includes therefore also those who may not work with the elderly.

8 Residential and nursing homes can be registered as dual purpose homes.

9 Trend toward hospital at home and community rehabilitation.

10 % in previous month.

11 First contacts per 100 aged 65 or over (district nursing + community psychiatric nursing) (6.0% seen in last month).

12 Clients per week per 100 aged 65 or over (8.0% seen in last month).

13 % who received private home help in last month.

14 3% of elderly aged 65+ received meals-on-wheels in last month.

15 Public old age homes. There are also profit homes, but no information is available on the number and characteristics.

16 Number of accommodation units per 100 65+.

17 Part of auxiliary services.

18 Home help in Ireland is predominantly part-time. Figures relate to both full- and part-time.

19 Figure refers to residential care.

20 The available figures are not classified by age. Total amount of places for all disabled was 6,300 in 1995.

21 Figures 1996: country report; for 1997: Gerste and Rehbein, 1998, Tables 8, 9.

both types of institutions will become the same. In Belgium, for this reason, arguments are being made in favour of establishing similar financing rules. Home help, which responds to instrumental ADL, is to a large extent publicly financed, although the differences between the countries are substantial. District nursing is publicly financed. The trends toward joint supply of these services will again, however, bring both schemes together, since they are sometimes performing the same activities.

There are substantial differences in financing between countries: old-age homes are substantially financed by the elderly themselves in Belgium, Spain and (to a growing extent) the Netherlands, but remain largely publicly financed in the Scandinavian countries. This is even more pronounced in nursing homes, following again the rationale that the more medical a service becomes, the more public financing is involved. For this reason, in most of the countries district nursing is strictly publicly financed (health insurance), while more personal or household help implies more co-insurance. Nevertheless, the level of public financing is high and approaches the health care figures (about 80 per cent to 85 per cent). In some countries there is even a convergence towards more public involvement in home help.

The exercise of using case studies to compare an older person with a certain degree of dependency and income (since some of these services are conditional on income or dependency), reveals significant differences in coverage. Particularly in an international comparison, such detailed analysis may be needed because it can change the first impression of certain levels of protection. For example, it is becoming clear that in some countries free old-age homes are compensated by a deduction from a person's pension, leaving the elderly with only pocket money. In doing so, this changes the initial perception of a system being generous into a situation where the system reveals itself as being more restricted. This is analysed further in chapter 4.

4   The Fading Borderline Between Housing Provision and Services

In the care systems, a distinction is very often made between housing, hotel cost, housekeeping, care and cure aspects. Services oriented to certain aspects are specialised from the beginning (for example, 'meals-on-wheels' is oriented only towards 'catering' for the elderly staying at home). Other services are tending to focus their activities more and more. For example, outsourcing occurs in residential services that want to concentrate only on housing aspects, with nursing aid provided from outside by district nurses. Some services reorient themselves or sometimes cluster once again, regrouping in 'multi-product' initiatives in which housing and care are integrated to a varying degree (the broadest type could be the so called 'multilevel services'). Those organisational shifts or differences have basic economic and financial implications. Housing and hotel costs are considered to be private expenditures and ought to be paid out of the pockets of the elderly themselves. Housekeeping and home care are somewhat less so and health care should be almost completely publicly financed. At the same time, however, housing receives substantial public support in almost all welfare states, and the same is true for social and health care. We will document how the boundaries between housing and services are fading, perhaps coming closer to the reality of the daily life of the elderly, where all those aspects are and should be integrated.

4.1   Elements of Social Protection and the Special Situation of Housing Costs

Social protection of the elderly is initially concentrated on income protection. The pension schemes range from the legal pension scheme, occupational welfare and guaranteed income, to private life insurance, individual pension savings accounts and other allowances (such as in-cash benefits). There is one element in this category that is sometimes forgotten as a factor of social protection, but which is of ultimate importance: housing conditions and housing costs. For those who own their home, this element can be defined as pension saving *avant la lettre*. For the others, the cost of renting a dwelling can be a significant burden on their income.

   A significant part of the total costs in the care sector go to financing housing accommodation for the dependent elderly in need either of temporary or permanent help, or in need of adapted housing. Parts of those costs are – or can be – covered by the general housing policy (including tax and other instruments for acquiring and owning a house, the organisation and financing of the social housing sector, or policy interventions with rent control or rent subsidies). The elderly can be a special target group within these fields. In Table 3.6 we reproduce some partial information on those aspects, collected from the national reports on social protection of the elderly and from some other sources.

   Significant portions of housing support and implicit income support are situated in social housing policies and budgets. Substantial public support for housing is also embodied in tax relief or subsidised loans for housing acquisition, mostly during the economically active period of the family life cycle. This disappears when the home is acquired, so that most of the elderly

Table 3.5   The financing of some specific services – on average information

Residential = Old age homes + Nursing homes. Community = Home help + Meals-on-wheels.

	Old age homes E	Old age homes P	Old age homes O	Nursing homes E	Nursing homes P	Nursing homes O	Home help E	Home help P	Home help O	Meals-on-wheels E	Meals-on-wheels P	Meals-on-wheels O	District nursing E	District nursing P	District nursing O
A 1989	20–30	60	10	20–30	60	20	20–30	60–70	5	20–30[5]	60–70	5	20–30	60–70	5
B 1993. Fl.	70	30		50	50					77[4]	23[4]				
1993. Wal.	65.3[3]	34.7		55.9[3]	44.1										
1994							14	86					0	100	
1994. Fl.															
DK 1989				2	98		20	80		40[1]	60	0	0	100	0
1993				20	80		0	100	0	5			0	100	0
1995				4	96		0	100	0				0	100	0
D						22	35	43					12	32	56[2]
GR															
E (1995)	50	50		20	80		30	70					20	80	0
FIN (1992)	19	81		12	88		7	93					0	100	
F	Income and institution-related						Income-related participation of the elderly			67[6]	33[6]		Social security		
IRL (1996)	25	75		100 / 40	0[8] / 60[9]	0 / 0	33[10]	66	0	33[10]	66	0	0	100	0
I	Income and institution-related						Local agreements								
L (1995)	+	+		+	+		33	66		+	+		0 (7)	100	0
NL 1989	10	90	0	5	90	0	50	25	25				15	85	0
1994	38	62	0	11	89	0		81					14	86	0
P	Income and institution related						Income-related participation of the elderly						Social security		
S 1995	12	88		12	88	0	6	94	0	6	94	0	0	100	0
UK 1994	30	70		30	70	0	9	91	0	60	40	0	0	100	0
N 1994	15	85		15	85	0	5	95	0				5	95	0

Table 3.5 cont'd

Notes

E   Percentages of costs paid by the elderly and their relatives.

P   Percentages of costs paid by government and social insurance.

O   Percentages of costs paid by others: private insurance, sponsors, charities.

1   Food cost.

2   Social security and volunteer organisations.

3   Is in reality higher since supplements for special services -- to be paid by the elderly -- are not included.

4   Only concerns meals distributed by public centres for social welfare (='OCMW').

5   The elderly pay at least the food cost.

6   Refers to auxiliary services.

7   Only for conventional nursing tasks; for corporal and hygienic care the elderly have to contribute.

8   Pure private nursing homes.

9   Maximum public subvention for private accommodation.

10 Varies by health board and by community care area.

Source: country reports.

Table 3.6   Number of elderly 65+, housing stock by tenure and spending on social housing

	Year	Number of the elderly 65+		Housing stock by tenure, total population, c. 1990				Public spending on housing (as % of GDP) (1991)	% of the elderly living	
		In 1,000 of inhabitants	% in total population	Owner-occupied	Social rented	Private rented	Other		in their own house	in social housing
A	1995	1,215	15.1	50	18	21	11	0.0	72.73 (Fl.; 1993)	
B	1995	1,596	15.8	65	6	28	1	2.5	50 (1990)	
DK	1996	795	15.1	52	24 (1)	18	6	0.7		
D	1995	12,542	15.4	38	15	43	4	0.9		
GR	1993	1,535	14.8	77	0	23	—	0.7		
E	1994	5,704	14.8	78	2	16	4			
FIN	1995	732	14.3	71	14	13	2	2.7		
F	1994	8,523	14.7	54	17	20	9	2.6		
IRL	1994	409	11.5	81	11	8	—	0.0		
I	1996	9,644	16.8	67	7	21	5	0.2		
L	1991	55	14.3	68	1	30	1	1.1	30	
NL	1994	2,021	13.1	45	40	15	—	0.0		
P	1995	1,467	14.8	58	4	35	3			
S	1994	1,536	17.4	43	36 (2)	21	—			
UK	1994	9,076	15.7	67	26	7	—	5.7	(1991) 47% of the older person households with one adult 60 or over; 68% of the older couples; 68% of the other older households	(1991) 45% of the older person households with one adult 60 or over; 27% of the older couples; 26% of the other older households
N	1996	694	15.9							

Notes

1   Includes 7% of the stock managed by cooperatives.   2   Includes 15% of the stock managed by cooperatives.

Sources: i) Figures on housing stock by tenure: estimated by the authors from variety of sources including European Commission, 1993; Ghékiere and Quilliot, 1991 and other official data; ii) Demographic figures: OECD Health Data and country reports on social protection for dependency in old age; iii) Spending on social housing: Commission of the European Communities, Directorate-General Employment, Industrial Relations and Social Affairs, Luxembourg, 1993.

are no longer receiving these benefits. The burden of this expenditure on public spending will lessen as populations get older. In some countries, social housing is explicitly mentioned as a part of the social protection system. This happens in a positive way in Ireland, where categories of social housing are explicitly mentioned: social housing from local authorities, sheltered housing and voluntary social housing. Also in Belgium (Flanders), an explicit category within social housing has been created for the elderly. In a negative sense we have to conclude that in the UK social housing is being reduced to an instrument of policy for reducing poverty.

Almost all countries use housing benefits and rent subsidies to improve the housing conditions of the elderly and/or to support income (see Table 3.7). As well as rent these benefits may include expenses of heating, water and electricity. Only fragmented information is available of the percentage of the elderly receiving this benefit, but it can be substantial in amount.

In our report we obtained some information of the relative importance. In Flanders rent subsidy is for low income groups (net taxable income below 12 509 ECU per year, situation in 1995) and is dependent on the paid rent and the actual income.[1] In Denmark low income groups of the elderly can benefit from a rent subsidy dependent on income and rent. About 50 per cent of the poorer elderly are entitled and a rule that rent can only be 10 per cent (before 15 per cent) of income is applied. We observed for Belgium that for the elderly who are not home owners the rent can increase to 30 per cent of disposable income. In Finland the rent subsidy is 261 ECU per month for older persons living alone on low income (428 ECU per month) and 153 ECU per month for older persons living alone on average pension income (of 858 ECU per month). For couples on low income (747 ECU per month) the housing allowance amounts to 293 ECU; for couples on average income (1,232 ECU per month) the housing allowance amounts to 129 ECU per month. These figures illustrate how substantial housing support can be. Also, a housing allowance exists for those owning their own house (41 ECU per month for low income pensioners living alone and 71 ECU per month for couples on low income).

In France the elderly with a low income can apply for a monthly housing allowance for social housing of about 107 ECU (which can be compared to a basic income of 945 ECU of a couple older persons). In the Netherlands the elderly below a certain income level receive a rent subsidy (income level is 18,500 ECU for couples and 14,000 for singles). For some countries (Greece, Ireland, Luxembourg and Spain) rent subsidies are not explicitly mentioned. Other important elements of housing are mentioned, for instance the existence of fuel allowance in Ireland, the heating benefits from social assistance in Austria. In those countries the housing support for the elderly is situated in the combat against poverty, again part of the 'social assistance' policy. Portugal is the only country where the existence of rent control is mentioned, but with substantial effects on the income position of the elderly, especially in the cities.

A third large category of social expenditure for the elderly is health and social services. We have concentrated here on the specific services for the elderly, and especially on the housing aspects. We distinguish three different types of services for the elderly: permanent residential services, temporary residential services and community care services. The latter sector includes adapted housing and other forms of support intended to help the elderly remain in their own homes.

4.2   Adapted Housing and Support Services for the Elderly

See Tables 3.7 and 3.8.

4.3   Relation with Services for the Elderly

The priority for community care explains the large number of services to support the elderly at home. The most important services are meals-on-wheels, district nursing and home care. Some services are especially aimed at improving the quality of the home environment, or at making the elderly feel more comfortable at home. Examples of such measures include those for home improvements and alarm systems, both of which are mentioned in almost all of the countries studied. Some of these innovations (although now already widespread), are being placed within the broader concept of adapted housing for the elderly (or handicapped persons). This form of housing is sometimes defined as an alternative to residential services, or often tends towards it. In between are the semi-residential or temporary services.

The residential and semi-residential services are ranked according to the decreasing degree of medical support that is available. Some slight differences might occur continuously in the dominant characteristics of the patients of each service, so the nature of the services can change over time. For example, services originally provided for independent older persons, such as the 'service flats' in Flanders, can change by nature when the elderly who enter the service flat become older, stay in the service and become more dependent. Even the difference in qualifications of the personnel in these services can imply that

Table 3.7   Support services for housing

	Rent subsidies (*name*, level (amount) and availability)	Home improvements (name)	Tele-alarm and telecommunication services (name and number of persons connected per 100 65+)
A	(Housing and heating benefits from social assistance).	Subsidies in some provinces.	Notruf (0.2 (1992))
B	*Huurtoelagen*: granted to low income pensioners (net taxable income below 12 509 ECU/year (1995)) when moving from unadapted to adapted housing Subsidies are dependent on the paid rent and the income (rent subsidy = rent x (12 713 ECU – income)/12 713).	Huursubsidie en installatiepremie Aanpassings- en verbeteringspremie La domotique: ± 100 houses in 1994	Personenalarmtoestellen/Bio-télévigilance FL.: 3,100 systems are subsidised (1987-1993); Wal.: 44 OCMW services (1994)
DK	*Rent subsidy*: dependent on income and rent. Flat max. 65 m² for singles and 85 m² for couples. For low income pensioners rent may not exceed 10% of income. For average income pensioners rent subsidy = 2,174 ECU for singles and 951 ECU for couples (1994). 50% of people renting apply for rent subsidies.	Boligændringer	Omsorgsalarmer
D	Subsidies for rent and other housing costs are dependent on income.	Improvements, housing accommodation	Emergency phone calls
GR	–		
E	–	Adaptación del Hogar	Telealarma (1 (1995))
FIN	*Eläkkeensaajan asumistuki* (26,266 pensioners in 1994): subsidies are dependent on the size of the dwelling, rent and other housing costs, income and place of residence Rent subsidy = 261 ECU/month for singles on low income (428 ECU/month); 153 ECU/month for singles on average pension (858 ECU/month); 293 ECU/month for couples on low income (747 ECU/month); 129 ECU/month for couples on average income (1.232 ECU/month) A housing allowance can also be granted to low income pensioners owning their own house (41 ECU/month for singles and 71 ECU/month for couples)	Parannus-ja kunnostustyöt	Hälytys-ja puhelinpalvelut (2.1 (1991))
F	*Aide au logement* (*Allocation logement à caractère familial, allocation de logement sociale et aide personnalisée au logement*): the allowance for social housing is dependent on income (± 107 ECU per month on average). (fuel allowance)	Amélioration du confort des logements	Télé-alarme

Table 3.7 cont'd

	Rent subsidies (*name*, level (amount) and availability)	Home improvements (name)	Tele-alarm and tele-communication services (name and number of persons connected per 100 65+)
IRL	+	+	+
I	–	Edilizia popolare	Telesoccorso
L		Services d'adaptation du logement	Télé-alarme
NL	*Individuele huursubsidie (IHS)*: dependent on income (14,000 ECU for singles and 18,500 ECU for couples) and rent (max. subsidy= 40% of rent)	Woningverbetering/renovatie/ aanpassing	Tele-alarm
P	Subsidy covers all rent increases. If invalidity is more than 60%, complementary rent subsidies are granted for a limited period		
S	*Housing allowance* (2,045 ECU/year on average, 1995) Subsidies are dependent on rent: 83% of the rent costs between 12 – 470 ECU per month are paid	Home adaptations (40,000 users in 1995)	Security alarm (54,000 in 1992) (3.5 (1992))
UK	*Housing benefit/Council tax benefit*: granted to persons receiving income support of max. 82.1 ECU per week. Subsidies are dependent on charges and income (Cold Weather Payments)	Improvement in housing conditions, 'staying put' schemes	Public, private or charitable providers. Fee depending on need and income
N	*Housing allowance*: subject to needs testing, income-related	Utbedringslån og-tilskudd	Omsorgsalarmer

Notes

+   existent

–   non-existent

Table 3.8   Special housing for the elderly

	Name	Number	Number of places per 100 65+
A (1993)	Seniorenwohnungen = Altenwohnungen	Small number	0.04
B (1993)	Bejaardenwoningen	Fl.: ±17,000	Fl.: 1.96
DK	Ældreegnede boliger[1]	43 300[1]	5.4[1]
D	–		
GR	–		
E (1995)	Hogares del Pensionist		0.03
FIN (1995)	Vanhusten asunnot		0.15
F	–		
IRL	+	Number increases	
I	–		
L (1995)	Pensions de famille	150	0.3
NL (1993)	Bejaardenwoningen	±215,000	10.4
P	–		
S	+		
UK	Special housing in Scotland developed since 1960. Less well developed in other regions		5
N	Trygdeboliger[2]		4.6[2]

Notes

+   existent   –   non-existent

1   Including housing for the disabled.
2   Including sheltered housing/service flats.

the character is different because, for instance, less qualified or less nursing personnel per group of residents is used.

The permanent residential and semi-residential services are generally available in all the countries. However, it should be noted that in some countries the large number of 'integrated' (independent) housing accommodation and care facilities, which are of a permanent but mostly semi-residential character, are increasingly replacing the purely residential services (see above).

4.4   Unbundling of Housing and Care in Theory and Integrated Services in Practice

We regroup the residential services in three categories (Figure 3.10): 'medicalised' housing (nursing homes, psychiatric nursing homes, housing for the disabled), traditional old-age homes and open housing (sheltered housing, service flats and multilevel homes). Many of the countries emphasise the distinction between care-intensive nursing places and housing. In these countries, the traditional old-age home is disappearing, though in some other countries it is still the dominant residential care system (Belgium, the Netherlands, Germany, France and Luxembourg). But in these countries, as well, plans exist to transform these traditional old-age homes either into nursing homes or sheltered housing. In Belgium, for example, the building of new old-age homes has declined and over the next five years one-third of all spaces in the existing old-age homes will be transformed into nursing home beds.

At the same time, and more precisely in Flanders, there is a strategy to shift from residential care to sheltered housing for the elderly: the so called 'service flats'. Those flats are meant for independent elderly, and their construction is subsidised by the Flemish government. New financial instruments have been developed in the last few years to stimulate investment by the elderly in this product (especially by tax exemption of the invested capital), though at the same time the public subsidy decreased. The promoters of these 'service flats' argued that there was a risk either of the product becoming unaffordable for lower income groups or of the project becoming unprofitable. At the same time, the question is being raised as to whether the service flat can be kept exclusively for the independent elderly, since those entering the system will become increasingly dependent after some years, thus requiring more in-house services.

It was decided in the Netherlands in 1990 that part of the old-age homes should evolve into nursing homes and the rest should evolve into sheltered home facilities. In 1994 a Commission on 'Modernising Care for the Elderly' studied the problem of maximum substitution and the relation between housing and care. They concluded that there were too many old-age homes since the elderly should stay longer at home. This implies that the rent subsidies should be raised. A new borderline was drawn between the elderly living in institutions and thus belonging to the care sector, and the elderly living at home and thus belonging to the sphere of public housing. The division between old-age home (social sector) and nursing home (medical sector) seemed to be of no relevance. Both are now covered by the Exceptional Medical Expenses Scheme, which also covers home care and district nursing (which integrated these services into a single providers system). We have the impression that decades of discussion about what are social services and what are medical services are coming to an end here, and even the housing aspects are covered (at least for the institutional part) by an 'Exceptional Medical' scheme.

In the UK, as well, from 1988 onward (quoted in Bond, 1998, p. 37) it has been recommended that housing and care needs should be treated separately. A similar movement has occurred already in Denmark where beginning in 1988 a strategy has been developed to disassociate housing and care (Gottschalk, 1991, pp. 25–7). The aim was to upgrade the housing function and to achieve a more flexible service system. In 1988 a large programme was launched to improve the quality of housing for the elderly. The nursing homes were replaced by modern housing, but some years later it was discovered that the new housing did not take into account the fact that the elderly living in this type of accommodation would need more service facilities after some years. More funding was made available recently to include more care facilities with this type of housing.

Staying put was launched in the UK as a strategy to cope with the reduction in public money on housing (of the elderly?), and sometimes described as an alternative to both sheltered housing and long-term institutional care.

4.5   Housing and Care: One Continuum

Together with the disappearance of the traditional old-age home, the emergence of increased demand for adapted housing can be observed. The further development of welfare states and the new market of an ageing population creates increasing variety in accommodation for the elderly, demonstrating the emergence of new care and housing combinations. This brings us to a new system of categorising housing for the elderly. The first group could be described as integrated housing and care facilities of an institutional type, oriented to (medical) care aspects. There will be a growing convergence between old-age homes and nursing homes. In many cases there may only be a difference in name and not in content of these services.

The second group also combines housing and care facilities, but these are independent housing types. It is mostly a grouped accommodation, but the elderly have their own apartment, combined with an alarm system, common rooms and facilities, and the presence of some staff. Sometimes more facilities such as kitchen, dining room and bathroom are shared, but they remain housing facilities. Historically, these services start with a low-care component and gradually develop a larger care component.

The third group of special accommodation for the elderly is adapted housing. Adapted housing is characterised by being barrier-free and having wide doorways and big bathrooms; it is adapted for wheelchairs (sometimes also in the kitchen). There is no in-house ward or service, but it is possible to

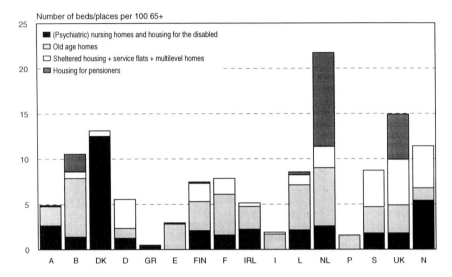

Number of beds/places per 100 65+

Legend:
■ (Psychiatric) nursing homes and housing for the disabled
□ Old age homes
□ Sheltered housing + service flats + multilevel homes
▨ Housing for pensioners

Countries: A B DK D GR E FIN F IRL I L NL P S UK N

Note: This graph is based on the figures in Table 3.4, therefore remarks accompanying this table should be kept in mind when interpreting this graph.. Number of places in sheltered housing in Ireland is underestimated: data are from 1986. Since then significant building has occurred in voluntary housing.

Figure 3.10 Availability of some services for the elderly (number of places per 100 65+)

call for home care and day and night help. The distinction is not always made between housing for handicapped persons and housing for the elderly. As this housing form appears, it will become less and less distinct from traditional housing, if one takes into account the new interest in lifelong housing which is to be found in the UK, the Netherlands and Flanders. Housing should be built which is adapted to all needs (or should be adaptable).

4.6   Housing as a Means of Financing Care

Several other aspects of the relationship between housing and care became evident in our comparative study. The way (social) housing providers are increasingly finding themselves confronted with an ageing population in their own premises is one of these aspects. This leads providers to become more involved in housing for the elderly and to recognise the need to organise care (either by themselves or in collaboration with care providers).

Housing is at the core of other aspects of care for the elderly. The question as to whether this aspect needs to be included in long-term care insurance is under discussion in many countries. However, this is only one issue. Whether people should use their assets, including their house, to finance the long-term care is another issue.

Proposals have been made in the UK in line with this concept, such as to institute reversed mortgages or (posthumous) recall on the inheritance. 'Only 50,000 of the 2.5 million owners over the age of 70 have taken up mortgage annuity schemes' (around 1990, see Bond, 1998, p. 38). There seems to be a clear opposition in public opinion to such a strategy. It is too reminiscent of means-testing solutions and social assistance instead of long-term care (social) insurance.

Up till now this reasoning has not been common in the welfare states of the EU, as it might be more accepted thinking in the USA (and also in Australia) (see Colloquium on Long-term Care Insurance in Sydney, August 1997). The old thinking in fact remains in force in the EU. One good example is the financing of 'service flats' in Flanders (see Pacolet and Lanoye, 1997). Although this financing vehicle was intended to attract private money, it stimulated savings by the 'seniors' through tax exemptions on the revenue and on the inheritance. This means that wealth can be transferred to the heir without being taxed, instead of using private assets. Perhaps this aspect can serve as a good example for other countries, since it is also aimed at increasing the (financing of the) supply of adapted housing for the elderly.

The possibilities of trade-offs between elements of income support, housing, and social and health care services are substantial. Housing is at the core of care for the elderly. A further analysis of these housing conditions is warranted. We have shown that there is an increasing variety of residential and community services where housing and care aspects converge. The increasing variety reflects the maturity of a welfare state, but at the same time it reflects the emerging maturity of the (mass-)market of (housing and services) for the elderly. Although in many EU Member States theoretical and political debates have taken place to distinguish the housing aspects from the care aspects – just as the same debate has taken place on the distinction between medical and social services – the reality is moving in the opposite direction. Housing combined with a varied (and increasing) care supply seems more and more to be the case, even though the experiment started with the emphasis on housing. The borderline between residential and community care, as well as between housing and care in general, is fading in organisational terms – and in some cases also in financial terms.

Table 3.9   Summary overview of fading borderlines

Services for the elderly: fading borderlines:
–   between professions and services in community care;
–   between residential and semi-residential care;
–   between providers of residential and community care;
–   between services and housing;
–   between cure, care and help.

5   Other Elements of Social Protection

In Table 3.10, finally, some other elements of support for the elderly are mentioned. They are grouped around two aspects: legal rights on the one hand and self help and informal care on the other hand. Mutual help, self help and informal care are the spontaneous support systems which are available to the elderly. They are supported and stimulated, however, by several instruments. The informal support can be in cash and/or in-kind.

6   Summary Overview of the Existing Services

See Tables 3.11–3.13.

Note

1   Rent subsidy per year = rent x (12 713 ECU – income)/12 713 ECU.

Table 3.10 Other elements of social protection

Type	A	B	DK	D	GR	E
1	**Legal protection**					
1.1	Charters of rights	Patiëntenrechten		Grundgesetz Sozialgesetzbuch		Derechos resiente
1.2	Right of representation (e.g. 'co-determination' in old-age homes)	Patiëntenraad/ Ouderenraad		Heimbeirat		Sistema representación
1.3	Right of appeal	Klachtencommissie bejaardentehuizen Klachtenregister in rusthuizen, serviceflats, dagverzorgingscentra en rust- en verzorgingstehuizen Recht om in beroep te gaan tegen beslissingen van het OCMW	Rights of appeal for cash benefits and home help	Court system		
1.4	Protection of wealth against fraud and misuse	Controlecommissie in rusthuizen Gevolmachtigde vertegenwoordiger of lasthebber		Penal law		Código Penal
1.5	Right of self-determination of care	Vrije keuze van zorgverlening		Freedom of choice with regard to institutional care		Derecho a elegir sistema atención
1.6	Right of determination of care by the family	+		Betreuer (legal representative)		
1.7	Advisory body at institutional level, municipal level, regional or	Bewonersraad in rust -huizen, RVTs en service flats Centrumraad in dagverzorgingscentra Bejaardenraden Adviesraad voor Gezondheids- en Welzijnszorg	Municipal elder councils	Seniorenbeirat		

Table 3.10 cont'd

Type	A	B	DK	D	GR	E
1.7 cont'd		Hoge Raad voor Thuis-verzorging Vlaamse adviescommissie voor ziekenhuizen en andere vormen van medische verzorging en begeleiding Gemengde Commissie Rustoorden en RVTs Nationale Raad voor zie kenhuisvoorzieningen, …				
national level						Consejo Estatal Mayores
2 Mutual help – self help						
2.1 Obligation to help		+		Obligation to self help Maintenance obligation		Obligación Ayuda Familia Plan atención
2.2 Care contract, care plan		Zorgenplan		Care contract with old-age homes, etc.		
3 Occupational additional protection						
4 Private insurances for						
a) in cash help						Seguro Privado
b) in kind help						

Type	FIN	F	IRL	I	L
1. Legal protection					
1.1 Charters of rights	laki perusoikeuksista laki potilaan asemasta ja oikeuksista sekä potilasasiamiesjärjestelmä laki sosiaalihuollon asiakkaiten asemasta ja oikeuksista	Charte sur les droits des personnes âgées		+ (informal charters)	

Table 3.10 cont'd

Type	FIN	F	IRL	I	L
1.2 Right of representation (e.g. 'co-determination' in old-age homes)				Tribunale di malati	
1.3 Right of appeal	valitus- ja muutoksenhakuoikeus Terveydenhuollon oikeusturvakeskus				
1.4 Protection of wealth against fraud and misuse	omaisuudensuoja			Diritto penale	
1.5 Right of self-determination of care	itsemääräämisoikeus			+	
1.6 Right of determination of care by the family					
1.7 Advisory body at institutional level, municipal level, regional or national level	kuntien neuvottelukunnat läänien neuvottelukunnat, komitealaitos, työryhmät, neuvottelukunnat				
2 Mutual help – self help				Obbligo degli allimenti	
2.1 Obligation to help	hoitosuunnitelma				
2.2 Care contract, care plan	hoitosopimus				
3 Occupational additional protection	toimintaterapia				
4 Private insurances for					
a) in cash help					
b) in kind help					

Table 3.10 cont'd

Type	NL	P	S	UK	N
1 Legal protection					
1.1 Charters of rights	Patiëntenplatform		Elder council	Patients' charter	Beboerråd (Council of residents)
1.2 Right of representation (e.g. 'co-determination' in old-age homes)	Bewonerscommissie in verzorgingshuis				
1.3 Right of appeal	Beroepscommissies		Right to appeal	Rights of appeal	Ankerett Control by county medical officer
1.4 Protection of wealth against fraud and misuse				Protection against fraud and deception	
1.5 Right of self-determination of care				Self-determination of care	Recommended quality criteria
1.6 Right of determination of care by the family	Familieraden				
1.7 Advisory body at institutional level, municipal level, regional or national level	Ouderenraad		+ +		Beboerråd Eldreråd (Senior Citizen Councils) Statens eldreråd (National Council for the elderly)
2 Mutual help – self help					
2.1 Obligation to help				Obligation for local authorities	
2.2 Care contract, care plan	Zorgplan		Care plans	Care plan	Omsorgsplaner
3 Occupational additional protection					
4 Private insurances for					
a) in cash help					
b) in kind help					

Table 3.11 Permanent residential and semi-residential services for the elderly: types and capacity

	Type	A	B	DK	D	GR	E
1	Nursing homes	Altenpflegeheim (30,195 places in 1992)	Rust- en verzorgingste-huizen/Maisons de repos et de soins Be.: 19,556 beds (1994)	Plejehjem (36,377 places in 1995)	(Altenpflegeheime (±151,800 places in 1992)		Residencias asistidas
2	Psychiatric nursing homes	(Geronto-) Psychia-trisches Pflegeheim (3,043 places in 1992)	Psychiatrische verzor-gingstehuizen/Maisons de soins psychiatriques Be.: 2,830 places (1994)	Psykiatriske plejehjem (5,781 places in 1994)		Therapeuteria chronion patheseon (chronic disease institutions) (2,000 in 1988)	
3	Housing for the disabled	Behindertenheim (2,023 places in 1992)	Tehuis niet-werkenden Fl.: 38 persons aged >65 (1989)	Plejeboliger (estimated: 14,450 dwellings in 1995) Ældreegnede boliger (estimated: 43,300 dwellings in 1995); including housing for pensioners			
4	Old-age homes	Altenheim, Senioren-heim, Pensionistenheim (27,541 places in 1992)	Bejaardentehuizen, rusthuizen, rustoorden/ Maisons de repos, maisons de repos pour personnes âgées, résidences Be.: 109,816 beds (1996) +		Altenheime (±132,000 places in 1992)	Gyrokomia (6,000 persons in non-profit 'homes', nineties)	Residencias de válidos
5	Multilevel homes for the elderly				Mehrgliedrige (mehrstufige) Einrich-tungen (±330,000 places in 1992)		
6	Sheltered housing	Betreutes Wohnen (<100 places)	Beschut wonen/ Habitations protégées, logements supervisés Be.: 2,386 initiatives (1994)	Beskyttede boliger (5,108 dwellings in 1995)	Altenwohnheime (±52,800 places in 1992)		Pisos asistidos

Table 3.11 cont'd

Type	A	B	DK	D	GR	E
7 Service flats	Seniorenwohnge-meinschaften (< 100 places) Seniorenwohnung in Sozialzentrum (100–200 places all over Austria)	Service flats and woning-complexen met dienstverlening/Senioreries Fl.: 5,161 housing units (1996)				Pisos con servicios comunes
8 Innovative services	Sozialzentren, Seniorenwohnungen und -wohngemeinschaften (<300 places)	Het beschermend zelfstandig wonen Fl.: 2 initiatives known (1992) Groepswonen Experimenten inzake woonformules Palliatieve ziekenhuis-eenheden (Fl.: 2 units with together 16 beds, 1994)				

Type	Finland	France	Ireland	Italy	Luxembourg
1 Nursing homes	terveyskeskuksen vuodeosasto (19,348 places in 1995)	Sections de cure médicale (138,791 places in 1996)	Private nursing homes (5,552 in 1991); Voluntary nursing homes (3,509 in 1991)	Residenze Sanitarie e Assistenziali (RSA) (6% of the elderly 65+ in 1992) (158,654 beds in 1991; 1.69 beds per 100 65+ in 1991)	Maisons de soins (1995: state: 784 beds; municipalities: 230 beds)
2 Psychiatric nursing homes	psykiatrian erikoisalan pitkäaikaishoito (823 older persons in 1994)		Psychiatric nursing homes/hostels (1,147 persons in long stay units characterised as chronic psychiatric; 1990)		Hôpital neuro-psychiatrique de l'Etat (170 patients in 1995)
3 Housing for the disabled	a) laitosasuminen b) vammaisten palveluasuminen				

Table 3.11 cont'd

	Type	FIN	F	IRL	I	L
4	Old-age homes	vanhainkoti (23,266 places in 1995)	Privé: maisons de retraite privées (179,600 beds in 1994) Public: maisons de retraite publiques et hospices (212,927 beds in 1994)	Health board welfare homes (1,589 public beds in 1991) + Health board geriatric hospitals (7,005 beds in 1991); long stay district hospitals (1,465 beds in 1991)		Maisons de retraite et centres intégrés pour personnes âgées (2,744 beds in 1995)
5	Multilevel homes for the elderly				Negligible number	
6	Sheltered housing	palvelutalo	Logements-foyers (153,050 places in 1994) (1.2% of households 60+ in 1990)	Sheltered housing (1,500 units in 1986; since 1986 significant building in voluntary housing)	Strutture protette (325 institutions; 20,062 beds in 1991)	
7	Service flats	palveluasum (together with sheltered housing about 14,683 places in 1995)	Résidence service		Some private experiments (very small number)	Logements aménagés pour personnes âgées (1995: 370 of the municipalities; 243 of the private sector)
8	Innovative services	ryhmäkodit	MAPAD (Maisons d'accueil pour personnes âgées dépendantes) Unités de vie Cantou MAPA; MARPA Résidence edilys MAPI (Maisons d'accueil pour personnes invalides) Appartement d'acceuil Domicile collectif			Projet de domiciles protégés pour malades Alzheimer

Table 3.11 cont'd

Type	NL	P	S	UK	N
1 Nursing homes	Verpleeghuizen (26,187 somatic beds in 1994)	Lares da 3° Lidade	Nursing homes (estimated 28,000 beds in 1995)	Nursing homes (148,000 in 1994) (England only)	Nursing homes (32,700 beds, 1995) (96% of the residents are 67+)
2 Psychiatric nursing homes	Psychogeriatrische verpleeghuizen (27,631 beds in 1994)	Hospitais psiquiatricos		Psychiatric hospitals (18,000 in 1994) (England only)	Psychiatric nursing homes (approximately 3,500 beds of which ± 50% are elderly, 1995)
3 Housing for the disabled	Adapted housing		See sheltered housing		Service housing (2,200 units, 1995) (85% of the residents are 67+)
4 Old-age homes	Verzorgingshuizen (131,000 beds in 1994; 121,064 elderly in old-age homes in 1994 = 6.4% of elderly 65+)	Lares para idosos (19,794 in 1986)	Old-age homes (estimated 45,000 beds/apartments in 1995)	Residential care homes (278,600 in 1994) (England only)	Old-age homes (10,000 beds, 1995) (96% of the residents are 67+)
5 Multilevel homes for the elderly		+	5 + 6 + 7 + 8: estimated 62,000 beds/apartments	+	Trygdeboliger (32,100 residents of which 80% are aged 67+, 1995) (see also housing for pensioners)
6 Sheltered housing	Aanleunwoningen (±45,000 in 1990)	Acollimento familiar		Sheltered and very sheltered housing (650,000 in 1991)	
7 Service flats	Service flats owners: ±100 service flats, 100% private renting: ±100 service flats, 50% private/50% state	Residenciais para idosos (167 in 1987)			
8 Innovative services	Woonzorgcomplexen	Turismo Social p/a 3° Idade Universidade da 3° Idade	Group homes for the demented	Respite care; 'Staying Put' schemes	Sheltered units/homes for demented in nursing homes

Table 3.12   Temporary residential and semi-residential services for the elderly: types and capacity

	Type	A	B	DK	D	GR	E
1	General hospitals	61,166 places in 1993	Algemene ziekenhuizen/ Hôpitaux généraux Be.: 292 hospitals (1994)	Somatiske sygehuse (23,905 beds in 1994)		Genika nosokomea	
2	Geriatric units in general hospitals	16,197 places in internal medicine units	Geriatrische diensten/ Services exclusivement gériatriques Be.: 6,206 beds (1994)	Geriatriske sengepladser (1,000 beds in 1994)	Geriatrische Abteilung in Sonderkrankenhaus		Unidades geriátricas hospitalarias
3	Long stay wards in general hospitals		Diensten voor langdurige zieken (V-ciensten)/ Services pour le traitement des malades atteints d'affections chroniques Be.: 3,500 beds (1994)				Estancias largas en hospitales generales
4	Medium stay wards in general hospitals		Gespecialiseerde diensten voor behandeling en revalidatie (Sp-diensten)/(spécialité) Be.: 500 beds (1994)				
5	Psychiatric wards in general hospitals	(Geronto-) Psychiatrische Abteilung (7,308 places in 1993; including places in psychiatric hospitals)	Diensten voor psycho-geriatrie (Tg-/Vp-diensten)/Psychogériatrie Be.: 667 (1994) Gespecialiseerde diensten voor behandeling en revalidatie (Sp-diensten, specialisme 'psychogeriatrische aandoeningen')/ spécialité Be.: 500 beds (1994) +	Psykiatrisk afdeling (4,300 beds in 1995)			
6	Geriatric hospitals				Gerontopsychiatrisches Krankenheim		Hospitales geriátricos
7	Psychiatric hospitals	Psychiatrisches Krankenhaus (6,445 places in 1993)	Psychiatrische ziekenhuizen/ Hôpitaux psychiatriques Be.: 71 hospitals (1994)	Psykiatriske sygehuse (2,265 beds in 1994)			Psiquiátricos

Table 3.12 cont'd

Type	A	B	DK	D	GR	E
8 Psycho-geriatric wards in mental hospitals		Diensten voor psycho-geriatrie (Tg-/Vp-diensten)/ Psychogériatrie Be.: 1.605 (1994)				
9 Rehabilitation homes	Rehabilitations-Anstalten	Revalidatiecentra Fl.: 164 centres (1993)				Centros de rehabilitación
10 Short-run nursing homes			Aflastningspladser	Kurzzeit Pflegeheim (±50,000 persons per year) +		Residencias asistidas
11 Short stay in old-age homes	<100 places	Kortverblijf/ centres de court séjour Fl.: 256 old-age homes (1993) (estimated)/ Wal.: 16 centres				Estancias cortas en Residencias
12 Geriatric day hospital	<100 places	Geriatrisch dagzieken-huis/Hôpital de jour Fl.: 77 places (1989)		Geriatrische Tages- oder Nachtkliniken		Unidades Geriátricas de Día
13 Day care	<100 places	Dagverzorgingscentra/ Services d'accueil de jour, centres de soins de jour, centres de jour Be.: 47 centres (1996); Fl.: 235 accommodation units (1996)	Daghjem (3,967 places in 1995)	Tagespflegeheime/ Tagesheime (±1,000 places in 60 institutions)		Centros de Día
14 Nightly care in old-age homes		Fl.: 82 old-age homes (1993) (estimated)	Natpladser			+
15 Social centres for the elderly		Dienstencentra/ Centres de jour Fl.: 102 centres (1995)/ Br. and Wal.: have regulation	Dagcentre (45,472 places and 105,352 persons in 1995)	Altentagesstaeten/ Altenbegegnungs-staetten (90,646)	Education/ recreation	Centros de Servicios Sociales
16 Innovative services	Kurzzeitpflege (<100 places) Tagespflege (<100 places)					
17 Preventive services						

Table 3.12 cont'd

	Type	FIN	F	IRL	I	L
1	General hospitals	yleissairaala		General hospitals (very low percentage of older people)	Ospedali generici (287,089 beds in 1994)	
2	Geriatric units in general hospitals	geriatrinen osasto		+ (percentage of older persons is very low)	Riparti geriatrici in ospedali generici (= geriatric units in general hospitals: 6,848 beds in 1994) Geriatric units in private clinics (but state connected): 1,262 beds in 1994	
3	Long stay wards in general hospitals	yleissairaalan pitkäaikaisosasto	Section d'hôpital de long séjour (77,871 places in 1994)	+	Long stay wards in general hospitals: 4,547 beds in 1994 Long stay wards in private clinics (but state connected): 6,859 beds in 1994	
4	Medium stay wards in general hospitals		Section d'hôpital de moyen séjour (39,814 places in 1994) (1990: 506,000 patients 60+ (=74% of total number of patients); 328,000 patients 75+)	+		
5	Psychiatric wards in general hospitals	psykiatrinen vuodeosasto	Services psychiatric d'un hôpital (20 000 patients 65+; 3,400 patients 85+) (75,915 beds (including psychiatric wards in psychiatric hospitals) in 1995)	+	Riparti psichiatrici in ospedali generici: 4,493 beds in 1994	
6	Geriatric hospitals	geriatrinen sairaala				
7	Psychiatric hospitals	psykiatrinen sairaala	+	7,005 beds (1991) 1991: 16% of total admissions; 1,139 admissions per 100 elderly	Concentrated in psychiatric wards in general hospitals 80 geriatric beds in psychiatric hospitals	
8	Psycho-geriatric wards in mental hospitals	psykogeriatrinen oasto		+	Concentrated in psychiatric wards in general hospitals	Service de psychogériatrie dans l'hôpital neuro-psychiatrique de l'Etat

Table 3.12 cont'd

	Type	FIN	F	IRL	I	L
9	Rehabilitation homes	kuntoutuskoti		+	Cliniche di riabilitazione	
10	Short-run nursing homes		Section d'Hébergement temporaire (2,985 lits et 173 logements, 1990 (concerns old-age homes and hospitals))	+		Quelques lits de vacance dans maisons de soins + de retraite
11	Short stay in old-age homes	lyhytaikaishoito	Section d'Hébergement temporaire (2,985 lits et 173 logements, 1990 (concerns old-age homes and hospitals))	+		
12	Geriatric day hospital	päiväkeskus/ päiväsairaala	Hôpital de jour	+	Day hospital di geriatria	
13	Day care	päivähoito (3,034 clients 65+, 1995)	Centre de jour	+	Centri diurni	Foyer de jour Alzheimer (3 centres with 22 places)
14	Nightly care in old-age homes	yöhoito		+		
15	Social centres for the elderly	vanhusten palvelukeskus	Clubs de personnes âgées	+	Centri sociali	Foyer de jour pour personnes âgées (18 centres)
16	Innovative services	innovatiiviset palvelut	+	+		
17	Preventive services	ehkäisevät palvelut				

Table 3.12 cont'd

	Type	NL	P	S	UK	N
1	General hospitals	Algemene ziekenhuizen (54.154 beds in 1994)	Hospitais Pentiais	Somatic hospitals (29,800 beds in 1995)		Somatic hospitals (14,500 beds, 1995) (65+ account for 50% of hospital days and 36% of discharges) + (a smaller number in some somatic hospitals)
2	Geriatric units in general hospitals	GAAZ		Geriatric wards (5,317 beds in 1995)	37,539 NHS places (1993/1994) Decline in number of hospitals providing long-term care since 1989 by one-third	
3	Long stay wards in general hospitals					
4	Medium stay wards in general hospitals					
5	Psychiatric wards in general hospitals	Psychiatrische afdeling algemeen ziekenhuis (2.089 beds in 1994)			+	
6	Geriatric hospitals			See geriatric wards		
7	Psychiatric hospitals	Psychiatrische ziekenhuizen (22.295 beds in 56 psychiatric hospitals in 1994)		Psychiatric hospitals (9,797 beds in 1994)	18,200 (1994) +	Psychiatric hospitals (3,300 beds, 1995) (few elderly patients)
8	Psycho-geriatric wards in psychiatric hospitals	Psycho-geriatric wards in psychiatric hospitals		– See psychiatric wards in	general hospitals	
9	Rehabilitation homes	±20% of the places in nursing homes are for rehabilitation				
10	Short-run nursing homes	Kortdurende opname (19,100 elderly in 1994)		Short-term stay in nursing homes and old-age homes	+	Short-term stay in nursing homes for respite care and rehabilitation
11	Short stay in old-age homes	Short stay in old-age homes		(5,442 beds in 1995)	+	
12	Geriatric day hospital	Dagbehandeling in verpleeghuis (1.868 somatic places, 1,980 psycho-geriatric places in 1994)		Available at 74 hospitals/clinics in 1993 with a weekly attendance of 5,200 visits	+	

Table 3.12 cont'd

	Type	NL	P	S	UK	N
13	Day care	Dagverzorging (in old-age homes (13,000 places in 1994)		Day care (50,000 visits/year)	+ (5% average of 65+ receive)	Day care in nursing homes
14	Nightly care in old-age homes	Nachtopvang		+		
15	Social centres for the elderly	Dienstencentra	Centros de dia (20,000 clients in 1987)	Day centres in every municipality	Day centres providing occupational therapy and meals 30,000 places in England (1990) 5% average of 65+ receive	Eldresenter (senior citizens centres/service centres) (± 20 centres, ± 150,000 users)
16	Innovative services		Apolo domiciliaria		+	
17	Preventive services				+	

Table 3.13 Community services for the elderly: types and capacity

Type	A	B	DK	D	GR	E
1 District nursing	Hauskrankenpflege Vienna: ±5,000 clients per year (1993) Austria: ±22,500 clients per year (1985)	Thuisverpleging/Soins infirmiers à domicile Be.: 15,000 district nurses (absolute terms) (1991)	Hjemmesygepleje (70% of clients are 67+)	Sozialstationen (>4,000) (See also home help services)	District nursing	Atención asistida
2 Paramedical care	Alten-/Pflegehelfer	Kinésithérapie/ Kinésithérapie Be.: 21,514 physiotherapists (1993)			Action therapy/ physiotherapy	
3 Mental health services	Psychosozialer Dienst Sachwalterschaft	Centra voor geestelijke gezondheidszorg/Centres de soins mentales Fl.: 93 centres (1995)/ Br.: 14 centres (1995)				Servicios Mentales
4 Health advisory services and health education	Modellprojekt 'Gesundes Krankenhaus'	GVO (Gezondheids voorlichting en -opvoeding)		Counselling services	Health advisory services	Educación para la salud
5 Social work	Sozialarbeit	OCMW/CPAS Be.: 589 centres (1995) Centra voor maat-schappelijk werk Fl.: 58 centres (1995)	+		Social work	Trabajo Social
6 Home help services	Heimhilfe (Vienna: 24,381 clients in 1991)	Gezins- en bejaarden-hulpdiensten/Les services d'aide aux familles et aux personnes âgées Be.: 14,352 helpers (absolute) (1990), 14,933 (*1,000) hours of home help subsidised (1990), 238 services (1990)	Hjemmehjælp (160,518 households aged 67+ in 1995)	Haus- und Familien-pflegestationen Gemeinde-, Kranken- und Altenpflegedienste Mobile soziale Hilfsdienste (Ambulante Pflegedienste (Wohlfahrtsverbände (80% market): 65,300 personnel or 47,600 FTE, including 'Sozialstationen')	Home help services	Ayuda a Domicilio (24,000 users in 1989)

Table 3.13 cont'd

Type	A	B	DK	D	GR	E
7 Cleaning services	Reinigungs- und Wäschepflegedienst (13,480 + 2,714 clients) (1991, Vienna)	Poetsdiensten/ Nettoyage, aide ménagère, maintenance de la maison, entretien du domicile Fl.: 4.550 helpers (FT) (1991); 5,823,453 hours of cleaning (1993) Wal.: 535,873 hours of cleaning (only offered by (72) OCMW's (1994))	Is part of home help			Servicios de Limpieza
8 Odd job services	Reparaturdienst (Vienna: 1,175 clients, 1991)	Klusjesdiensten/Petits travaux, dépannage à domicile Fl.: 109 services (of which 100 OCMW services) (1991); 78 helpers (FT) in OCMW services (1993)/Wal.: 69 services offered by OCMW	Havearbejde, snerydning			Servicios multidisciplinares
9 Domestic help	cf. Heimhilfe				KAPI (= Centres for the Open Protection of the Elderly) (135.000 clients in 1988)	
10 Meal distribution	Essen auf Rädern (Vienna: 6,757 clients in 1991)	Maaltijden aan huis/ Repas à domicile, distribution de repas Fl.: 4.3 million meals (1991) Wal.: 2.760.397 meals (only offered by (206) OCMWs) (1992)	Madudbrindning	Essen auf Rädern	Meal distribution	Comedores
11 Foyer restaurant	—		Cafetaria	Meal services in institutions		

Table 3.13 cont'd

	Type	A	B	DK	D	GR	E
12	Transport services	Fahrtendienst, Behindertentaxi	Vervoerdiensten voor bejaarden Fl.: 165 transport services (1995) Treinreducties (Rail Europe Senior-kaart, Golden Railpass, verminderd tarief openbaar vervoer, ...)	Befordring			Servicios de transporte
13	Care of terminally ill relatives		Palliatieve zorg/ Soins palliatifs Palliatieve thuiszorgteams 11 palliative teams in Fl. (1994) Palliatieve netwerken Fl.: 15 palliative networks (1996)	Plejeorlov			Atención a enfermos terminales
14	Family placement		Gezinsopvangdienst (Gast-, inwoon-, toezichtgezinnen)/ Service d'Accueil Familial pour Personnes Agées; Comité d'accompagnement (Familles d'accueil) Fl.: 1 service subsidised (1992)/Wal.: exists		Family placement		Familia Sustituta
15	Sitting/respite services	Pflegeurlaub	Bejaardenoppasdienst/ Accompagnement Fl.: 9 sitting services (1993)/Wal.: exists	Hjemmehos			+
16	Housing for pensioners	Seniorenwohnungen = Altenwohnungen	Bejaardenwoningen Fl.: ±17,000 houses in 1993	see housing for the disabled			Hogares del Pensionist

Table 3.13 cont'd

	Type	A	B	DK	D	GR	E
17	Home improvements	Subsidies in some provinces	Installatiepremie Aanpassings- en verbeteringspremie La domotique Be.: ±100 houses in 1994	Boligændringer		Improvements, housing accommodation	Adaptación del Hogar
18	Tele-alarm and telecommunication services	Notruf	O.a. personenalarmtoe-stellen/ Bio-télévigilance Fl.: 3,100 number of systems are subsidised (1987–93) Wal.: 44 OCMW services (1994)	Omsorgsalarmer	Emergency phone calls		Telealarma
19	Aids, facilities Technical aids Telephone Purchase of wheelchair	Telefon, Radio- und TV-Gebührenbefreiung (about 150,000 pensioners)	Sociaal telefoontarief	Technical aids			Reducción de tarifas telefónicas
20	Social benefits and other initiatives	Wohnungsbeihilfe, Sozialhilfe, Heizbeihilfe, etc. Seniorenklubs (4.500–5.000 local groups)	Parkeerkaart voor invalide bejaarden Rusthuis Info-foon 'Senioren-foon' Bijeenkomsten van thuisverzorgers, vzw Werkgroep Thuisverzorgers Lessen in gezondheidszorg en verzorging van bejaarde patiënten Fitnesscentra voor bejaarden (aanbod van ontspannende en educatieve activiteiten)				Restaciones económicas puntuales

Table 3.13 cont'd

Type	A	B	DK	D	GR	E
20 cont'd		Bejaardengroeperingen Vrijstelling van kijk- en luistergeld Plus-3-pas Sociaal elektriciteits- en gastarief				Servicio de Termalismo
21 Other innovative services		Samenwerkingsinitia-tieven/Centres de Coordination et de Soins et Services à Domicile Fl.: 83 initiatives (1995); Wal.: 56 initiatives (1993) Teams voor thuisverpleging Fl.: 264 teams (1996)		Living communities for elderly, social commission to co-ordinate help		
22 Preventive services or activities	–		Opsøgende besøg – Domiciliary visits	+		Servicios de Prevención Vacaciones Tercera Edad Asociacionismo de mayores

Type	FIN	F	IRL	I	L
1 District nursing	kotisairaanhoito	Soins infirmiers à domicile (31/12/1996: 1.547 services offer 56.650 places; 16.400 employees or 11.000 FTE) auxiliaires de vie (1992: 1 million hours for 13.000 persons of whom 6.500 are aged 65+; 1.864 FTE)	+	Assistenza Domiciliare Inegrata, ADI (257.552 clients, 1992)	Services de soins à domicile
2 Paramedical care		Pédicure libéral Kinésithérapeute libéral	+	Assistenza paramedica	
3 Mental health services	mielenterveyspalvelut		+	Servizio di Salute Mentale	

Table 3.13 cont'd

	Type	FIN	F	IRL	I	L
4	Health advisory services and health education	terveysneuvonta ja terveyskasvatus		+	Consultori familiari	
5	Social work	sosiaalityö (10,234 social workers in 1994)	+	+	Assistenza sociale	
6	Home help services	kotipalvelu (12,914 employees in 1994)	Aide ménagère (490,000 old persons and 74 million hours, 1994) ±50 000 FTE	Home help services (12,021 beneficiaries: 9,515 >65 in 1986) (3.5% of the elderly 65+ receive home help, 1995)	Assistenza domiciliare	Services d'aide à domicile (services d'aides seniors)
7	Cleaning services	siivousapu	Services de nettoyage			
8	Odd job services	tukipalvelut	Ramassage et lavage du linge; Services de petits travaux d'entretien à domicile	+	Assistenza domiciliare	
9	Domestic help	kotipalvelu	Employés de maison	+	Assistenza domiciliare (Small number)	
10	Meal distribution	ateriapalvelu	Portage de repas	+		Repas sur roues (1995: in 111 municipalities of the 118 municipalities)
11	Foyer restaurant	ateriapalvelu	Foyer restaurant			
12	Transport services	kuljetuspalvelut	Services de transport	Free travel	Carta d'argento (transport reduction)	Services de transport
13	Care of terminally ill relatives	saattohoito		+	Cure palliative	
14	Family placement	perhehoito	Placement familial	Boarding out (122 elderly persons in 1986)		
15	Sitting/respite services	kaitsemispalvelu	Gardes à domicile	Respite care		
16	Housing for pensioners/places	vanhusten asunnot		+		Pensions de famille (150 in 1995)
17	Home improvements	parannus- ja kunnostustyöt	Amélioration du confort des logements	+	Edilizia popolare	Services d'adaptation du logement
18	Tele-alarm and telecommunication services	hälytys- ja puhelinpalvelut	Télé-alarme	+	Telesoccorso	Télé-alarme

Table 3.13 cont'd

Type	FIN	F	IRL	I	L
19 Aids, facilities Technical aids Telephone Purchase of wheelchair	apuvälineet, tekniset apuvatineet	+			Services d'aides techniques
20 Social benefits and other initiatives					
21 Other innovative	innovatiiriset palvelut	Hospitalisation à domicile services (HAD) (3,950 places, 1992)		Ospedalizzazione Domiciliare	
22 Preventive services or activities	terveyskasvatus, – valistus, liikuntakampanjat, verenpainemittaukset, valistustilaisuudet, ravintoneuvonta				

Type	NL	P	S	UK	N
1 District nursing	Wijkverpleging (1994: 236,628 clients of which ±50% elderly)	Nursing services	Home nursing care (46,000 clients in 1995)	5% aged 65 or over receive district nursing	Hjenmesykepleie (31/12/95: 66,300 patients of which ±80% are 67+)
2 Paramedical care	a.o. physiotherapist (11,500 professionals in 1994)		Occupational therapists (1,695 persons in 1994); physiotherapists (966 persons in 1994)	+	Physiotherapy, etc.
3 Mental health services	RIAGG (254,900 clients; 61 institutions, 1993)		Counselling services	1% aged 65 or over see community psychiatric nurse	Counselling in service centres etc.
4 Health advisory services and health education	Gezondheidsadviesdiensten			1% aged 65 or over see health visitor	
5 Social work	Maatschappelijk werk (1994: 161 institutions; 502,876 clients of which 7% 65+)	Socia work	Social work	Social work	Social work

Table 3.13 cont'd

	Type	NL	P	S	UK	N
6	Home help services	Gezinsverzorging (1994: 234,000 clients of which ±75% elderly 65+)	Ajuda domiciliaria (4,240 clients in 1987)	Home help services (169,000 clients 65+ in 1995)	Home help 9% average of 65+ receive	Hjemmehjelp (31/12/95: 116,300 clients of which ±85% are 67+)
7	Cleaning services					= part of home help
8	Odd job services					= part of home help
9	Domestic help	Gezinszorg		= part of home help	= part of home help	see home help
10	Meal distribution	Maaltijdverstrekking	Meal distribution	Meals-on-wheels (8,000 clients in 1992)	Meal distribution: 26 million meals distributed in England in 1994 – 2% average of 65+ receive	Matombringing
11	Foyer restaurant	+				
12	Transport services	Treinreducties Vervoersdienst voor gehandicapten Car adaptations Wheelchairs Transport allowances	Passe de 3° Idade	Transportation services (432,000 clients in 1995)	Subsidised travel on public transport in some areas	Transporttjeneste + favourable price on taxi/public transport
13	Care of terminally ill relatives			Integrated part institutional and home-based care	Care of terminally ill relatives Available from public, private or charitable providers. Fee may be required, depending on individual need and level of income	= part of home nursing
14	Family placement		Acollimento familiar			
15	Sitting/respite services			= part of home help	Available from public, private or charitable providers. Fee may be paid depending on individual need and level of income	Besökstjeneste (visitors)
16	Housing for pensioners	Bejaardenwoningen (±215,000 in 1993)		+	Special housing in Scotland developed since 1960. Less well developed in other regions	see sheltered housing/service flats

Table 3.13 cont'd

Type	NL	P	S	UK	N
17 Home improvements	Woningverbetering/ renovatie/aanpassing		Home adaptions (40,000 users in 1995)	Improvement in housing conditions, 'staying put' schemes	Utbedringslån og-tilskudd
18 Tele-alarm and telecommunication services	Tele-alarm		Security alarm (54,000 in 1992)	Available from public, private or charitable providers. Fee may be paid depending on individual need and level of income	Omsorgsalarmer
19 Aids, facilities Technical aids Telephone Purchase of wheelchair	Aids and facilities provided by home nursing organisations		Technical aids	+	Tekniske hjelpemiddler
20 Social benefits and other initiatives				+	
21 Other innovative services				+	Senior Citizen Centres (service centres) Universities of III age
22 Preventive services or activities	+			Annual screening of people aged 75 and over by general practitioner	Senior Citizen Centres

4 Differences in Treatment of Similar Categories of Need

1 Methodology

The focus of the study on the elderly who are (1) dependent, (2) over normal retirement age, and (3) in need of long-term care constitutes the general framework within which the case studies have been developed.

Since an exhaustive study of the availability of services exclusively based on case studies was considered impossible, we have chosen for a full description of the available services (which services – in cash and in kind, formal and informal – who finances, who utilises, who is eligible to utilise), supplemented with the description of the social protection arrangements of a limited number of specific cases. The reasons for including these case studies are twofold: firstly, it is a very convenient methodology for comparing the level of social protection and the eligibility of services for elderly persons in different countries, and secondly, it makes the report easier to understand. The examination of case studies can also help to reveal hidden features of the welfare system.

It should be made clear, however, that the case studies are only illustrative and cannot be supposed to represent the entire elderly population. Therefore we make no claim to be comprehensive. However, in choosing the case studies, we selected those which probably appear most frequently in practice. In this way, despite the lack of comprehensiveness, a large share of the elderly population is covered by the case studies.

In defining the cases, our goal was to distinguish, on the basis of the most relevant subdimensions, a limited number of categories of elderly people, on the basis of which the differences in social protection arrangements for the elderly in the considered countries (legal rights and financing of services) should become clear.

This chapter gives a synthetic analysis of the information we have about those several cases. The basic information is reproduced in a separate volume, the 'Statistical and Institutional Annexes' (see 'List of Publications on Social

Protection for Dependency in Old Age in the EU and Norway' at the end of this volume).

2   The Choice of Case Studies

Dependency has four dimensions (see also chapter 1):
– physical dimension;
– mental dimension;
– economic dimension, with reference to:
   *   the financial situation of the older person;
– availability of personal assets and income;
– availability of resources from family (in case of insufficient income of the older person):
   *   insurance record of the elderly person;
– social dimension with reference to the elderly person's living arrangements and the availability of a social network.

  The following 13 case studies have been defined on the basis of this observation (see Figure 4.1). One case study has been defined as optional. The others should be representative of the situations of dependent elderly people.

3   Defining the Dimensions of the Case Studies

The following definitions of and remarks about the dimensions of dependency underlie our choice of the 13 case studies and should be kept in mind when reading the information on each country.

3.1   *Physical Dimension*

Because the focus of the study is on dependent people in need of long-term care, each case study in the present research project refers to elderly persons who are to a large extent disabled or physically dependent. For a clear description of who is 'to a large extent disabled or physically dependent', we refer to chapter 1.

  In the case studies of couples living in the community, only one of the two older persons is considered to be fully disabled.

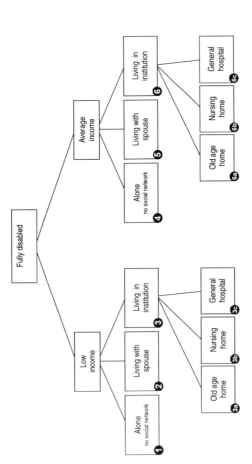

7   Widow, female, +80 years, 'survivor' (has never been in employment), income spouse low, fully disabled (in need of long-term care), living alone, no social network.

8   Demented elderly person, physically able, average income, living with spouse.

9   Immigrant, elderly person with foreign nationality who has stayed in the country for a shorter period than needed for insurance record or shorter than minimum period of membership, further to be defined by the country according to rules (facultative).

Figure 4.1   Definition of types of cases

3.2   Mental Dimension

Only one case study takes into account the mental dimension: case study 8, which includes persons who have been medically assessed as demented patients.

3.3   Economic Dimension

Two categories were retained in defining the cases:
– low income category;
– average income category.

Only the pensions the elderly receive are taken into account when the term 'income' is referred to. In order to keep the case studies simple, no other personal incomes or assets and other personal resources are taken into account. Income is thus defined in a more limited way than in chapter 2, which aims to give a global view on the financial situation of the elderly in each country (in terms of pension and other incomes or resources). Moreover, if other personal incomes or resources have to be drawn upon by the elderly in case of insufficient pension (the low-income cases), this is mentioned in the description of the cases.

The low income category is supposed to receive the minimum income legally guaranteed in each country to single elderly persons or to two older persons, depending upon the case study considered. By comparing the legal minimum guaranteed income with the poverty lines according to EU norms, the degree of social protection in terms of cash benefits can be assessed. The average income category is the group of elderly persons who receive approximately the average income in each country for retired private sector wage earners who have retired at the legal pension age (complete career).

The differences in low and average income represent differences in the insurance record of the older person, since the pension level is to a large extent determined by the previous occupation of the older person or his/her spouse. In every case study, except the special 'widow' case study, one (and only one) older person is supposed to have a personal insurance record. This means that, in the case studies of persons living alone, the person him- or herself has been in employment. In cases involving couples, only one of the older persons is supposed to have been in employment. We assume that this is the most common situation for dependent older couples at the present time (male worker who has been in employment while his wife is financially dependent). We realise, however, that in the future these 'single career' pensions will be getting less representative.

Because this group of elderly persons appears frequently in reality and because it is especially vulnerable to poverty, the case of a very old widow is included in order to represent the large group of female 'survivors' who have never been in employment and thus have no personal insurance record.

3.4   Social Dimension and Living Situation

The following categories are included because they are considered to refer to the most common living situations of elderly people:
–   living alone, no social network available: the older person cannot rely upon relatives for help and care or financial assistance;
–   living as a couple in the community;
–   living or staying in an institution:
  –   living in an old-age home;
  –   living in a nursing home;
  –   staying in a hospital.

3.5   Age

Age is normally considered to be the best index of dependency, though it is usually combined with the physical dimension: the older the person, the more he/she becomes physically dependent; especially after the age of 85 the need and use of care services because of physical dependency increases rapidly. It is not age in itself, but rather the increase in physical dependency that usually accompanies ageing, that is relevant for the research.

Because only highly disabled people are considered and because no discrimination on the basis of age (in any case, not above the age of 65) is supposed to be made for the availability of services, further distinctions based on age – which would multiply the number of case studies – are considered unnecessary. However, if relevant for the description of services or their availability, additional remarks about the age of the older persons are made.

3.6   Gender

No distinctions have been made on the basis of gender (except for the case of the widow, but even here it is not the gender, but rather the fact that the older person is a 'survivor' that is important). The omission of gender is again inspired by our efforts to limit the cases, since in terms of the right to social security, differences might exist in practice. So, again, if relevant for the description of services or their availability (which will probably be the case in the description of the pension rights), additional remarks are made about the gender.

4 Social Protection of Different Categories of Dependent Elderly People in Austria

4.1 The Definition of Case Studies (see Appendix 2)

In Austria the assessment of dependency does not rely on ADL criteria but only on the number of hours a dependent person needs care. According to the number of hours needing help and care, a certain level at the attendance allowance scheme is accorded to the dependent person, e.g. level 4 means: at least 180 hours monthly care needs. The assessment is done by medical doctors, and is very much based on physical disabilities, meaning that demented persons usually are classified in lower levels of the attendance allowance scheme.

It is important to note that differences in the level of the attendance allowance might occur even within the group of 'persons needing exceptional care'.

Ninety-nine per cent of the inhabitants are health insured (persons with a private voluntary health insurance do have some advantages). Most older persons are covered by the pension system (be it by means of paid employment or as widows/widowers). Those who never had the chance to get into the pension system can rely on social assistance. These latter persons have the same right to receive attendance allowances.

A low income pensioner is defined as a person receiving a compensatory supplement on top of an old-age or invalidity pension which is below the set standard rate (standard rates in 1996: 587 ECU for singles; 838 ECU for couples). Thus, the sum of the pension entitlement, other income and the compensatory supplement does not exceed the amount of the standard rate.

Two hundred and eighty thousand persons or 16.7 per cent of the pensioners are receiving a compensatory supplement on top of their pension. Seventy-two per cent of them are women. Approximately 250,000 persons are receiving attendance allowances above the age of 65.

The data on average pensions in Austria are only partially telling. Firstly, a cumulation of pension entitlements is possible. Secondly, different pension systems have to be taken into account. In the General Social Security Law

(ASVG), the highest pension is about 2,010 ECU (old-age pension), respectively 1,191 ECU (survivor pension). The average old-age pension for male white collar workers is 1,303 ECU (for women: 774 ECU (December 1994)). For male blue collar workers, the average old-age pension is 849 ECU (for women: 424 ECU (December 1994)). The average invalidity pension (*Pension wegen geminderter Arbeitsfähigkeit*) is 737 ECU (all pension systems, excluding civil servants). For civil servants the average pension for men and women (*Ruhensbezüge*) is about 2,278 ECU per month.

Approximately 450,000 pensioners have a pension entitlement above 1,303 ECU. There are 902,021 persons who receive more than the median pension (all pensions: 737 ECU (December 1994)), out of which about 750,000 are above the age of 60. 580,000 are above 65. Only one-third of women receive a pension higher than 737 ECU as against about 85 per cent of all men (all direct pensions).

It is important to mention that all Austrian pensions and benefits, except the attendance allowance, are paid 14 times a year.

4.2   Social Protection of the Case Studies

4.2.1 Case study 1: fully disabled, low income, living in community, alone without social network A dependent person is defined as a person needing more than 180 hours of care per month (corresponding with level 4 of the attendance allowance).

Of the persons 65+, receiving an attendance allowance, 8 per cent get level 4. In 1996 there were ±30,000 persons receiving level 4 of the attendance allowance.

If the person is taking advantage of social care services, he is obliged to pay a part of his income (including the attendance allowance) as a contribution per service-hour received. In many provinces, there are minimum contributions (e.g. Vienna: 5.36 ECU per hour) and additional contributions calculated from the client's net income (about 1 per cent). In the case of persons receiving very low pensions (standard rate) most provinces only cash from the attendance allowance.

In reality, fully disabled persons with a range of care needs corresponding with level 4 (or higher) of the attendance allowance, won't be able to live at home any longer if there is no social network to support them.

4.2.2 Case study 2: fully disabled, low income, living in community with spouse (which is the main carer) Dependency is defined as needing more than 180 hours of care plus need for continuous presence of a helper. This corresponds with level 6 of the attendance allowance. In 1996, approximately 6,000 persons were receiving level 6 of the attendance allowance. This is about 2 per cent of all persons receiving attendance allowance above the age of 65.

Whereas health and social care services and living conditions and legal rights are concerned, no differences are noticed between people living alone and pensioners living with their spouse.

4.2.3 Case studies 3a and 6a: fully disabled, low income or average income, living in an old-age home A dependent person is defined as a person needing more than 180 hours of care per month (corresponding with level 4 of the attendance allowance).

In 1993, approximately 25,000 persons above the age of 65 were living in 'old-age and nursing homes' (but not occupying 'nursing beds').

Most pensioners moving into long-term care institutions have to pay their whole pension (except some pocket money) and their attendance allowance to cover the costs. Eighty per cent of the pension will be transferred to the provider to pay for the old-age home. Also 80 per cent of the real attendance allowance (in this case: level 4) is paid directly to the provider (usually the provincial government). The person entitled to the attendance allowance will receive a lump sum of 85 ECU (1995), i.e. 20 per cent of level 3 of the attendance allowance, as additional pocket money. Since 1 May 1996, this lump sum has been reduced to 10 per cent of level 3, thus 42 ECU per month.

Only 30 to 40 per cent of persons living in institutions are able to cover the total costs. Depending on the provincial Social Assistance Acts, personal wealth and/or co-payment of siblings are to be used before social assistance subsidies are granted (principle of subsidiarity). In relation to this latter aspect, some provinces are more strict than others to let siblings pay for institutional care of other family members.

4.2.4 Case studies 3b and 6b: fully disabled, low income or average income, living in a nursing home In 1993 approximately 30,000 persons above the age of 65 were living in 'old-age and nursing homes', 'nursing homes' or geriatric hospitals occupying 'nursing beds'.

The sources of income of residents in nursing homes are the same as of people living in old-age homes and the rules of the pocket money are the same.

The real cost of a nursing home is usually higher than the cost in an old-age home. However, as many old-age homes are more and more becoming nursing homes, real costs are hardly available. Badelt et al. (1995) estimated the costs for institutional care as follows: between 521 and 744 ECU per month in case of no or slight dependency, but between 1,303 and 3,052 ECU per month in case of severe disability.

4.2.5 Case studies 3c and 6c: fully disabled, low income or average income, staying in a general hospital (since more than four weeks) The attendance allowance is not paid in case of a hospital stay which exceeds four weeks.

Co-financing for a hospital stay is 4.5 ECU per day. Persons with an income below 587 ECU (for singles, 1996)/838 ECU (for couples) are exempted from paying this amount.

4.2.6 Case study 4: fully disabled, average income, living in community, alone without social network This case is almost like case 1 except that these pensioners have an average income. Contrary to the case studies concerning low income pensioners, it is now relevant to distinguish according to gender, because the average pensions of women are generally much lower than those of men. It is also relevant to make a distinction according to the social security situation, because average pensions of persons in the general Social Security Law are much lower than those of civil servants, i.e. even the highest possible ASVG-pension is lower than the average pension of civil servants.

If the person is taking advantage of social care services, he is obliged to pay a part of his income (including the attendance allowance) as a contribution per service-hour received. In many provinces, there are minimum contributions (e.g. Vienna: 5.36 ECU per hour) and additional contributions calculated from the client's net income (about 1 per cent). Suppose for instance a pensioner living in Vienna with an income of 1,340 ECU and 447 ECU housing costs. His net income is 893 ECU. He will pay 1 per cent of his income to social services (or 9 ECU) plus 5.36 ECU or in total 14 ECU per service-hour.

4.2.7 Case study 5: fully disabled, average income, living in community with spouse A dependent person is defined as a person needing more than 180 hours of care and needing exceptional care, e.g. infusions, artificial respiration. This degree of dependency corresponds with level 7 of the attendance allowance. In 1996 approximately 4,000 persons were receiving level 7 of the attendance allowance. Of the persons above the age of 65 receiving an attendance allowance the percentage of persons getting level 7 was about 1.5 per cent. This percentage shows that the number of beneficiaries in this level is very small. In reality, most of these persons might live in a nursing home.

And even in the latter case the medical doctors assessing the person might be inclined to concede level 4, 5 or 6 only.

In this case it is assumed that also the wife has her own pension entitlement.

The large difference with case 4 is that it usually will be the spouse who will care for the husband.

4.2.8 Comments on other case studies

Case study 7: fully disabled widow, female 'survivor', 80+, living in community, alone without social network The situation of a widow without any career on the labour market is very similar to the situation of an elderly single person with low income. Dependency is defined as needing more than 180 hours of care plus needing exceptional care, e.g. infusions, artificial respiration (level 7 of the attendance allowance).

The average pension of widows is currently not higher than 460 ECU (December 1994) which means that widows of husbands with low income will in any case receive not more than the standard rate of the compensatory supplement for single persons (574 ECU (1995)).

In December 1994, 280,000 persons were receiving compensatory supplements. Seventy-two per cent of them (202,000) are women. 25 per cent of women receiving widow pensions are receiving compensatory supplements.

For this case study it is relevant to distinguish according to gender and according to social security situation. The latter is true because, firstly, average pensions of persons in the general Social Security Law are much lower than those of civil servants. Secondly, the share of widows who have to rely on compensatory supplements is at 36 per cent for farmers, but only at 3 per cent for white collar employees.

Case study 8: senile older person Elderly people suffering from dementia are in principle treated like physically disabled elderly people.

4.3 Overview

The differences in protection between some of these cases are very small. The differences that do arise mostly relate to income protection.

Social services require a consumer co-payment, which is mostly income-related.

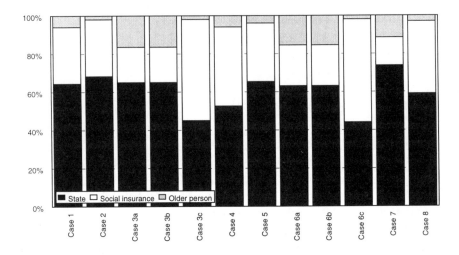

Figure 4.2   Overview of the case studies: the costs of additional needs (*) of dependent older persons and the estimated contribution of different actors

*   Only the financing of additional needs of dependent persons (in cash and in kind) are highlighted, i.e. the financing of pensions was not taken into account.

5   Social Protection of Different Categories of Dependent Elderly People in Belgium

5.1   The Definition of Case Studies (see Appendix 2)

All case studies involve elderly who have reached the age of 65. Elderly above the age of 65 made up 16 per cent of the Belgian population at 1 January 1996, and 15.4 per cent in 1993.

All pensioners considered in the case studies are physically disabled. For a description of physical dependency, an index of six activities is used (dressing, continence, feeding, bathing, toileting and transfer). A person is considered to be physically dependent if he is at least dependent in bathing, dressing, transfer and/or toileting (= category B and C). No information is available on the present state of physical disability among the elderly as a whole (i.e. living in community and residential services) in Belgium (Leroy, 1995). However, we do have information according to the living situation.

Table 4.1 shows the number of physical dependent elderly persons in old-age homes, nursing homes and elderly persons living in the community in Belgium.

Table 4.1   Number of physical dependent elderly persons in Belgium according to the living situation

Target group	Year	Degree of (physical) dependency	Number
Elderly persons in old-age homes	30.9.1996	Fully dependent:[1]	39,116
		B category:	17,474
		C category:	22,116
Elderly persons in nursing homes	30.9.1996	Fully dependent:[1]	18,034
		B category:	2,553
		C category:	15,481
Elderly persons living in the community[2]	1992	Fully dependent:[1]	30,793
		A category:[3]	18,671
		B category:[3]	12,122

Notes

1   According to Vanden Boer (1992), elderly can be considered as fully dependent when reaching the dependency conditions of elderly in nursing homes (namely B or C category of dependency).
2   Concerns elderly persons aged 75 and more.
3   The conditions for the A and B category in the community are the same as respectively those for the B and C category in old-age homes and nursery homes.

Sources: Leroy, 1995; RIZIV statistieken (30 September 1996).

The income of a single older person is considered to be 'low' if it is lower than 11,596 ECU/year (1 May 1996). This amount is the income limit for a WIGW (Widows, Invalids, Pensioners and Orphans) to have a preferential status in the health insurance. If a pensioner has a spouse to support, the income limit is increased with 2,147 ECU/year. This income differs considerably from the guaranteed minimum income for elderly, which is 6,382 ECU/year for a single and 8,509 ECU/year for a couple (1 October 1997).

The making of a distinction between female and male elderly is irrelevant where the social protection arrangements are concerned.

District nursing and home help utilise profiles of clients, taking the presence of a social network into account. Moreover, meals-on-wheels and home help will preferentially be provided for people who are on lower incomes and have higher levels of disability. The availability of other social services for elderly persons living in the community does not differ according to presence of a social network or spouse.

In Belgium private insurance to cover fees or shares of total costs that are not covered by social security or state financing exists but is not widespread. It is expanding, however.

5.2   Social Protection of the Case Studies

5.2.1 Social and fiscal franchise Before discussing the social protection arrangements (health and social services) of the case studies 1, 3a, 3b, 3c, 4, 6a, 6b and 6c, social and fiscal franchise are described.

Since 1 January 1994, higher consumer co-payments were introduced to economise for the rising costs of health care. To make this socially acceptable, arrangements were made to restrict consumer co-payments per person to a certain ceiling (i.e. franchise). Two types of franchise were introduced, namely social and fiscal franchise. The former is defined as follows: some patients with a low income, such as WIGW with a preferential status in health care and persons with a guaranteed minimum income for elderly, pay 381 ECU consumer co-payments a year at most. Contributions above 381 ECU are all paid back by the health insurance. Persons who are not belonging to this group, benefit from fiscal franchise. All out of pocket payments above a ceiling, which depends on the income, are paid back by the treasury: low incomers get back all contributions above 381 ECU; the ceiling for the highest incomes is 1,271 ECU. The reimbursement by the treasure can take more than one year. According to data of 1994 of LCM (Christian health insurance organisation), more than 70 per cent of the out of pocket payments of persons benefiting from social franchise are contributions for stay in a hospital. The other consumer co-payments were mainly for physiotherapy and consultations and visits to general practitioners and specialists (Diels, 1996).

5.2.2 Case study 1: fully disabled, low income, living in community, alone without social network Elderly persons living in the community can call upon general practitioners or specialist health care services. When using these ser-vices, low income pensioners pay 8 to 14 per cent of the fee, which is higher for specialist care than for general care and which depends upon whether or not the visit is paid to the patient's home. The national social security insurance pays the additional 86 to 92 per cent of the fees (90 to 91 per cent in 1994).

For hospital services, a hospitalisation fee has to be paid for each day the patient stays. In general hospitals, this hospitalisation fee amounts to 175

ECU per day in 1994 (89 ECU per day in 1987 for all types of wards). The state (Ministry of Health) covers 25 per cent of the cost of the stay in a common room (more than two persons); Social Security covers the remaining 75 per cent. The consumer co-payment differs according to the length of the stay in the hospital and whether the patient is a low income earner (lower consumer co-payment for a low income earner). The fee of a low income earning pensioner represented only approximately 2.5 per cent of the total cost in 1987. The patient has to pay all costs of facilities (stay in a single or double room, TV, telephone, etc.). As in 1994, older persons are exempted from cost-sharing for ambulatory hospital services, except for clinical biology and radiology. Elderly persons have to pay 42.5 per cent of total costs and a lump sum for ambulatory clinical biology and a lump sum for ambulatory radiology. The national social security insurance pays the additional costs.

Pharmaceuticals are paid for by the elderly themselves and partly reimbursed by the national social security insurance. The reimbursement rates are still 0 per cent, 85 per cent, 50 per cent, 40 per cent and 20 per cent. Those rates are based on the therapeutic aspects.

For physiotherapy, the elderly have to pay still 10 to 20 per cent of the total costs; for dental services 0 to 38 per cent. District nursing is still almost provided free of charge – contributions of the elderly represent only 0 to 1 per cent of total costs – but is only provided upon prescription by a physician (except for ADL help).

For social services, personal fees are higher and are – in contrast to already mentioned services – rising. For home help services, contributions of 20 per cent in Flanders (while 13 per cent in 1993) and 14 per cent in Wallony and for meals-on-wheels in the public sector, contributions of about 77 per cent (while about 70 per cent in the whole sector in 1991) of the costs have to be made (low or middle income earners). Personal contributions depend upon the level of income and not only upon the low versus middle income status. In contrast to the health care services, social services are very little/not co-financed by public institutions at the national level, but rather at the regional or local level, or else by social assistance.

5.2.3 Case study 3a: fully disabled, low income, living in an old-age home At 1 October 1992, 33,271 B and C category persons lived in old-age homes in Belgium (2.1 per cent of the 65+ population) (Ministerie van Sociale Zaken, 1994); at 30 September 1996, 39,590 B and C category persons or 2.4 per cent of the 65+ population (RIZIV-statistieken, 30 September 1996). This concerns elderly persons with low and middle incomes.

People living in old-age homes can call upon the same health care services as people living in the community except, of course, for district nursing. Financing arrangements are almost identical to those for people on low income living in the community.

The cost for the stay in an old-age home itself is divided into the cost of care and the cost of stay. The cost of care is – in theory – completely financed by the national social security insurance. The contribution paid by the RIZIV (health insurance) depends upon the level of disability of the person admitted to the old-age home. It does not depend upon the level of income of the older person. Bogaert and De Prins (1996) shows that in reality the elderly pay 13 per cent to 42 per cent of the cost of care. The VVI-KBG survey (VVI-informatie, November 1995) mentions 16 per cent. The cost of stay (rent of the room, meals, etc.) is normally not publicly financed. In the first place the resources of the older person him- or herself (including savings, personal assets and any kind of inheritance) are drawn upon. Since the pensioners only have a small income, it is assumed that these resources are insufficient to cover expenses. In this case, contributions from certain members of the family are demanded. It is only when contributions from relatives are either unavailable or insufficient that social assistance (OCMW) will cover the additional expenses. It is important to note that the OCMWs have the duty to pay 'pocket money' to the pensioner if his/her income is completely used to cover old-age home expenses. On average, this 'pocket money' per pensioner amounts to 729 ECU per month in 1993 (Van Velthoven and Boeckxstaens, 1993).

Research has shown that, as in 1988, about 30 per cent of the elderly in old-age homes in Flanders is financially supported by OCMW in 1993 (Bogaert and De Prins, 1996).

5.2.4 Case study 3b: fully disabled, low income, living in a nursing home At 1 October 1992, 17,768 B and C category persons lived in nursing homes in Belgium (1.1 per cent of the population aged 65+) (Ministerie van Sociale Zaken, 1994); at 30 September 1996, 18,034 B and C category persons or 1.1 per cent of the population aged 65+ (RIZIV-statistieken, 30 September 1996). It is not possible to make a distinction according to the level of income.

The fees that are paid by the RIZIV (health insurance) to cover the costs of care are higher for the nursing homes than for old-age homes; (the costs for physiotherapy, which for persons staying in an old-age home have to be covered personally, are included in the costs of care and paid for by the RIZIV). Again, the costs of stay (hotel costs) have to be covered by the older person/family/ social assistance. 'Pocket money' is also applicable to people living in nursing homes.

As in 1991, 31 per cent of the population living in nursing homes in Flanders is in 1993 financially supported by OCMW (social assistance) (Van Camp and Van Rensbergen, 1995).

Nursing homes provide a combination of nursing and social care. Therefore, people staying in these institutions do not need other social services.

Where other health care services are concerned (except for physiotherapy), there are no differences with case study 3a.

5.2.5 Case study 3c: fully disabled, low income, staying in a general hospital Pensioners on low income staying in a general hospital for a longer time pay the usual daily fee that pensioners on preferential status pay (a small share of the hospitalisation fee). Until 1994, older people staying a longer period in general hospitals were hospitalised in special wards (V-wards). In these wards the same basic care was provided as is provided in nursing homes; (differences in care were attributed to medical specialist treatment). People staying in nursing homes, however, have to cover a higher share of the costs. Since long-term care for elderly persons in hospitals is much more expensive from the viewpoint of the state and social security, these wards were being completely cut back. From 1994 onwards, older people can be hospitalised in specialised beds for treatment and rehabilitation (Sp-wards). Treatment in these wards is extendable, but however temporary.

As in 1994, elderly persons with a low income are exempted from cost-sharing for supervision by a GP or specialist, radiology, technical medical acts and special technical medical acts (general special services) (except lump sum). Personal contributions for clinical biology are not free and, however, are higher than personal contributions for ambulatory clinical biology. Personal contributions for dental services are also not free. Financial arrangements for physiotherapy are identical with those for elderly persons on low income living in the community and in an old-age home.

Elderly persons staying in a hospital pay a daily lump sum of 0.64 ECU for pharmaceuticals.

5.2.6 Case study 4: fully disabled, average income, living in community, alone without social network The contributions for health care services of elderly persons living on an average income are higher than those of the low income earners: 30 per cent for a consultation with the GP, 35 per cent for a visit from the GP and 40 per cent for a consultation with a specialist. For physiotherapy, average income earners have to pay twice as much as pensioners with a preferential status. The contributions of the elderly represent 25 per cent[1] of total costs of district nursing and 10 to 50 per cent of total costs of dental services. Not 85 per cent but 75 per cent of the costs are reimbursed by the national social security organisation when pharmaceuticals are bought in a pharmacy; other reimbursement rates remain the same.

Contributions for the use of hospital services are also higher: 7 per cent of the hospitalisation fee has to be privately paid (in 1987); contributions for technical medical acts and for ambulatory special technical medical services can be 15 to 25 per cent of the fee. As of 1 January 1994, pensioners without preferential status are also asked to pay an additional fixed amount of 25 ECU when they enter the hospital. Contributions of middle income earners for ambulatory clinical biology and radiology are the same as of those of low income earners (except a lump sum).

As already mentioned, home help services are delivered by preference to low income earners. On average, 20 per cent and 14 per cent of the costs have to be covered privately in respectively Flanders and Wallony. For meals-on-wheels (organised by the public sector) people living on higher income pay more than 77 per cent of the total costs. Personal contributions for home help services and meals-on-wheels do depend upon the level of income and not only upon low versus middle income criterion.

Except for the rising contributions of home help services and meals-on-wheels, the situation of the other services remained the same as in 1993/1994.

5.2.7 Case study 6a: fully disabled, average income, living in an old-age home As in 1994, for the provision of health care services (except for district nursing), the financing arrangements for average income earners in the community are valid (case study 4). For physiotherapy in old-age homes, average income earners also have to pay twice the contribution of low income earners.

The public contributions (costs of care) made for the stay in an old-age home of a pensioner on average income is the same as the contribution made for people on low income. The contribution does not depend on the income of the pensioner, but rather on disability. The costs of stay which are not publicly paid will be covered by the pensioner himself.[2]

5.2.8 Case study 6b: fully disabled, average income, living in a nursing home Public contributions for a stay in a nursing home (costs of care) do not depend upon income. Physiotherapy is included in the costs of care and does not have to be paid for privately. Since the pensioner has an average income, the costs of the stay in the nursing home will be covered by him- or herself.

No special remarks have to be made regarding the health care services. Contributions for these services are the same as in case study 4 (except for district nursing and physiotherapy).

5.2.9 Case study 6c: fully disabled, average income, staying in general hospital
Pensioners on average income pay the usual daily fee of pensioners without preferential status. For pensioners on average income, a stay in the hospital is more expensive than for pensioners on low income, while there is no such difference for a stay in a nursing home. The contributions for the hospital services, however, stay a small share of the total cost of a hospital stay and are much less than the daily fees in a nursing home.

For general and specialist services, the pensioner has to cover 35 per cent of the total costs. Personal contributions for physiotherapy, technical medical acts and dental services are higher than – and for other health services are equally high as (except lump sum) – for elderly persons with a low income. The situation remained the same as in 1994.

5.3   Overview

In Belgium, most health and social services for the elderly require a consumer co-payment. These co-payments differ according to a persons income: the lower the income, the lower the consumer co-payment; or the lower the income, the larger the social protection concerning health and social services. Consumer co-payments (social protection) also differ according to the case study. These differences can be small, e.g. between an elderly person who lives in a nursing home and an elderly person who lives in an old-age home.

Granting a guaranteed minimum income for the elderly, a housing subsidy, or allowance for help for older persons and 'pocket money' is income- or means-tested. Income support can also differ according to the case study: e.g. the level of a minimum income differs between a family and a single person.

6   Social Protection of Different Categories of Dependent Elderly People in Denmark

6.1   *The Definition of Case Studies (see Appendix 2)*

The principle of Danish policy for elderly people is, that accessibility to cash benefits and public services for the elderly should be the same irrespective of which type of housing they live in. At the same time most health and social services are tax financed and without any user payment. Therefore there are little differences between people with low income and people with average income and between people living independently and people living in an institution. Besides average income is just a little higher than low income which consists of public pension because rather few retirees have income in excess of public pension.

All elderly persons considered in the case studies are dependent as regards performance of the four instrumental activities: cooking, shopping, cleaning and transportation. Furthermore the elderly are dependent on assistance as regards carrying out one of the following six personal activities: eating, dressing, bathing, toileting, continence and walking.

Low income means that the elderly person has only public pension (the basic amount and the full pension supplement) and potentially ATP (compulsory occupational pension).

6.2   *Social Protection of the Case Studies*

6.2.1 Case study 1: fully disabled, low income, living in community, alone without social network About half the people aged 65+ lives alone and about 10 per cent of the people aged 70+ is dependent on assistance for going out-of-doors, walking stairs, getting about the house, washing, dressing or cutting toenails (Platz, 1989). This means that less than 5 per cent of elderly people aged 65+ both lives alone and is dependent on help for PADL. About half the pensioners living alone has an income almost only consisting of the public pension.

The pensioner gets full public pension and receives a personal allowance for heating, medical drugs and for expenses for possible glasses. The old person also receives a rent subsidy so that he will only pay a rent of 10 per cent of his income if he lives in a flat not exceeding 65 m^2. Rent above 7,010 ECU a year (1996) is not subsidised.

Health care services such as visits to general practitioners, specialists, hospital services and district nursing are delivered free of charge. Medical drugs are subsidised by the national government. The local authorities mostly grant a personal allowance for financing the medicines. Only a small share remains to be paid by the pensioners. In general, the use of health care services depends on prescriptions from or referral by the general practitioner.

Pensioners living alone with severe disabilities receive home help for housework and personal care probably more times a day and every day in a week. Home help, technical aids and alarm systems are provided free of charge and irrespective of income. For meals-on-wheels the elderly have to pay at least the cost of food but some local authorities charge, too, for a share of the labour costs. Also if the pensioner is staying in a day centre once or twice a week, or if he stays in a day-care home, he has to pay for the services he uses (hairdressing, pedicure, meals, use of raw materials for needlework, etc.). All social services are tax-financed and granted irrespective of potential possibilities of help from family. Access to social services is dependent upon referral by the local authority. It is important to note that, even though the pensioner lives on a low income, he has to pay the same user charge as a person whose income reaches an average level and/or who has other resources available.

If the house or flat of the pensioner is not suitable, considering the pensioners incapacities, the local authority might offer an adapted dwelling. Rent in this dwelling is subsidised according to the same rules as rent in ordinary housing, this means that the pensioner pays a rent of maximum 10 per cent of income. For this kind of housing there is no limitation on the size of rent that is subsidised.

6.2.2 Case study 2: fully disabled, low income, living in community with spouse

About 40 per cent of the married couples where both are pensioners have an income consisting almost only of public pension and ATP, which will be the minimum income.

The two partners of a married couple have each a lower public pension than the single pensioner. The pension supplement is higher to pensioners living alone than to pensioners living with a spouse. The married pensioner will get personal allowances and rent subsidies like a single pensioner (in this case 85 m^2 are subsidised) and access to health services is the same.

When allocating home help to a married pensioner, the local authority will consider the ability of the spouse. If the spouse can do the housework, home help will not be allocated for that, but probably home help is allocated for personal care unless the spouse is willing to take care of that. If the spouse can cook, meals-on-wheels are not supplied and normally an emergency alarm is not installed if the spouse is well. Other social services are offered if the local authority finds it appropriate.

The married pensioner has access to adapted dwellings in the same way as do single pensioners.

6.2.3 Case studies 3b and 6b: fully disabled, low income or average income, living in a nursing home In 1995 in total 32,500 people aged 65+ lived in a nursing home. The number is still diminishing because nursing homes are changed into adapted housing. Housing for elderly people is no longer built under the concept of nursing homes.

The sources of income of residents in nursing homes are the same as of people living in ordinary housing and the rules of the public pension are the same. Residents pay a rent dependent on the size of income, the standard of the nursing home and the size of the area that the residents have at their disposal. Besides the residents pay for heating and electricity. Normally the residents will have to pay for cleaning, meals and laundry. The price varies because of differences in costs. Help for personal care and participation in day centre activities is free of charge.

People living in nursing homes have access to health services on the same conditions as other citizens.

6.2.4 Case study 4: fully disabled, average income, living in community, alone without social network This case is almost like case 1 except that these pensioners have an income in excess of public pension and ATP (compulsory occupational pension). About 25 per cent of the single pensioners have an income about average. If the income in excess of the public pension does not exceed 5,814 ECU (1996) the pensioner is granted the basic pension as well as the full supplement. This will be the case if the pensioner has an average income.

The pensioner will get a personal allowance for heating, but the allowance will be reduced because of income above the level of the public pension. The pensioner with an average income will get a rent subsidy and pays a rent of 10 per cent of income if the flat does not exceed 65 m^2.

As far as access to health care, social services and housing are concerned, there are no differences between pensioners with an average income and low income pensioners. Average income pensioners will get smaller personal allowances for medical drugs and because of a higher income they will have to pay a higher rent in an adapted dwelling.

6.2.5 Case study 5: fully disabled, average income, living in community with spouse About 25 per cent of the married couples where both are pensioners have an income around average. This case is very like the case of a married pensioner with low income. The pensioner of course has a higher total income but he has experienced no deduction in the public pension. He will just under special circumstances receive personal allowance for heating. The pensioner has to pay a rent of 10 per cent of income up to 19,005 ECU (1996) and 20 per cent of income above this amount. If actual rent exceeds that and the flat is not above 85 m² he will receive a rent subsidy to pay the rest.

He will have access to health services, social services and adapted housing on the same conditions as the low income pensioner. Rent in adapted housing is subsidised according to the same rules as rent in ordinary housing but there is no limitation on the size of rent that is subsidised. Payment for medical drugs is higher because the pensioner usually does not receive a personal allowance for medicine.

6.2.6 Comments on other case studies

Case study 7: fully disabled widow, female 'survivor', 80+, living in community, alone without social network The situation of a widow without any career on the labour market is very similar to the situation of an elderly single person with low income. In this case, however, the widow has no benefits from ATP (compulsory occupational pension) and her income, therefore, is a little lower.

She has the same access to services and housing as other low income pensioners.

Case study 8: senile older person Elderly people suffering from dementia are in principle treated like physically disabled elderly people. If the demented person and his spouse cannot cope with the situation, they are entitled to get help. Most commonly they will get help in the community: home help, district nursing, day-care home, etc., depending on the severity of the illness. If the well spouse cannot cope with the situation, the ill spouse may be allowed to a nursing home.

Traditionally demented people have been given the same type of offers as physically disabled persons, but now there is a tendency to create sheltered units, special housing and special day centres for people suffering from dementia.

Case study 9: immigrants Immigrants will usually not be entitled to a full old-age pension since full public pension is only granted after being resident in Denmark for 40 years. The right to have a reduced pension is obtained after 10 years of residence. Immigrants with a reduced public pension may apply for a personal allowance. The personal allowance obtained will frequently supplement the pension paid to the immigrant up to the same amount as the normal old-age pension (Social Commission, 1993a).

Immigrants have access to the same social services, health services and housing facilities as Danish citizens.

6.3   Overview

Since the Danish health and social system is based on the principle of equal rights, irrespective of the former labour market career, the differences in protection between some of these cases are very small indeed. The differences that do arise relate mostly to income protection. Supplementary old-age pensions and rent subsidies are means-tested.

Most health care services are free. Social services are either free or else the amount paid depends on the extent to which the services are used. Social services are generally not means-tested.

7   Social Protection of Categories of Dependent Elderly People in Germany

7.1   The Definition of Case Studies (see Appendix 2)

All pensioners have reached the legal pension age, which is 65 for men and women. The fact that the pensioner has reached the pension age means that it is assumed that he/she no longer receives any income from labour market participation.

All pensioners in the case studies are fully disabled. According to the German universal health insurance system, people 'with the highest grade of dependency' are those people who in the opinion of physicians, due to sickness or disability, need help to a great extent in performing the normal and frequently recurring tasks of everyday life.

Low income earners have an income which is below the social assistance limit. These persons receive additional benefits to top up their income.

7.2   Social Protection of the Case Studies

7.2.1 Case study 1: fully disabled, low income, living in community, alone with or without social network The pensioner has been active on the labour market and is presumed to have been a member of the universal health insurance system and to have kept this insurance after having reached the pension age. When the pensioner has been insured on a continuous basis, he can fulfil the eligibility conditions for health and social services.

When the pensioner lives alone and has no social network and thus nobody who can care for him or her, the health insurance organisation calls upon home nursing aid, which the pensioner receives in kind. The amount of help depends on the degree of dependency of the pensioner. A fully disabled pensioner (level 3) receives home care for an amount of 1,467 ECU per month.

The statutory health insurance benefits can possibly be supplemented with nursing help benefits (*Hilfe zur Pflege* or *Eingliederungshilfe für Behinderte*) from social assistance, if special conditions are fulfilled and if the need is not yet covered by the social care insurance. These nursing help benefits are income-related and means-tested.

If the older person can count on relatives or friends to care for him or her or to help with household activities, the older person can receive home nursing care in cash (681 ECU per month (level 3)) instead of home nursing care in kind. It is also possible to receive a combination of in cash and in kind benefits. In that case a percentage in cash (e.g. 80 per cent = 545 ECU) and a percentage in kind (e.g. 20 per cent = 293 ECU) is granted.

7.2.2 Case study 2: fully disabled, low income, living in community, with spouse This case study is comparable with the case of pensioner living alone with a social network. While the contributions of the social care insurance are not income-related, the contributions of social assistance (*Eingliederungshilfe für Behinderte* and *Hilfe zur Pflege*) are. The income which is taken into consideration is the income of the pensioner together with the income of his spouse. The latter contributions are also need-dependent.

7.2.3 Case study 3a: fully disabled, low income, living in an old-age home This case is comparable with case 1. The pensioner receives home nursing aid in kind or in cash.

7.2.4 Case study 3b: fully disabled, low income, living in a nursing home For this case it is supposed that the pensioner receives nursing aid up to an amount of 1,467 ECU. As far as the nursing costs do not include hotel costs and stay below the fee the institution charges for, supplementing *Hilfe zur Pflege* is taken into account. This means that *Hilfe zur Pflege* compensates for the nursing costs and that also additional pocket money is granted.

7.2.5 Case studies 3c and 6c: fully disabled, low and average income, staying in a general hospital A stay of a pensioner in a general hospital is completely covered by health insurance funds (social security). During maximum 14 days the pensioner has to pay 6 ECU per day to the hospital. Also in this case low income pensioners can call upon *Hilfe zur Pflege* and *Eingliederungshilfe für Behinderte*.

When the pensioner is not insured (= exception) and when he lives on low income, social assistance interferes.

7.2.6 Case studies 4 and 5: fully disabled, average income, living in community, alone or with spouse Normally, pensioners living on average income will not receive supplementary contributions from *Hilfe zur Pflege* or *Eingliederung-shilfe für Behinderte*. This is the only difference with case studies 1 and 2, as contributions from the social care insurance are not income-related.

7.2.7 Case studies 6a and 6b: fully disabled, average income, living in an independently managed residential or nursing home Case study 6a is identical to case study 3a, except whereas the *Hilfe zur Pflege* and the *Eingliederung-shilfe für Behinderte* are concerned.

It is of no importance if the nursing home is independently managed or not: social care insurance pays part of the costs and social assistance interferes if necessary.

7.2.8 Comments on other case studies

Case study 7: fully disabled widow, female 'survivor', 80+, income spouse low, living in the community, alone without social network For this case, it is supposed that the female survivor disposes of an old-age pension, a survivor pension or another income source or gets social assistance. When she lives outside an institution, she can get contributions of the social long-term care insurance.

For this case, social help for the elderly (*Altenhilfe*) can also be taken upon, which is meant to help preventing/overcoming/alleviating difficulties, caused by old-age and to help the elderly to participate at life in community.

Examples of help are: help with providing/maintaining housing for pensioners, help with visiting organisations or institutions, which offer sociability, entertainment or training, meet cultural needs of elderly persons, or enable the elderly to maintain their relationship with family members.

Case study 8: senile older person The only difference with case study 7 is that next to contributions of social care insurance, also contributions of health insurance and *Eingliederungshilfe für Behinterte* are provided.

Case study 9: immigrant Persons with German nationality from Eastern Europe are equally treated as inhabitants of Germany. The same is true for German persons of the EU, Island, Liechtenstein and Norway. Elderly persons, who came as pensioners to Germany, can only rely on social assistance if health insurance and social care insurance in their country of origin is insufficient.

   For other immigrants, the legislation on social security of the country of origin prevails. Social assistance cannot be taken up.

7.3   Overview

The differences that do arise between the cases relate mostly to income protection. The availability of a social network or the spouse determines the way home nursing aid is granted: in kind or in cash.

8   Social Protection of Different Categories of Dependent Elderly People in Spain

8.1   The Definition of Case Studies

People considered in the case studies have reached the normal retirement age, which is 65 for both men and women.

   All persons in the case studies are fully disabled: this means that they have very serious difficulties in performing personal care, domestic activities and external relations (shopping, visits to relatives, etc.) and they need permanent care of relatives or social services for at least eight hours per day.

   The income of a single person is considered to be low if lower than the minimum wage (422 ECU per month). Therefore, elderly people with a noncontributory pension, which is 332 ECU (including an increase because of dependency) per month for a single person, are considered as the low income category. Average income is an income between the minimum income and twice and a half the minimum income. An average income pensioner is defined as a person receiving the contributory pension, which is 498 ECU (including an increase because of dependency) per month for a single person.

The making of a distinction between female and male elderly is irrelevant where the social protection arrangements are concerned.

8.2   Social Protection of the Case Studies

8.2.1 Case studies 1 and 4: fully disabled, low and average income, living in community, alone without social network In 1993, 16 per cent of the people aged 65 and above lived alone The low income pensioner receives 332 ECU per month (noncontributory pension); the average income pensioner 498 ECU per month (contributory pension). One third of the contributory pension is in fact an increase of the pension because of dependency; it is a variable amount in the noncontributory system. This increase is meant as an attendance allowance. It is paid to those who have become disabled as a result of illness or injury prior to their retirement, i.e. during working age.

Health support (district nursing,etc.) provided by the public sector (national health system) and pharmaceuticals are free of charge for all elderly persons. The costs are covered by the state and social security system. Only those who turn to the private health care sector have to pay market prices.

Both the regional and local authorities (respectively Autonomous Communities and Councils) and the social security system provide a varied spectrum of social services among which home help, day centres, etc. Access to social services varies between the different regions, and is in general dependent upon economic, personal and family circumstances.

Clients with low income using home help services make up 0.93 per cent of the population 65+; clients with average income 0.16 per cent. The average annual cost of home help was 1,815 ECU in 1995. Consumer co-payments represent 4.0 per cent of the costs. Social security covers 21.4 per cent. The state (municipalities, regions, counties, etc.) pays the additional costs.

8.2.2 Case studies 2 and 5: fully disabled, low and average income, living in community with spouse Elderly people living in the community with spouse made up 57 per cent of the population aged 65 and above in 1993.

While the noncontributory pension for an elderly couple is not higher than the noncontributory pension for a single person, the contributory pension is. Therefore, the noncontributory pension is the same as in case study 1. The contributory pension amounts to 586 ECU per month. Each pension incorporates an increase because of dependency.

The case studies are similar to case studies 1 and 4 in terms of access to and consumer co-payments for health and social services. Moreover, the right to free health care support is also conceded to the spouse provided that they live together and at the expense of the partner.

8.2.3 Case studies 3a and 6a: fully disabled, low and average income, living in an old-age home No difference with persons living in the community (case studies 1 and 4) where income situation is concerned. However, the increase because of dependency can be substituted for lodging and care in an institution at the expense of the social security system.

These case studies are also similar to case studies 1 and 4 in terms of access to and consumer co-payments for health services and pharmaceuticals.

Old-age homes are provided by the social security system and local authorities. Access is dependent upon economic, personal and family circumstances. The average cost was 838 ECU per month in public old-age homes and 571 ECU per month in private old-age homes. The charge to the elderly is equivalent to 75 per cent of their pension and it covers 29 per cent of the cost in public old-age homes. 71 per cent of the cost is then covered by the social security system and the state (central and regional).

8.2.4 Case studies 3b and 6b: fully disabled, low and average income, living in a nursing home This case study is similar to case studies 3a and 6a in terms of income and to case studies 1 and 4 in terms of access to and consumer co-payments for health services and pharmaceuticals.

Nursing homes are as in the case of old-age homes provided by the social security system and the regional and local authorities. Therefore, access is conditioned on economic, personal and family circumstances in general and differ between the regional authorities. Average cost in 1995 was 1,350 ECU per month in the public sector and 980 ECU per month in the private sector. The cost in public nursing homes is totally covered by the social security system and the state (central and regional). The cost in private nursing homes is covered in two ways according the contracting-out system: either the state, social security system and the elderly peopleor only the elderly people cover the costs.

8.2.5 Case studies 3c and 6c: fully disabled, low and average income, staying in a general hospital No differences with persons living in old-age homes exist where income is concerned.

The cost per month in general hospitals is 5,880 ECU. Public hospital services are totally free for the elderly population. The state covers 70 per cent of the cost and social security 30 per cent. The pensioner is only charged for some extra costs for special room or facilities. Private hospital services are not free for elderly people; they have to pay the market prices.

8.2.6 *Comments on other case studies*

Case study 7: fully disabled widow, female 'survivor', 80+, income spouse low, living in the community, alone without social network Where income is concerned, a widow has right to 45 per cent of the pension of the spouse which is in this case 45 per cent of the noncontributory pension of the spouse.

Where access to and consumer contributions for health and social services are concerned, we refer to case study 1.

Case study 8: senile older person This case study is similar to case study 5 where income and access to and consumer co-payments for health and social services is concerned.

8.3 *Overview*

Public ambulatory and hospital health support and pharmaceuticals are free for all persons aged 65 and above, irrespective of whether he/she lives at home or in an institution and of income. Only those who turn to the private ambulatory or hospital sector, have to pay market prices for health care.

Access to health and social services differ between the regions. In general, access is dependent on economic, personal and family circumstances.

9   Social Protection of Different Categories of Dependent Elderly People in Finland

9.1   *The Definition of Case Studies (see Appendix 2)*

People considered in the case studies have reached at least the normal retirement age, which is 65 for both men and women. In the case studies concerning couples, the spouses are also assumed to be over 65 years old. Only one of the spouses is considered to be fully disabled i.e. in need of external help in daily living and mobilisation.

The low income category encompasses pensioners whose income only consists of the national pension, which is available to all residents regardless of work history. This national pension comprises a basic amount (66.8 ECU) and an additional amount (361 ECU) (figures refer to pension rights prior to January 1996). About 14 per cent of the pensioners receive only national pension (the majority of the pensioners receive pensions from employment pension schemes). Low income pensioners usually also get a housing allowance, which affects the amount of disposable income considerably. For each case study additional information is given about the situation for those living in rented housing and for those living in their own homes. The latter is the most common form of living for the elderly in Finland: 80 per cent of the elderly households (65+) own their own apartment or house.

For the cases it is supposed that a single client lives in a 40 m^2 apartment and that he pays a rent of 346 ECU a month. If he owns the apartment, the running expenses are estimated at 86 ECU a month. For a couple, the assumption regarding the size of the apartment is a 60 m^2 apartment. The couple pays rent 519 ECU a month. If they own the apartment the running expenses are estimated at 130 ECU a month.

Average pensioners receive a pension of 858 ECU per month.

It is not relevant to distinguish according to gender for any of the services in question.

In the case studies it is assumed that a fully disabled person living with the spouse receives some help from him or her, and therefore the need for auxiliary services, like home help, cleaning, home nursing, etc. is smaller than for people living alone.

Co-financing of social services is income-related for home help and institutional care. Property is not taken into account.

For home help there are two forms of client's co-payment. The first one concerns the continuous use of home help while the other one for those needing occasional use.

A client of continuous home help gets the service free of charge if his income before taxation is less than 433 ECU a month. If the client's income is more than 433 ECU a month, his co-payment is at maximum 35 per cent of the difference between client's income and 433 ECU. Also, couples earning less than 796 ECU a month do not have to pay a contribution. If the couple earns more, the rate of co-payment is 22 per cent at highest (municipalities may charge less). The client co-payment for home help also aggregates continuous use of home nursing, i.e. if the client already pays for home help, he does not have to pay separately for home nursing. The exact amount of the client fees is decided by the local authorities. The fees are based on the client's income, the size of the household and the number of visits.

For occasional home help use municipality can charge moderate co-payment. For occasional home nursing municipalities can charge at maximum 8.6 ECU for doctor's visits and 5.2 ECU for nurses' visit.

For long-term care in an institution with full board the client has to pay 80 per cent of his income after taxation. The only restriction is that the pensioner has to receive at least 77 ECU as 'pocket money' every month.

The highest possible fees for short-term care in a hospital or in an old-age home are 22 ECU a day, and for day or night care 11 ECU a day. Other service fees vary across municipalities, e.g. for one meal, a municipality may charge between 2.6 and 5.2 ECU.

Municipalities can never charge more from the client than the actual production cost of the services.

9.2   Social Protection of the Case Studies

9.2.1 Case study 1: fully disabled, low income, living alone in community (no social network) The pensioner of this case study receives the national pension, a pensioner's care allowance and a pensioner's housing allowance. As the person is living alone without a social network, the care services provided by the care system will consist of a relatively 'heavy' package. The average monthly service package for this type of client can be as follows: 70 home care visits, including four home nurse visits; meals-on-wheels every day of the month; cleaning four times a month; laundry four times a month; bathing service once a week; day care a day a week; intensive day care three times a week in one month period twice a year; and interactive alarm system. The contents and intensity of the package vary across the municipalities.

Health care services are given at the local health centre, either free of charge or with a yearly client fee of 26 ECU (or a fee of 8.6 ECU per visit for maximum three visits). For pharmaceuticals and expenses for private sector's medical expenses the person receives a refund from the sickness insurance. For specialist care the client needs a referral from the health centre. Home nursing is given free of charge to the patient once a week, paid by the local authorities.

For social services the client's co-financing is higher. Home help is the only service where the local authority does not charge a client fee (as the income of the pensioner in this case study is too low). For meals-on-wheels the client's share in average is highest (75 per cent).

9.2.2 Case study 2: fully disabled, low income, living in community, with spouse Here it is presumed that both the client and spouse receive only national pension, although this is rare. Because marital status changes the additional part of national pension, individually they receive a smaller pension than a pensioner living alone. For both of them the national pension is 373.7 ECU a month and the total pension of the couple is 747.4 ECU a month. Again, depending on housing conditions, a housing allowance is offered.

Because the client is fully disabled, he gets the care allowance from SII (239 ECU a month). In addition, the municipality can pay home care allowance for the spouse. Municipalities classify the clients in different home care allowance classes, with the highest class reserved for the most disabled persons. In 1994 average home care allowance in the highest class was 445 ECU.

Due to the presence of the spouse and care allowance, the service package for the disabled person is much smaller than in case 1. Usually if persons receive care allowance, they don't get any home help at all although they still get four home nursing visits. They could receive cleaning services once a week, bathing service once a week, return transportation to day care via eight taxi vouchers and interval care for two weeks twice a year.

9.2.3 Case study 3: fully disabled, low income, living in an institution Long-term care is mostly given in old-age homes and primary health care hospital bed wards (the latter may be considered as similar to 'nursing homes'). Nowadays it is very rare that an elderly person lives permanently in a specialized hospital, except for psychiatric patients. Still, there are elderly people waiting for other care form in the specialised hospitals.

About 25 per cent of the elderly over 85 years of age and about 13 per cent of the elderly over 75 years of age are in long-term institutional care.

As national pension's additional amount is payable at a reduced rate after three months in an institution, client's income is reduced to 222 ECU a month. Besides the person has to pay a share of the costs for institutional care. As the person is a low income pensioner, he is left with only a pocket money of 77 ECU a month after having paid the maximum amount allowed.

9.2.4 Case study 4: fully disabled, average income, living in community, alone without social network The client's average pension income is 858 ECU a month comprising of aggregated national pension and employment pension. He also receives pensioner's care allowance, as it is assumed that he has some expenses due to disability. The income of the pensioner does not affect the decision on access to services. Therefore the fully disabled person with average income receives the same package of services as the low income pensioner (case 1). However, due to differences in income client fees are different.

Another difference to case 1 is the amount of housing benefit, as this is calculated partly with information on income.

9.2.5 Case study 5: fully disabled, average income, living in community with spouse There are four cases, because although client's income is average, the spouse's income could be either low or average and they can live either in a rented or an own apartment.

a) Suppose that the income of the fully disabled person is 858 ECU a month (average employment pension) and that the spouse's income is 373.7 ECU a month (national pension). Total monthly income of the couple is then 1,231.7 ECU. In addition depending on their housing situation, there are two cases. Either the family pays 519 ECU rent a month, in which case they get 129 ECU housing allowance. Or, the family has an own apartment. In that case they are not entitled to housing benefit as their income is deemed sufficient.

b) In another, more representative case both of the spouses receive employment pension. Total income of the couple is then 1,716 ECU a month. In this case the income of the couple is high enough so neither in rented housing nor own apartment they are entitled to housing allowance.

Because the client is fully disabled, he gets the pensioner's care allowance from SII. Also, the municipality pays the carer home care allowance.

As far as health and social services are concerned, no differences with case study 2 are noticed.

9.2.6 Case study 6: fully disabled, average income, living in an institution The client's pension is 858 ECU a month. This case is similar to case 3 with regard to services available and getting them. As the income is taken into account when deciding about the charges for client co-funding, the client fees are respectively higher than in case 3. The client pays a certain percentage of his income (80 per cent) contributing to the costs of care. The rest of the costs is paid by the local authority.

For instance in the old-age home the share of client fees makes up 24 per cent of total costs. This is calculated from the co-financing rule: 80 per cent of income after taxation (which means that the client pays 547 ECU a month).

This leaves the person with a disposable income of 137 ECU a month. The same amount (547 ECU a month) is paid by the pensioner in primary health care hospitals and district hospitals, but the share of the client fees in total costs is now lower, as these two latter services are more expensive than old-age home care.

9.2.7 Comments on other case studies

Case study 7: fully disabled widow, female 'survivor', 80+, living in the community, alone without social network This case is basically similar to case 1. Pension rights are individual, not derived, so the pension of the widow is not dependent on the spouse's income. In Finland the surviving spouse's pension is only available for widows under 65 years of age.

Case study 8: senile older person This case is very similar to case 5 with regard to income situation. Granting the pensioner's care allowance depends on the dependency of the demented person and the costs incurred from this dependency. If the person is severely demented so as to need help in daily routines and there are expenses rising from this need he will get the special care allowance, 239 ECU a month. If the dementia is not very severe and does not lead to additional expenses, the care allowance might not be granted.

As in case 5 municipality can pay home care allowance for the carer. In the home care allowance scheme the carer has a right of having a day off every week, which is granted by the municipality, that is obliged to give substitution for the carer during days off.

The service package has been adapted to special needs arising from being a demented person. Services are given here almost as in case 1 to give the carer some rest. In addition there is the service of a day centre or day hospital, where the demented person can visit twice a week. This service is intended both for the demented person but also for the carer to get a chance to rest. If the demented person is difficult to take care of at nights, it is possible to get him to a nursing home or old-age home for night care and thus give the carer off duty time during the night. As there are experiences from this solution not being a best possible alternative for the demented person, the municipalities probably prefer increasing respite care instead. In addition, once a year the demented person gets two weeks short-term care in an old-age home to give a 'vacation' for the carer.

Case study 9: immigrant An immigrant is considered to be a person without Finnish or EEA citizenship living in Finland. This is a very rare case, as there are not many immigrants in Finland.

The national pension is payable to residents in Finland according to the years of residence. In the case of immigrants it is not very likely that a person has lived in Finland for 40 years (required period to be eligible for full national pension) without citizenship. Therefore it is assumed that the immigrant is not entitled to full pension. In this case he is entitled to the last resort guaranteed minimum income scheme. From the beginning of 1997 he is also entitled to pensioner's housing allowance. Before that date immigrants got their housing allowance from the general housing allowance scheme.

Some services have consumer co-payments. If the immigrant is not able to pay them, it is possible either to waive the co-payments or give additional income support. The Ministry of Social Affairs and Health recommends in these cases the co-payments are waived.

The services will be given to the immigrant on the same basis as a national.

9.3   Overview

The differences in the protection of pensioners living alone or with their spouse are not very great, as the pension rights are based on individual earnings and services are given according to need. However, to live alone usually increases the need for some services. The only eligibility criterion for services is need assessment.

Social services in Finland are mostly financed by taxes and the services are mainly produced by the local authorities. Client fees are used in most of the services.

10   Social Protection of Different Categories of Dependent Elderly People in France

10.1   The Definition of Case Studies (see Appendix 2)

People considered in the case studies have reached at a minimum the normal retirement age, which is 60 for both men and women.

All persons in the case studies are fully disabled: this means that they are either bound to bed or chair, or else not bound to bed or chair but in need of help for toileting and dressing.

The low income category encompasses pensioners whose income is less than the minimum guaranteed income for the elderly, which on 1 January 1997 was 539 ECU per month for a single person and 945 ECU per month for a couple. Pensioners living on an average income are defined as having revenues which lie between the third and seventh decile.

It is not relevant to distinguish according to gender for any of the services in question.

10.2   Social Protection of the Case Studies

10.2.1 Case study 2: fully disabled, low income, living in community, with spouse Case study 2 represents 0.28 per cent of the French population aged 65 and above.

A couple living in the community is guaranteed the minimum income for pensioners, which is 945 ECU per month. The basic pension which the couple receives is topped up with benefits publicly financed at the national level until the minimum guaranteed income is reached.

Health care services are provided by self-employed physicians or nurses. Since the pensioners have to cover 30 per cent and 40 per cent of the costs of the services of the self-employed physicians respectively nurses, it is unlikely that (nursing) care will be exclusively provided by self-employed nurses when the resources of the pensioners are restricted as in case study 2. The residual respectively 70 per cent and 60 per cent of the costs are covered by the universal social security system. It covers home nursing services completely, but services can only be called upon if they are available in the neighbourhood and if places are available. The number of visits a nurse pays to an older person varies from once every two days to three times per day. Home nursing services are prescribed in terms of number of times for a certain period. The reimbursement of home nurses depends on the social security system situation of the pensioner. The number of home nurses depends on their term on the reimbursement: according to the reimbursement, there will be more or less home nurses. The number of home nurses has increased in recent years.

Home help services are provided if the pensioner is in need and if the partner is unable to care for his or her partner. For home help services, personal contributions from 0 to 2 ECU have to be made. The volume of home help (up to 90 hours per month) depends on the social security situation of the pensioner and the department in which the pensioner lives. If the income of the pensioner is below a certain limit, departmental social assistance covers the remaining share of the costs.

Tele-alarm, meal distribution and sitting services are informal care services for which the pensioner makes only small contributions. The largest share of the costs is covered by contributions from departmental social assistance, local collectives and the social security system (CNAVTS). Social assistance can be appealed to only after income-testing.

Low income pensioners receive allowances for social housing (in general the rent is low). Attendance allowances are granted if a third person is needed for essential activities in daily life. The granting of the attendance allowance depends largely on the income of the pensioner.

10.2.2 Case studies 4 and 5: fully disabled, average income, living in community, alone without social network (case study 4) or with spouse (case study 5) Case study 4 represents 0.7 per cent of the population aged 65 and above. Case study 5 represents 1.2 per cent of the total population aged 65 and above.

Pensioners who have an average income are considered to have a basic legal pension exceeding the minimum guaranteed income of pensioners (539 ECU per month for a single person and 945 ECU per month for a couple). Since pensioners who live on low incomes are assumed to have an income which is less than acceptable, there is no means-testing for – or income-related co-financing of – services for them. For the others, however, there are resource conditions for the attendance allowance and income scales have been defined for the co-financing of home help and other in kind services financed by social assistance or CNAVTS.

In France, pensioners on average income seem more often to be privately insured to cover eventual health care expenses than is the case with pensioners on low income. Iit will not, thus, be the pensioner him- or herself, but rather private insurance that will co-finance the health care services. There are no differences in the extent to which health care expenses are publicly financed.

The extent of home help services is 90 hours per month at most. Private contributions depend upon the income of the pensioner. The rest of the costs are covered by the pension scheme of the pensioner and varies from 1 to 12 ECU. Each pension scheme sets its own conditions of eligibility.

Personal contributions for informal care services are higher than contributions of low income earners. The real cost of the service, however, rapidly exceeds the personal contribution.

Average income earners do not qualify for social housing allowances and attendance allowances largely depend on income.

10.2.3 Case study 3c: fully disabled, low income, staying in a general hospital, long stay unit Case study 3c represents 0.1 per cent of the total population of people aged 65 and above.

No differences with persons living in the community exist where income is concerned: pensioners living on low income are guaranteed the minimum income for pensioners of 539 ECU per month for a single person and 945 ECU per month for a couple.

The cost of long-term cure and care in the hospital is completely covered by the universal social security system by means of a fixed sum. To cover the hotel costs, however, the following arrangements are in place: the pensioner pays 90 per cent of his income. Relatives have an alimentary duty and pay according to their income. If previously mentioned contributions are insufficient, income and departmental social assistance intervenes. For a longer stay in a general hospital, a person has to prove the impossibility of staying at home, the insufficiency of resources and the impossibility of moving into an authorised home.

People staying in a general hospital and living on low income receive allowances for social housing and attendance allowances.

10.2.4 Case study 6a: fully disabled, average income, living in an old-age home Case study 6a represents 0.62 per cent of the total population of people aged 65 and above.

Old-age homes aim at providing care for pensioners for longer periods of time. They sometimes also have beds at their disposal for the temporary housing of pensioners.

Health care services can be delivered by self-employed physicians or nurses who pay visits to the old-age home. Health insurance pays 70 per cent (on average) of the service fee; the pensioner himself or private insurance covers the remaining 30 per cent of the costs.

A fixed amount which is intended to cover the cost of daily care provided for pensioners in an old-age home is paid by the health insurance (social security), while hotel costs are covered in one of the two following ways, depending upon the hypothesis:

– hypothesis 1: recourse to social assistance (depends on the hotel costs; very variable in France): same arrangements as studies 3a, 3b and 3c;
– hypothesis 2: no recourse to social assistance: the costs are covered by the person himself or by a dependency assurance and by complements of the family (these complements are usually negotiated with the family).

People living in an old-age home qualify for attendance allowances.

10.2.5 Case study 6b: fully disabled, average income, living in a nursing home Case study 6b represents 0.64 per cent of the total population of 65+.

Nursing homes aim at providing care for pensioners for longer periods of time but, again, they sometimes also have beds at their disposal for the temporary housing of pensioners.

The lump sum which is paid by the health insurance (social security) for daily medical care provided to pensioners living in a nursing home is much higher than the fixed sum for daily care provided in an old-age home.

The financing rules for the hotel costs do not differ from the financing rules in an old-age home.

10.2.6 Comments on other case studies

Case study 7: fully disabled widow, female 'survivor', 80+, living in the community, alone without social network Case study 7 represents 0.14 per cent of the elderly population above the age of 65.

The only difference between case study 2 and case study 7 is the legal widow's pension. Legal home help is provided for a dependent widow in any case since there are no other persons in the household who can help her. This is in 'contradiction' with case study 2, where legal home help can only be appealed to in case the spouse of the dependent person cannot provide informal help for his or her partner.

10.3   Overview

For health services, patients usually pay flat-rate fees. The cost of long-term cure and care in the hospital and for daily medical care in old-age and nursing homes is completely covered by the universal social security system by means of a fixed sum. For social services, on the contrary, there is means-testing or income-related co-financing.

11   Social Protection of Different Categories of Dependent Elderly People in Ireland

11.1   The Definition of Case Studies (see Appendix 2)

A low income pensioner is likely be in receipt of a noncontributory old-age pension, which is 82.5 ECU per week. Payment for people aged 80 and over is slightly higher (by 6.5 ECU). An average income pensioner is a person likely to be in receipt of a contributory old-age pension or retirement pension of 95 ECU per week. Payment is 13 ECU more for people aged 80 or over.

Persons with no income other than a noncontributory pension are eligible for a Medical Card, i.e. have Category 1 eligibility to public health care. This entitles them to free general practitioner care and prescription medicines, free general out-patient care in public hospitals, and free in-patient care in public wards of these hospitals. Other persons are unlikely to qualify for a Medical Card, they will have Category 2 access to public health care.

Dependency is interpreted in a flexible manner and varies across the country, but is mainly based on ADL measurement. People living at home are functionally disabled, i.e. they require assistance with mobility and personal care, as well as having medical and psychological problems. Dependency in old-age homes is defined on the basis of ADL and social measures. Dependency in nursing homes is assessed on the basis of an activity of daily living (ADL) scale, mental capacity, and social factors. Medium dependency describes a person whose independence is impaired to the extent that he or she requires nursing home care because the appropriate care cannot be provided in the community. His or her mobility would be impaired to the extent that he or she would require supervision or a walking aid. A highly dependent person is defined as a person needing nursing care but not bed bound. The person may have a combination of physical and mental disabilities, may be confused at times and be incontinent. He or she may require a walking aid and physical assistance to walk. Maximum dependency requires constant nursing care. The person is likely to have very restricted mobility, require assistance with all aspects to physical care or be confused, disturbed and incontinent.

The availability of personal care services for elderly persons differs according to presence of a social network or spouse. In general, the health authorities ration personal care services on the basis on need, linked to household composition: the inclusion of spouse reduces the likelihood of some public service provision, particularly home help services.

11.2 Social Protection of the Case Studies

11.2.1 Case study 1: fully disabled, low income, living in community, alone without social network The proportion of elderly persons living alone in private households is 24 per cent in 1991.

A national survey by O'Connor et al. (1988) mentioned that there are over 66,000 old people living at home in Ireland requiring some degree of care. This is approximately 17 per cent of all old people in the country. They are functionally disabled, i.e. they require assistance with mobility and personal care, as well as having medical and psychological problems. Of people requiring care in the community, 36 per cent need 'a lot of care', 38 per cent 'some care' and 26 per cent 'occasional care'.

About 23 per cent of all dependent elderly living at home are cared for by persons outside the home.

An old person in this case study is likely be in receipt of a noncontributory old-age pension. Old people aged 66 years or over, not in receipt of a contributory pension or a retirement pension, with insufficient resources, are eligible for the noncontributory old-age pension. There is a means-test to determine eligibility for the scheme. Reliance on the social welfare system is greatest among the elderly living alone. People in this category are less likely to have income from either occupational pensions or from savings.

Entitlement to free or subsidised health care in Ireland depends on income. Old people in this case study are likely to have 'medical care' cover, which entitles them to free general out-patient care in public hospitals, and free in-patient care in public wards of these hospitals. The vast majority of elderly people (over 80 per cent) qualify for medical card coverage. Old people in this case study are also likely to be on the 'at risk' register of the community public health nurse, and therefore are in receipt of regular visits from that source. They are also likely to be receiving the services of a home help. While this service is not automatic, the practice is to allocate this relatively scarce resource to vulnerable people, particularly highly dependent elderly people living alone.

The old person described in this case study is also likely to be in receipt of meals-on-wheels, particularly if he/she is living in an urban area. Access to other community care services, e.g. paramedical care, is likely to be low and variable. Access depends on the particular circumstances of the old person and the policy of the health board, within whose catchment area the old person is living. More than likely, highly dependent old people living alone receive visits from voluntary agencies, particularly if they are living in an urban area. If day hospital care or day care facilities are available locally, then, more than likely the old person is attending both, but these services, particularly the former, are sparingly provided.

11.2.2 Case study 2: fully disabled, low income, living in community with spouse This case study is similar to case study 1, in terms of the eligibility of the old person for free public provision. However, the inclusion of spouse in this case study reduces the likelihood of some public service provision, particularly home help services. People living with spouse are less likely to receive home help services than people living on their own. In general the health authorities ration personal care services on the basis of need, linked to household composition. This means that old people living on their own receive priority treatment.

Income in this household may also increase as a result of family caring arrangements. The spouse may receive a Carer's Allowance, which is a means-tested payment to carers who are providing full-time care and attention to incapacitated people in the same household. The objectives of the Carer's Allowance are to give official recognition to the role to the carer and to provide a secure and independent source of income. However, only 5 per cent of payments from this budget goes to carers aged 65 or over, although an estimated 25 per cent of carers are in that age bracket. There is also a slightly higher probability that the spouse, particularly if male, has an occupational pension.

11.2.3 Case study 3a: fully disabled, low income, living in an old-age home
The best estimate of the total number of old people in long-stay care in Ireland is approximately 19,000 people, or close to 5 per cent of the elderly population. Just over half of those are living in old-age homes, taken to mean in this case study, health board geriatric hospitals, health board welfare homes, and health board district hospitals.

There is quite a variation in the distribution of dependency across public long-stay institutions. Overall figures for the dependency mix are not available, though estimates based on a number of individual cases studies suggests that the proportion of low dependency old people in public institutions may be as high as 20 per cent of the total resident population. Most people in health board geriatric hospitals are classified as chronically ill, though significantly, 17 per cent of patients are classified as social cases. In welfare homes, almost two-thirds of residents are classified as social cases.

On admission to an old-age home, the pension of the old person is paid directly to the institution. The old person receives pocket money from the institution, which varies considerably, but rarely exceeds 25 per cent of the full pension; the remainder of the pension is retained by the institution. The weekly cost of care in typical, low technology, long-stay public old-age homes is just over 254 ECU per week. The resident, as described in this case is not liable for any of the cost of care, except for the retention of his/her pension, referred to above.

11.2.4 Case study 3b: fully disabled, low income, living in a nursing home
Nursing home care is either provided privately, or by the voluntary, mainly religious, sector. Just under 30 per cent of all long-stay beds are in private nursing homes, while 18 per cent of beds are in the voluntary sector.

Private nursing homes provide for-profit care for old people right across the dependency spectrum, but not usually for people with medical complications. Many residents are admitted to nursing homes for social reasons. The data on dependency suggest that 50 per cent of people in long-stay private homes are ambulant without assistance, while 63 per cent are mentally alert.

The voluntary sector is not-for-profit care, mainly provided by religious orders. Just under half of residents in voluntary homes are chronically ill, about one third are there for social reasons.

The admission of low income, high dependency, elderly people to private nursing homes is governed by the Nursing Homes (Subvention) Regulations of 1993. Public subvention of residents is determined by a means-test linked to an assessment of dependency. Dependency is assessed on the basis of an activity of daily living (ADL) scale, mental capacity, and social factors. For the calculations of means, the relevant health board takes into account both the income and assets of the person making the application for subvention. The income of family members is also taken into account in the assessment of means, for the payment of nursing home subvention. Once a person has qualified for assistance under the means-test, three types of payment are possible, depending on the classification of dependency. People assessed as medium dependency qualify for a subvention of 89 ECU per week; high dependent people qualify for a subvention of 121 ECU per week; while maximum dependency persons receive the maximum subvention of 152 ECU per week. Average weekly costs in private nursing homes are difficult to estimate given the differentiated nature of provision. However, costs are likely to lie within the region of 229–279 ECU per week. The combination of subvention and public pension is unlikely to cover the full cost in private nursing homes for low income highly dependent old people, particularly in urban areas. Any shortfall must be met from the private resources of the individual, or their families.

11.2.5 Case study 3c: fully disabled, low income, staying in a general hospital
The number of old people in acute general hospitals is estimated at approximately 4,500 or just over 1 per cent of the total elderly population.

Elderly people are entitled to hospital care on the same basis as everyone else. As mentioned earlier, the majority of elderly people are likely to be in category 1. This entitles them to all in-patient acute hospital services in public wards, including consultant services. Generally speaking, elderly people who have recovered from treatment do not remain in general hospitals. Both admission to hospital and length of stay do, however, tend to increase with age. The elderly still account for a disproportionate share of acute bed-days relative to their overall share of the population.

There has been a historical concern about the role played by older people in 'blocking beds' in acute care hospitals. A lot has been done in recent years to encourage a faster turnover of elderly beds. The increase in the number of consultant geriatricians has resulted in a better use of acute hospital geriatric beds. Hospitals with a designated department of geriatric medicine tend to have a shorter duration of in-patient stay for old people than hospitals without such a facility. Day hospital provision also tends to encourage out-patient care for old people. Better communication between the hospital and community care providers, through the use of liaison officers and coordinators of care, has also encouraged the earlier discharge of old people from hospitals. Some social cases remain in acute beds, but the problem is not now so severe as it has been. If for whatever reason an elderly person, as described in this case study, remains in acute care for a prolonged period, the state continues to bear the cost of care.

11.2.6 Case study 4: fully disabled, average income, living in community, alone without social network People in this case study are likely to be in receipt of a contributory old-age pension or a retirement pension. They may also have an occupational pension. The latter depends on the type of job held while they were in the labour force.

They are unlikely to qualify for a medical card because of their income level, so they will have Category 2 access to public health care. They are likely to be insured for private health care, either in a private hospital, or in semiprivate and private rooms in public hospitals.

Although not having Category 1 eligibility for community care services, old people described in this case study are likely to receive public health nurse services free at the point of use, on the basis of a special need status. Living alone, they are also likely to receive home help services. The likelihood is that they are asked to make a contribution to the cost of this service. They may also have access to public and voluntary day care facilities. A contribution would also be expected for the use of this service. Private community care provision is not a feature of the Irish health care system.

11.2.7 Case study 5: fully disabled, average income, living in community with spouse The major effect of the 'living with spouse' condition is to reduce the likelihood of any public involvement in the care of the old person. The rationing of public resources is done on the basis of need. Non-Category 1 people with average income, living with a carer spouse, are likely to rank low on the priority list relative to other categories of need, particularly people on low incomes living alone. While access to public health nurses is least likely to be affected, the utilisation probability for home helps, day care, and other publicly provided community care services will be reduced significantly, if not zero.

11.2.8 Case study 6a: fully disabled, average income, living in an old-age home Only a small number of old people on average income are likely to seek admission to a public long-stay institution. The majority of this group tend to use private nursing home care. For those who do receive care in a public institution, charges are levied to cover the cost of care. An assessment is made on the basis of means, including consideration of both income and assets, and charges are levied accordingly. Accommodation in a public institution is more likely if an alternative private accommodation is not available locally. Alternatively, there may sometimes be competition between the public and private sector for fee-paying patients, particularly if the public institution is well-regarded locally.

11.2.9 Case study 6b: fully disabled, average income, living in a nursing home Old people in this category are unlikely to qualify for public subvention. They will have to bear the full cost of nursing home care from their own resources and from the resources of their family. Long-term care insurance is not available in Ireland for private nursing home care.

11.2.10 Case study 6c: fully disabled, average income, staying in a general hospital All citizens, irrespective of income and wealth, are entitled to all in-patient public health services in public wards, including consultant services. People in Category 2, i.e. those not entitled to a medical card, must, however, pay an accommodation charge of 25.4 ECU per day, for a maximum of 10 days, or 254 ECU per year. People who want private care in a private hospital, or in private and semiprivate beds in public hospitals must take out private insurance. Private insurance also guarantees faster access to non-emergency care, as well as providing a choice of consultant. The vast majority of people take out insurance under a state-sponsored monopoly (up to recently) non-profit provider of health insurance called Voluntary Health Insurance (VHI).

Insurance cover for acute care is community-rated in Ireland. This remains the situation even though an additional insurer has now been allowed to operate in the country. Long-term nursing home care is, however, not covered by private insurers.

11.2.11 Comments on other case studies

Case study 8: senile older person Dementia is likely to affect about 2 per cent of the elderly population, rising to 20 per cent for those aged 80 years and over.

People with mild dementia but with no significant physical disease, or illness, are likely to be treated by their general practitioner with minimal involvement by the specialist geriatric or psychiatric services. The carer spouse is likely to receive some support, mainly in the form of day care relief provided by either the health board, or at the instigation of the Alzheimer's Society of Ireland. The latter provides both information and more direct forms of intervention for the affected household. Dementia groups exist throughout the country. Counselling services for carers are also available in some locations.

The availability of general community care services, such as community nursing and home help, is likely to depend on the approach to the rationing of these services in specific health boards. Once again, priority is likely to be given to at risk people living alone. The needs of old people with mild dementia living with spouse are likely to receive less attention than the needs of people living alone.

The support available for people with severe dementia living at home in the community is not adequate in Ireland. While clear objectives exist for the provision of home care programmes for people with dementia, adequate funding has not always been provided. Consequently, the structure of care is weak in the community. In the majority of cases, families may have no alternative but to seek institutional care in nursing homes, psychiatric hospitals, and in general hospitals. Not all nursing homes accept patients with dementia. Where institutionalisation does occur, it is not always suited to the needs of the patients with dementia.

Case study 9: immigrant Eligibility for health care in Ireland is available to immigrants on the same basis as Irish citizens. Immigrants must, however, satisfy the relevant health authorities that they are ordinarily resident in the country. Once the authorities are satisfied with respect to residence, coverage under either Category 1 or 2 is automatic. Similarly, immigrants are entitled to social assistance payments on the same basis as Irish citizens.

11.3   Overview

The differences in protection between the cases are mostly related to income.

Low income elderly people are eligible for a Medical Card i.e. have Category 1 eligibility to public health care. This entitles them to free general practitioner care and prescription medicines, free general out-patient care in public hospitals, and free in-patient care in public wards of these hospitals. Other persons are unlikely to qualify for a Medical Card, they will have Category 2 access to public health care. They have to pay a contribution to the cost of health services, except for district nursing.

Community care services are free for low income elderly people. Average income elderly people are asked to make a contribution.

Health and social services in Ireland are mostly financed by taxes.

12   Social Protection of Different Categories of Dependent Elderly People in Italy

12.1   The Definition of Case Studies

The assessment of dependency is based on ADL criteria. A uniform definition of dependency between the regions is however lacking. Not all regions use the same evaluation schemes for dependency and, moreover, even within some regions different schemes are used. In general, 22 per cent of persons aged 65 and above was in 1994 dependent in at least one activity, 10 per cent was in at least three activities. About 2–3 per cent was completely dependent. A sample of 8,745 elderly people showed that 4 per cent was in 1994 dependent upon seeing, hearing and speaking and 10 per cent upon moving.

In case the pensioner has worked, low income is defined as the minimum pension which is about 363 ECU per month. In case he has not worked, the minimum pension is the social pension.

The availability of home help for elderly persons living in the community differs according to presence of a social network or spouse.

12.2 Social Protection of the Case Studies

12.2.1 Case study 1: fully disabled, low income, living in community, alone without social network
10.3 per cent of the male elderly persons aged 60 and above are living alone, while 31.4 per cent of the female elderly persons are.

Social services of the city or village administration will intervene. It is however most unlikely that fully disabled elderly persons without a social network will be cared for at home.

12.2.2 Case study 2: fully disabled, low income, living in community with spouse
49.6 per cent of the male elderly persons aged 60 and above are living in the community with spouse, while for females elderly persons the proportion is 32.1 per cent.

Where full dependency is demonstrated, the carer will receive an attendance allowance of 389 ECU a month.

In some regions, especially in the north, nursing and other services can be requested. At first, it will however be the spouse, with the help of the children, that takes care of the disabled person. As women generally live longer and as men more often than women create a new family in the case of widowhood or divorce, men are more often cared for in the family than women. Women are less likely than men to receive care from their spouse. It implies also that women more often than men care for a person.

12.2.3 Case studies 3a and 3b: fully disabled, low income, living in an old-age home + nursing home
Actually, 6 per cent of the elderly population (65+) lives in Health Assistance Residences (Residenze Sanitarie Assistenziali, RSA).

The charges of the residential services differ between regions. The health aspects related to dependency are paid for by the state. The rest has to be paid for by the client. In case the client has no/not enough means to pay, the communes intervene. Generally, the communes 'try' to receive money of relatives. Regional laws determine the responsibilities of the offspring.

Institutionalisation is generally considered as the last possible solution.

12.2.4 Case study 3c: fully disabled, low income, staying in a general hospital
If the prognosis of the hospitalised person is long-term chronicity, relatives will be invited to bring the patient home or to look for a place in a Health Assistance Residence (old-age and nursing home). As the number of beds and the presence of Health Assistance Residences are limited in almost all Italy, heavy burdens are often supported by the families.

12.2.5 Case study 4: fully disabled, average income, living in community, alone without social network Since becoming disabled is usually a step-by-step process, the average income permits to appeal first to paid informal care like cleaning the house, private or public nurses, medical care, etc. The average income does not permit, as high income does, to appeal to a person for complete care. Even if home care is available, it is not directed to fully disabled people living alone.

12.2.6 Case study 5: fully disabled, average income, living in community with spouse Where the attendance allowance and gender aspects are concerned, we refer to case study 2.

The integration of public services, if available, the presence of a first carer and the (especially emotional) help of generally living near children imply a rather ideal caring situation for the dependent person. Moreover, the average income permits to integrate the heavy family contribution with informal paid help (e.g. private nurses, help in house cleaning, etc.) especially if services like home care are missing.

12.3   Overview

In Italy, the spouse and the social network have an important task in taking care for the dependent elderly persons.

13   Social Protection of Different Categories of Dependent Elderly People in Luxembourg

13.1   The Definition of Case Studies

People considered in the case studies have reached at a minimum the normal retirement age, which is 65 for both men and women.

All persons in the case studies are fully disabled: this means (according to the Luxembourg legislation) that 'they are dependent in one or more physical or mental functions to that extent that they need the help or constant care of a third person'.

The low income category encompasses pensioners whose income is less than 955 ECU per month. This is the minimum pension to which a person who has worked during 40 years has right. Average income is defined as the average pension on 31 December 1995, which was 1,273 ECU per month.

The state subsidises the working and personnel costs in public old-age, nursing homes and day care centres and part of the personnel costs in community services (district nursing and home help). This intervention allows the use of 'social fees'. The state fixes 'leading' prices, which do not correspond to the actual cost. The difference between those 'leading' prices and the actual cost is met by the state in the same manner for the whole population. Those 'leading' prices can be considered as being 'social' prices, since they have to allow a pensioner with an average old-age pension to be able to pay the cost of stay in a specialised institution.

In any case, the dependent person can apply for state contributions for special settling-in expenses and for technical aids and facilities of specialised services.

A dependent person can deduct exceptional charges, costs of assistance and taking care of a dependent person from his taxes.

13.2 Social Protection of the Case Studies

13.2.1 Case study 1: fully disabled, low income, living in community, alone without social network Elderly living in the community benefit from services in cash and in kind.

The *allocation de soins* is a service in cash and is in theory meant for a third person who is helping a dependent person for free. In practice, this allocation can also be meant for a dependent person living alone on condition that the allocation is applied for taking charge of the dependency (e.g. by appealing to a hospital attendant, the use of a community service or day care centre). The *allocation de soins* is means-tested: the income of the dependent person, i.e. the old-age pension, the rent of immovable property, savings, etc. dependency of the older person. The allocation amounts to 360 ECU and is normally only paid in case the older person is living at home.

The pensioner of this case study can also benefit from services in kind or community services, such as district nursing and home help. Traditional district nursing acts are prescribed by the general practitioner and covered by health insurance. Personal hygiene performed by district nurses is on the contrary not covered by health insurance and stays at the expense of the dependent person. District nursing is applying 'social' fees, i.e. a lump sum of 7.37 ECU per day at most.

Home help services are provided if the dependent person does not need the traditional nursing care, but needs help in housekeeping and in performing the daily life activities among which personal hygiene. Home help is in theory limited to two hours per day. Personal fees are income-related, whereby the *allocation de soins* is also considered as income, and vary between 3.05 and 12.71 ECU per hour or 6.10 and 25.42 ECU per day (two hours).

The dependent person of this case who is living alone can apply to a day care centre. Health insurance does not cover these centres. The contributions of the elderly persons are income-related and vary between 12.71 and 30.50 ECU per day. Next to this, at least 1.27 ECU is charged for transport per day.

The *allocation de soins*, the provision of district nursing and home help and the application to a day care centre can be cumulated. In that case, the *allocation de soins* covers about the minimum required request for home help for one hour per day (during seven days a week) and the minimum required request for a day care centre for one day (five days a week) or 371 ECU per month. Consequently, there is nothing left for, e.g., help during the night.

Medical acts, acts performed by physiotherapists and medical drugs are not to that extent covered by health insurance.

13.2.2 Case study 2: fully disabled, low income, living in community with spouse The dependent person of this case study benefits from the same services in cash and in kind and under the same conditions as the dependent person of case study 1. The *allocation de soins* is meant for a third person, which is the spouse in this case.

A person who engages personnel for taking care of a dependent house-mate can deduct the expenses from his taxes.

13.2.3 Case study 3a: fully disabled, low income, living in an old-age home There are two cases: either the dependent person is staying in a public either private old-age home.

In the first case, the pensioner has to pay the cost of stay which is fixed by legislation. The cost of stay (1,361 ECU per month) is divided into a basic amount of 1,055 ECU in 1995 and the additional costs caused by dependency of 306 ECU. Since the pensioner has only a pension of 955 ECU per month, other resources of the older person him- or herself (savings, personal assets, etc.) and contributions from relatives are drawn upon. It is only when contributions from relatives are either unavailable or insufficient that social assistance will cover the additional expenses. Anyway, the pensioner has to maintain pocket money in order to meet personal needs. The pocket money was fixed at 165 ECU per month in 1995.

In the second case, the pensioner can apply to the *allocation de soins*, which is normally only paid where the older person is living at home. His income then amounts to 1,315 ECU per month. Since the cost of stay in a private old-age home is the same as in a public old-age home – the religious congregations who are owners of most of the private old-age homes have tuned their 'leading' prices in to those of the public old-age homes – the pensioner lacks 46 ECU to meet the cost of stay. The resources of the older person him- or herself and contributions from relatives are only little drawn upon.

For dependent elderly persons living in an institution, health insurance covers medical and paramedical acts performed by professionals, normally working outside the institution. These professionals are paid by way of fees. When the professionals are salaried personnel from the institution, their remuneration is part of the global working costs. Health insurance covers medical drugs.

13.2.4 Case study 3b: fully disabled, low income, living in a nursing home
Since all nursing homes are public, prices are all the same. The cost of stay is fixed by legislation and is not related to dependency. It amounts to 1,500 ECU per month in 1995. This is much higher than the income of the pensioner, since the *allocation de soins* is never paid to a pensioner living in a nursing home. Therefore, other resources of the older person (savings, personal assets, etc.) and contributions from relatives are drawn upon. Social assistance covers the additional expenses when contributions from relatives are either unavailable or insufficient. The older person can maintain pocket money (165 ECU per month in 1995) as in old-age homes.

We repeat that for dependent elderly persons living in an institution, health insurance covers medical and paramedical acts performed by professionals, normally working outside the institution. These professionals are paid by way of fees. When the professionals are salaried personnel from the institution, their remuneration is part of the global working costs. As in old-age homes, health insurance covers medical drugs.

13.2.5 Case study 3c: fully disabled, low income, staying in a general hospital
There are two cases: either the dependent person is staying in a general hospital, nor in a neuropsychiatric hospital of the state.

In the first case, the hospitalised dependent person is waiting to be admitted to a more suitable institution. After a period of three to six months, the medical control declares the person 'cas de simple hébergement'. This means that cost of stay, which was about 2,288 ECU per month in 1995, is no more covered by health insurance, but by the person him- or herself. The state

(Ministry of Health) can under certain conditions cover the difference between the cost of stay and the old-age pension without appealing to the resources of relatives and without withdrawal on the legacy.

In the second case, the older person has been treated in a neuropsychiatric hospital of the state and is admitted to a long stay service 'maison de soins interne' after the acute stadium. In that case, persons aged 60 and over are automatically considered as 'cas de simple hébergement': they have to pay the cost of stay themselves which was 1,933 ECU per month in 1995. Contrary to the former case, there is no intervention of the state even when the person is on the waiting list for admission to a public nursing home. Therefore, the difference between the cost of stay and the income of the old person is charged to the relatives or is met by the state (with withdrawal on the legacy).

Health insurance covers for dependent elderly persons living in an institution medical and paramedical acts performed by professionals, normally working outside the institution. These professionals are paid by way of fees. When the professionals are salaried personnel from the institution, their remuneration is part of the global working costs. Medical drugs are covered by health insurance.

13.2.6 Case study 4: fully disabled, average income, living in community, alone without social network This case is similar to case study 1.

13.2.7 Case study 5: fully disabled, average income, living in community with spouse This case is similar to case study 2.

13.2.8 Case study 6a: fully disabled, average income, living in an old-age home There are 2 cases as in case study 3a.

In the first case, the pensioner has to meet the cost of stay, which is 1,361 ECU per month. His income is 1,273 ECU per month. The shortage of 88 ECU is covered by relatives or by the state (with withdrawal on the legacy).

In the second case, the older person can benefit from the *allocation de soins*. His income is then 1,633 ECU per month, which allows the pensioner to pay totally the cost of stay.

13.2.9 Case study 6b: fully disabled, average income, living in a nursing home As in case study 3b, the old-age pension (1,273 ECU per month) is still not enough to pay the cost of stay. The shortage of 227 ECU per month is covered by relatives or by the state (with withdrawal on the legacy).

13.2.10 Case study 6c: fully disabled, average income, staying in general hospital This case is similar to case study 3c.

13.2.11 Comments on other case studies

Case study 7: fully disabled widow, female 'survivor', 80+, living in the community, alone without social network We assume that the husband received a minimum old-age pension. Therefore, the female survivor has a minimum survivor's pension of 774 ECU per month (1995).

Since she stays at home, she can apply to the *allocation the soins* and benefit from district nursing, home help and the services of a day care centre. Personal fees are modest and can be covered by the *allocation de soins*.

Case study 8: senile older person This case is similar to case studies 2 and 7.

Case study 9: immigrant Two cases are assumed: firstly, the pensioner has worked during 25 years in Luxembourg; secondly, the pensioner has worked during 15 years in Luxembourg.

Where the first case is concerned, the older person has right to a minimum old-age pension. The amount is defined pro rata the years worked more than 20 years, which is 597 ECU per month.

Where the second case is concerned, the older person has no right to a minimum old-age pension. He can, on the contrary, apply for guaranteed minimum income, which was 792 ECU per month in 1995.

The person has a right to services in kind and in cash of common right in either case. He or she has access to all institutions under the same conditions as the natives.

13.3   Overview

For elderly persons living at home only acts done by nurses are paid for by health insurance; medical acts, acts performed by physiotherapists and medical drugs are not to that extent covered. District nursing attracts a lump sum fee, which is not income-related.

For dependent elderly persons living in an institution, health insurance covers medical and paramedical acts performed by professionals, normally working outside the institution. These professionals are paid by way of fees. When the professionals are salaried personnel from the institution, their remuneration is part of the global working costs.

The cost of staying in an old-age and nursing home is fixed by legislation and is not income-related. In the first place, the resources of the older person him- or herself (including savings, personal assets and any kind of inheritance) are drawn upon. It is only when contributions from relatives are either unavailable or insufficient that social assistance will cover the additional expenses.

14   Social Protection of Different Categories of Dependent Elderly People in the Netherlands

14.1   The Definition of Case Studies (see Appendix 2)

All case studies refer to pensioners who have reached the normal pensionable age, which is 65 for both men and women.

All pensioners are 'severely disabled'. The term is based on a combined index of impairment of ADL and IADL activities, reduced to a compact division into four categories (Huijsman and de Klerk, 1993):
–   little or no impairment: the older individual has no ADL problems and can perform IADL activities almost totally alone;
–   moderate impairment: the individual is capable of performing all ADL items alone but has obvious difficulties with IADL activities;
–   severe impairment: the individual can no longer perform some ADL activities and simultaneously has difficulty with many housekeeping activities;
–   very severe impairment: the individual has difficulty with many ADL activities and can no longer perform any of the housekeeping tasks.

Low income is defined as the minimum income legally guaranteed by the General Pension Act ('AOW') to all residents 65+. Income from other sources (assets, rent subsidy) are not taken into account.

Average income is defined as approximately the average income in each country for retired private sector wage earners who have retired at the legal pensionable age. Contrary to low income pensioners, do average income pensioners also dispose of an occupational pension and other private income. 79 per cent of 65+ households has occupational pensions.

Case studies 3c and 6c will not be described, as general hospitals are not meant to be long-term institutions in the Netherlands.

14.1 Social Protection of the Case Studies

14.2.1 Case study 1: fully disabled, low income, living in community, alone without social network

In 1994 there were 657,000 households consisting of a single pensioner; 35,000 received only the legal pension (5.3 per cent). The person in the case study has been chosen to be female but in the description of the case study no reference is made to eventual differences in social protection arrangements according to gender.

The share of the elderly population (65+) represented by case study 1 is less than 2 per cent.

Services of general practitioners, pharmaceuticals, specialist health care services and hospital care (max. one year) of 'low income earners' are covered by Public Health Insurance and provided as provision in kind. Pensioners with a low income pay a contribution of 1.4 per cent of the 'AOW'-benefit.

If medical care in a hospital is needed for more than one year, it is financed by AWBZ, and no longer Health Insurance.

To receive district nursing, membership of a district nursing organisation is required. The contribution amounts to 22 ECU per year. The services are free of contribution. They are based on need assessment.

Home help services, meals-on-wheels and transport services are social services that are based on need assessment. Pensioners have to make personal contributions, the amount of which is related to the income level. The costs of home help are covered by a special social insurance scheme (AWBZ), which is obligatory to all residents. Meals-on-wheels are financed by subsidies at municipal level.

It is important to note that all pensioners can utilise intensive home care for a maximum period of six months.

In general there are a number of day care facilities available, in nursing homes, in homes for the aged and in regional welfare centres. For institutional care, old-age homes and day care, people have to be assessed before they can use the service.

14.2.2 Case study 2: fully disabled, low income, living in community with spouse

In 1994 there were 529,000 households consisting of couples with at least one pensioner 65+ (of these couples 71 per cent were both 65+); 7,000 households received only the legal pension (this is 1.3 per cent of total households of couples 65+). The person in the case study has been chosen to be an impaired man (fully disabled, grade 6) but in the description of the case study no reference is made to eventual differences in social protection arrangements according to gender.

The share of the elderly population (65+) represented by case study 2 is approximately 2 per cent.

Whereas health and social services are concerned, no differences occur with pensioners living alone in the community (case study 1).

14.2.3 Case study 4: fully disabled, average income, living in community, alone without social network In 1994 the average gross income for a single person with an additional pension was 16,686 ECU. For the age group 65–69 the amount was 17,294 ECU and for the age group 75–79, 16,265 ECU. The average gross income for female singles was 16,219 ECU.

The share of the elderly population (65+) represented by case study 4 is less than 4 per cent.

This case study concerns a fully disabled (grade 5) woman. In case of extreme housing costs, Social Assistance intervenes. Services of general practitioners, pharmaceuticals, specialist health care services and hospital care (max. one year) are covered by private health insurance, as people on higher incomes are probably insured privately to a greater degree with the health insurance companies or insured for higher levels of personal risks. The contributions that people on higher income have to make also depends on their choice of the level of personal risk. For district nursing, no differences with low income pensioners are noticed.

Since for the social services, personal contributions have to be made which depend on the income level, the only difference between pensioners on low and average income will be the level of personal contribution. For home help, the contribution of a single household with a net income of 1,075 ECU per month is 93 ECU per month. The personal contributions for home help are limited to a certain amount per month. The maximum contribution is 467 ECU per month for a single household with a net income of 2,103 ECU per month.

14.2.4 Case study 5: fully disabled, average income, living in community with spouse The person in the case study has been chosen to be an impaired man (fully disabled, grade 7), living with spouse. 40 per cent of 65+ households is 'living with partner', but not all of this 40 per cent is disabled.

In 1994 the average gross income for couples with an additional pension was 24,538 ECU. For the age group 65–69 the amount was 26,595 ECU and for the age group 75–79, 24,024 ECU.

In case of extreme housing costs, Social Assistance intervenes. Whereas with health and social services, the only difference with case study 4 is the level of the personal contributions for social services. For home help, the contribution for a household consisting of more than one person with a net income of 1,075 ECU per month is 43 ECU per month. The maximum contribution per month is 430 ECU for a household consisting of more than one person with a net income of 2,103 ECU per month.

14.2.5 Case studies 3a and 6a: fully disabled, living in an old-age home This case study refers to a fully disabled woman (grade 5), living on average or low income.

In 1994, 6.4 per cent of the 65+ in the Netherlands lived in old-age homes. 80 per cent of them are female. It is not possible to determine how many of these people are disabled or who lives on low or average income.

For the financing of a stay in an old-age home, people have to invest their own assets and incomes and pay as long as there are income and assets available. People with a low income may keep a certain amount as pocket money. As soon as there are no assets available and the individual is not able to cover the costs with his/her income (public and private pension), social assistance will add the amount which is missing. From 1 January 1997 on, homes for the aged will be financed within the framework of AWBZ. From that date on, co-financing will only be income-related (now hotel and care costs are means-tested and income-related).

14.2.6 Case studies 3b and 6b: fully disabled, living in a nursing home This case study refers to a fully disabled woman (grade 8), living in a nursing home.

2.7 per cent of the 65+ in the Netherlands lives in nursing homes. 1.3 per cent in somatic nursing homes; 1.3 per cent in psycho-geriatric nursing homes.

For a stay in a nursing home, people have to contribute a share of their income (maximum 1,028 ECU at the moment), not of their assets. Next to this fixed amount from private income, there is a supplemented contribution of the Exceptional Medical Expenses Insurance Scheme (AWBZ).

14.2.7 Comments on other case studies

Case study 7: fully disabled widow (grade 6), female 'survivor', 80+, living in community, alone without social network Single women, 80+, not living in institutions make up 8.3 per cent of the population 65+.

Women in these situations receive a public pension (minimum income for unmarried woman). They can apply for social assistance in case of extreme housing costs.

They have the same access to services as other low income pensioners living alone.

Case study 8: senile older person The share of the elderly population (65+) represented by this case study is 5 to 10 per cent.

There are no differences from case study 5 as far as income, health and social services are concerned.

14.3   Overview

Social services demand personal contributions that vary according to the level of income. Even persons in low income categories pay contributions, but if their income is insufficient, they receive cash benefits from the Social Assistance Act. In case of old-age homes, the cash benefit is paid directly to the institution.

15   Social Protection of Different Categories of Dependent Elderly People in Portugal

15.1   The Definition of Case Studies

All case studies assume that the people considered have reached the normal retirement age, which is at present 65 years for both genders.

All pensioners of the case studies are fully disabled. In. Portugal the assessment of dependency does not rely on the Katz index of ADL based on instrumental and personal capabilities, but on the amount of external help a dependent person needs (i.e. the Social Security criteria). Fully disabled is defined as needing permanent external help in order to satisfy basic needs and housekeeping. The assessment of the level of dependency is made by a social worker belonging to the staff of the local social service agency.

The Minimum Guaranteed Income (equivalent to the Minimum National Salary), which was 280 ECU per month for a single person in 1997, is the borderline between low and average income. A low income pensioner is defined as a pensioner whose income is less then the Minimum Guaranteed Income, an average income pensioner whose income is more.

The average pension (old-age, invalidity and survival pension) was 238

ECU per month in 1994. About 87 per cent of the pensioners receives a pension of less than 205 ECU per month. Consequently, a vast majority of the retired people has a monthly pension of less than the Minimum Guaranteed Income. Only nearly 13 per cent are entitled to a monthly pension of more than the Minimum Guaranteed Income.

There are different pension systems. In the General Regime, the average monthly pension (old-age, invalidity and survival pension) was 204 ECU in 1994; in the Regime for Agricultural Activities, 130 ECU; in the Regime of Non-Contributors 162 ECU and in the Regime for Civil Servants 614 ECU. The distinction between a low and an average income pensioner is the same as between retired civil servants and other professional classes.

It is not relevant to distinguish according to gender for any of the services and social protection arrangements in question.

15.2   Social Protection of the Case Studies

15.2.1 Case studies 1 and 4: fully disabled, low and average income, living in community, alone without social network If the pensioner has been active on the labour market, he/she is entitled to a full old-age pension from the General Regime or any other Regime. If the pensioner has been active on the labour market for a short period he/she is entitled to an invalidity pension. If he/she has never contributed to the social security system, the pensioner can claim for a survival pension.

If living in a rented house, the pensioner can benefit from a rent subsidy to compensate for any (extraordinary) increase of the rent. In order to claim this right, the pensioner has to introduce yearly a specific demand to the Social Security Centre of his region. Furthermore, if he suffers from an incapacity level of more than 60 per cent, he can benefit from a complementary rent subsidy for a limited period.

All retired people, disabled or not, are entitled to the National Health Service irrespective if they have contributed or not during their working life. Health care services are free to all pensioners, except for drugs. The state contributes partially or fully the cost of pharmaceutical products, depending upon the need of the pharmaceutical product to support life (e.g. insulin for diabetics is free to the pensioners) and /or upon the social protection regime of the pensioner. Consumer co-payments for drugs vary from 0 to 50 per cent (40 per cent in case the drugs are prescribed by a doctor).

A pensioner who does not meet the minimum conditions to stay alone and who does not have family or relatives who can take care of him/her, is entitled to home care services in kind. These services include nursing care, home help and cleaning, cooking arrangements (if not beneficiary of meals-on-wheels), treatment of clothes (dry cleaning), assistance for intake of pharmaceuticals, company for small walks, etc. The contributions to these social services are means-tested. The contribution of the pensioner for services in a day centre is 40 per cent of the per capita income (or 50 per cent if a daily meal is served) and for house help also 40 per cent (25 per cent for meals-on-wheels, 5 per cent for personal care, 5 per cent for house cleaning and 5 per cent for laundry). In general, the pensioners pay at least 70 per cent of their monthly income for these facilities, even 85 per cent for the more severe cases of disability. The per capita income is the gross income of the whole family aggregate, including the reform pensions, minus the fixed expenses (including pharmaceutical drugs), divided by the number of persons composing the family.

15.2.2 Case studies 2 and 5: fully disabled, low and average income, living in community, with spouse There are no differences with case studies 1 and 4 where the pension and rent subsidy are concerned. An elderly couple in these case studies is entitled to a monthly guaranteed minimum income.

Next to this, a pensioner is entitled to a supplement to his/her pension of 23 ECU per month in 1997 in case the spouse has never contributed to the social security pension fund.

Pensioners who are fully dependent on the help of another person to satisfy their basic needs (whatever the degree) are entitled to a subsidy for the help of a third person of 52 ECU (General Regime) and 44 ECU (Agricultural Activities Regime) per month. The subsidy for the help of a third person is not income-related.

The supplement and subsidy for the help of a third person can be exchanged for social security facilities and the intake of meals usually associated with it.

A retired couple, who are both dependent, can be temporary or definitively integrated by the Social Assistance services into a family if no places in nursing homes are available. The family takes care of them and are paid for by Social Security. In 1996, Social Security paid 280 ECU per person in case of full dependency.

No differences are noticed with case studies 1 and 4 where health care services are concerned.

15.2.3 Case studies 3a and 3b/6a and 6b: fully disabled, low/average income, living in an old-age home /nursing home There are no differences with case studies 1 and 4 where the pension is concerned.

The number of (beds in) nursing homes are very scarce. This means long waiting lists of sometimes two or three years. Entitlement is considered in case of severe disability, i.e. the pensioner is unable to care for him-/herself and manage daily life without help, and cannot count on the help of relatives.

Personal contributions for care and lodging in old-age and nursing homes are means-tested. In old-age homes, 75 per cent of the per capita monthly income is automatically withdrawn, in nursing homes (the more severe cases of disability) this amounts to 85 per cent. The pensioner is left with the remaining 'pocket money'.

15.2.4 Case studies 3c and 6c: fully disabled, low income or average income, staying in a general hospital There are no differences with case studies 1 and 4 where the pension is concerned.

Health and hospital care services are free to all pensioners, except for services in private hospitals and clinics, if they are agreed by one of the National Health Services, and drugs. Services in public hospitals and health centres (or private ones, if chartered) as well as auxiliary diagnostic and therapeutic means and other the like exams are free. We refer to case studies 1 and 4 where contributions to the cost of drugs are concerned.

15.2.5 Comments on other case studies

Case study 7: fully disabled widow, female 'survivor', 80+, living in the community, alone without social network Where the income is concerned, several cases are possible:
- if the spouse has made contributions to the pension system for at least 36 months and she has been married for at least one year, she is entitled to a survival pension;
- if the spouse has never made contributions, she is entitled to a widow pension, which is 60 per cent of the social old-age or social invalidity pension or, in case she has an income of less than 30 per cent of the Minimum National Salary, she is entitled to an Elderliness social pension.

Next to this pension, the widow has right to a subsidy for the help of a third person.

This case study is the same as case studies 1 and 4, where health and social services are concerned.

Case study 8: senile older person Demented pensioners are entitled to free consultations, treatments and drugs prescribed by psychiatric doctors. In case of severe dementia, the pensioner can only go to private mental hospitals and clinics, because there is a lack of psychiatric beds in general hospitals. Since hospitalisation in private hospitals is not free, only pensioners with very high income can afford hospitalisation.

The case of permanent dementia is not assumed by the Social Security Services. Therefore, these cases mean an overcharge for the family and relatives. Solutions are looked for in private nursing homes and clinics, which only accept to care for such cases against extra charges. However, due to the general depression of the supply of such establishments and the long waiting lists and taking into consideration that a mental disease requires immediate treatment and care, it is evident that there are no solutions available for people with those characteristics.

Case study 9: immigrant Immigrants have right to a full pension if they meet the minimum contributive period which is necessary to be entitled to it. As they can not practice jobs from the Central Admin-istration as civil servants, they are restricted to the General Regime or the Agricultural Activities Regime and cannot subscribe to the Social Security Regime of Civil Servants, the most favourable one.

Immigrants have the same rights to all social services and nursing homes as Portuguese citizens.

Some immigrants have their rights restricted, namely detached workers (law of their state of origin is implemented), workers of international transport (laws of the country of the employer are implemented) and workers having professional activities in several countries and workers of free trade areas (laws of the country where their enterprises have their head offices are implemented).

15.3 Overview

The availability of social services is theoretically 100 per cent. However, in practice the availability depends on the region, the cultural level (access to information) and the insertion of family and relatives. The disparities are tied to the regional density of the network of Social Security regional centres, the availability of personnel and, if available, the level of training of personnel.

Health and hospital services are free for all pensioners, except for services in private hospitals and clinics. Consumer co-payments for drugs amounts to 50 per cent.

Social services are means-tested.

16   Social Protection of Different Categories of Dependent Elderly People in Sweden

16.1   *The Definition of Case Studies (see Appendix 2)*

Most health care services are heavily subsidised and the patient usually pays a low flat-rate fee, which in fact covers only a fraction of the actual costs. Each county council sets its own fees. To limit the costs incurred for the patient, there is a 'high cost ceiling'. A patient who has paid 258 ECU (1997) for (out-patient) medical care and for pharmaceutical preparations is entitled to free care and free medicines for the reminder of 12 months, which is calculated from the first visit to a doctor or the first purchase of medicines.

Social services are paid according to the extent to which the services are used and are partly means-tested (70 per cent of the municipalities is using this combined system). This means that the differences between the different cases are mainly related to the income level and to a lesser extent to the level of dependency. Further, there are no differences in terms of fees, whether the person lives in an old-age or a nursing home (other than what is motivated by differences in housing standard). However, as the municipalities are free to decide about the fees for housing, services and care, there are substantial inter-municipal differences in terms of fees. Persons with equal level of dependency and income, could be charged very differently, in one municipality as compared to another.

Another factor that has an impact on the level of patient fees, is whether the person is single or cohabiting/married. If one spouse needs, e.g., home help, the level of the fees, will usually be determined on the basis of half the total income of the household.

These general principles count irrespective of whether the dependent is senile (case study 8) or whatever the reason for dependency.

Regarding the case studies, the most important dimension of social protection from the Swedish perspective is whether the elderly person is living at home (case studies 1, 2, 4 and 5) or in an institution (case studies 3a, 3b, 6a and 6b).

A low income pensioner is defined as a person receiving the basic pension, which was 5,641 ECU/year in 1995, and the pension supplement of 2,315 ECU/year at maximum (in 1996). Average income is defined as the supplementary pension (ATP), which was 9,496 ECU/year in 1995 for a single pensioner.

Table 4.2 gives a view of the degree of disability of elderly in Sweden according to their living situation.

Table 4.2   Degree of disability of elderly in Sweden according to the living situation

Target group	Degree of disability
Elderly persons in old-age homes	Unknown
Elderly persons in nursing homes	A category: 5%
	B, C, D category: 9%
	E, F category: 58%
	G category: 25%
	Others: 3%
Elderly persons living in the community	
– aged >65	
	B category: 11.3%
	E category: 2.4%
– aged >75	B category: 13.7%
	E category: 3.1%

16.2   *Social Protection of the Case Studies*

16.2.1 *Case studies 1 and 2/4 and 5: fully disabled, low/average income, living in community, alone without social network/with spouse* Elderly persons living in the community can call upon general practitioners or specialist health care services. When using these services, low income pensioners (as everybody) pay a flat fee, which is higher for specialist care (varies between 12 and 31 ECU) than for general care (varies between 7 and 16 ECU). If the doctor pays a call to the patient's home, there is usually an extra 6–12 ECU charged.

For hospital services, a hospitalisation fee has to be paid for each day the patient stays. The fee represents only approximately 3–4 per cent of the total cost. The state covers approximately 10 per cent of the rest of the costs. Regional taxes pay the additional costs.

Pharmaceuticals are paid for by the elderly persons themselves and partly reimbursed by the national social insurance. Contributions of the elderly amount to 23 per cent of the costs.

As mentioned before, there is a 'high-cost coverage', which means that the patient is charged for medical consultations and drugs prescribed, up to an annual limit (258 ECU in 1997).

District nursing as well as physiotherapy is usually provided free of charge, but in some places patients could be charged 6–12 ECU per treatment.

For social services, personal fees are higher: they depend on the level of income and the amount of services needed. For home help services, the contributions amount on average to 8 per cent. For security alarm, the recipient pays between 12 and 16 ECU per month.

In some municipalities, there is an option for an attendance allowance. The allowance is a cash payment that is not taxed. It is paid to the dependent (at least in theory) of case studies 2 and 5 and is based on the need of the dependent. It is used as reimbursement for care given by the spouse, the daughter or whichever person actually responsible for the caring. The level of payment is however very modest, especially compared with the time and effort most carers put in, and holds only token value. The payment varies between 141 and 588 ECU per month.

The spouse (carer) of elderly persons of case studies 2 and 5 can receive a remuneration for his/her caring, i.e. carers allowance. The term is used for those situations where a family member is employed by the municipality to care for a next of kin. The payment is seen as a remuneration of any other salaried worker (tax-wise, social protection, etc.).

16.2.2 Case studies 3a and 3b/6a and 6b: fully disabled, low/average income, living in an old-age home/nursing home The pensioner in this case study is living in an old-age or nursing home in which the general old-age pension is not withdrawn in part-payment for housing, care and services. Since the older person lives on a low income, he only receives the general old-age pension and pension supplements. Those receiving the supplementary pension will generally reach average income and above.

Since 1993 it has been possible for the municipality to collect fees for the services in a nursing home and all other types of municipal institutional facilities. As a matter of policy, the persons are charged for these services at the same rate as if they had been living in the community. The resident pays for the care and meals and pays a rent for the housing costs. The rent depends on the standard of housing in the facility and, thus, can differ substantially between different institutions. As with persons living in the community, means-tested rent subsidies are available.

The amount left to the pensioner after paying all services must be at least as high as the 'pocket money' which the pensioner would have disposed of if the social pension had not been paid. In general, the residents pay about 70 per cent of their total income for housing, care and other services which may be paid for, including cleaning, hairdressing and pedicure. A 'last resort' for a low income pensioner with high costs for service and care needs, is to claim social assistance. This is very seldom done by the pensioners in Sweden.

Only about 2 per cent of all people claiming social assistance are retired people.

Nursing homes etc. are required to provide care that meets the needs of the residents. Health care services (i.e. physiotherapy, doctors visits, dental care), provided to persons living in a nursing home are in principle identical to those provided to elderly persons living in their own home and are paid for the same way.

16.2.3 Case studies 3c and 6c: fully disabled, low income or average income, staying in a general hospital If a person is admitted to a general hospital, he pays a daily fee of 5–9 ECU. This fee covers both 'housing' and care (including pharmaceuticals). If the sick person is in a terminal stage of his illness, a family member could stay out of work for a maximum of 60 days to attend the sick person. The family member is paid for by social insurance. The payment is the same as if the family member was sick. In order to claim this (statutory) right, there must be approval by a physician and the patient and the arrangement is only possible for a person in working age (up to 65 years).

16.2.4 Comments on other case studies

Case study 8: senile older person This case study is similar to case studies 2 and 5 where the attendance allowance is concerned.

Case study 9: immigrant Immigrants, who have not lived long enough in Sweden (the minimum is three years) might have problems to receive pension. In that case, the immigrant has to claim social security for income support.

16.3   Overview

The Swedish pension system provides the overwhelming majority of elderly Swedes, with a basic economic security and generally nobody has to abstain from services and care. Since the Swedish health and social system is based on the principle of equal rights, irrespective of the former labour market career, the differences in protection between some of the cases are very small indeed. The differences that do arise mostly relate to income and subsequently the amount of out-of-pocket payment the service user has to pay. For health services patients usually pay flat-rate fees. The personal contributions for social services, on the contrary, are related to income. No differences occur in terms of fees for persons living in old-age homes and in nursing homes.

17 Social Protection of Different Categories of Dependent Elderly People in the UK

17.1 The Definition of Case Studies (see Appendix 2)

All case studies refer to people who have reached the normal pensionable age, which is 65 for men and 60 for women.

The pensioners in question are considered to be fully disabled, which means that they are 'short or critical-interval dependent'. The dependency of these people has been assessed using an Activities of Daily Living (ADL) score which includes both personal and instrumental activities (Isaacs and Neville, 1976; Bond and Carstairs, 1982). 15 per cent of the estimated number of people aged 65 and over in Britain are 'short or critical-interval dependent'.

By 'elderly living on low income' is meant individuals or households that are in receipt of income support, the official UK government poverty line. Approximately 10 per cent of older people in the UK live on income below the income support level. Over 50 per cent of pensioner households are below 50 per cent of the average household income (DSS, 1996). The minimum income represents the theoretical income level at which a large number of means-tested benefits and services are available free of charge to those senior citizens who need them.

Although data is available relating to social networks of frail elderly people, the type of social network (availability of relatives who do not live in the same household as the pensioner) has no effect on the eligibility of an individual for social protection. The key difference is whether or not the subject lives with a spouse, since this is what affects pension levels.

There are no differences in the social protection afforded to female and to male pensioners. There is, however, some evidence that men living alone in the community are more likely than single women to receive personal social services, particularly home care services such as home helps (Charlesworth et al., 1984). In addition, home care services are more likely to be given to older couples when the woman has the higher degree of disability than when the man has the higher degree of disability.

17.2 Social Protection of the Case Studies

17.2.1 Case study 1: fully disabled, low income, living in the community, alone without social network Case study 1 represents 10 per cent of the short or critical-interval dependent elderly.

For older people living alone on low income, income support will underpin their standard of living. The actual level of benefit received will depend on other kinds of income, in particular state retirement and occupational pensions. Only people who have less than 9,801 ECU savings and whose income is less than the 'applicable' amount are eligible for income support. One in five of those eligible for social assistance in 1985 did not claim it (DSS, 1996). Income support for older people consists of a personal allowance and a pensioner premium, the amount of which depends on the age of the person.

Pensioners in receipt of income support are eligible for additional benefits such as benefits from the Regulated Social Fund (for example, cold weather payments) and from the Discretionary Social Fund (for example, community care grants), housing benefit and council tax benefits.

Some older people who are 'severely disabled' receive attendance allowance, which also makes them eligible for the severe disability premium. However, entitlement to these benefits largely depends on subjective professional judgements. Hence, not all disabled older people will receive these benefits.

Invalid care allowance (ICA) is payable to people who care for someone who is in receipt of attendance allowance, provided the carer is not 'gainfully employed' and was under pensionable age at the time of the first claim. Those eligible for ICA also qualify for a carer's premium with income support, although the person receiving the care loses any entitlement to a severe disability premium. A 'better-off' calculation would be necessary in order to ascertain whether it would be in the people's best interest to receive ICA.

Visits to general practitioners, hospital services and district nursing are free to all citizens in the UK. All pensioners, regardless of income level, receive free drug prescriptions. Other health care services, such as dental and ophthalmic services and chiropody, are means-tested services but are free to pensioners on income support.

All personal social services, which are means-tested, are free to these persons also, but they are rationed according to need by social service professionals.

17.2.2 Case study 7: fully disabled widow, female 'survivor', 80+, living in the community, alone without social network Case study 7 is similar to case study 1. A widow whose spouse has been in employment and has met the contribution requirements receives the same state retirement pension as pensioners in case study 1. Graduated retirement benefits depend on the spouse's graduated contributions.

17.2.3 Case study 2: fully disabled, low income, living in the community, with spouse Case study 2 represents 10 per cent of the short or critical-interval dependent elderly.

There are no substantial differences in social protection between case study 1 and case study 2 except in the level of financial support which couples are eligible for (personal allowance and pensioner premiums for couple, severe disability premium for couple (if both partner and spouse are eligible for attendance allowance)).

17.2.4 Case study 4: fully disabled, average income, living in the community, alone without social network Case study 4 represents 13 per cent of the short or critical-interval dependent elderly people.

Receiving an average income implies that the older person will not be eligible for income support or any other means-tested cash benefit. The person is still eligible for attendance allowance, which is not an income-related benefit but rather depends on the level of disability as assessed by a medical practitioner.

The pensioner receives a basic pension and in some cases a graduated retirement pension. The basic pension as received in the case study requires that the recipient has made the necessary contributions. Recipients can also apply for a graduated retirement benefit based on graduated contributions made between 1961 and 1975. Women are discriminated against under the contribution conditions of this benefit. Men are entitled to 0.10 ECU per week for every 9.19 ECU paid whereas women are entitled to the same amount for each 11.03 ECU paid (*Rights Guide to Non-means-tested Benefits*, 1996).

Occupational pensions depend on participation in the labour force but, among current pensioners, substantial occupational pensions are scarce (restricted to recent pensioners). All occupational pensions are dependent on contributions and are paid in addition to the basic state retirement pension.

Some health care services (general practitioner services, hospital services and district nursing) are free to all citizens. However, depending on the level of their income, they pay part of the costs of the means-tested health care services. All pensioners receive free prescriptions, regardless of income level.

All personal social services – with the exception of social workers and in some authorities respite and day care – are means-tested and thus charged for pensioners on average income. However, where charges are rendered, the service is still substantially subsidised through general taxation (personal contributions constitute only 5–10 per cent of total costs).

17.2.5 Case study 5: fully disabled, average income, living in the community, with spouse Case study 5 represents 20 per cent of the short or critical-interval dependent people.

Case study 5 is similar to case study 4. The key difference is the increased pension for a married couple in contrast to a single pensioner.

17.2.6 Case studies 3a and 3b: fully disabled, low income, living in an independently managed residential or nursing home Case studies 3a and 3b represent 14 per cent of the short or critical-interval dependent elderly.

In the UK, independently managed nursing or residential homes can be private and for-profit or managed by a voluntary organisation and not-for-profit. Older people are eligible for admission to a home in the independent sector if assessed by professionals as needing that level of support.

People on low incomes admitted to residential or nursing homes prior to 1 April 1993 are funded through income support up to a ceiling charge defined by the Department of Social Security (depending upon type of home and type of care received) and housing benefits. Relatives of older people are able to top up this amount to secure better facilities (e.g. a single room). However, in practice older people on low incomes living in the independent sector are more likely to be sharing a room with one or more others. Since April 1993, support of low income older people in residential or nursing homes is funded through the local social services department or health authority.

Financial support for people in residential and nursing homes means that they lose eligibility for the state retirement pension or income support and receive just 16.8 ECU per week 'pocket money'.

People in the situation of case studies 3a and 3b receive no means-tested benefits except, in some cases, housing benefit. People receiving attendance allowance will stop receiving it after they have lived in a publicly funded home for more than 4 weeks.

17.2.7 Case studies 6a and 6b: fully disabled, average income, living in an independently managed residential or nursing home Case studies 6a and 6b represent 15 per cent of the short or critical-interval dependent people.

When people have average incomes or savings of at least 9,801 ECU, residential and nursing home care will be paid for out of their personal resources (income and savings), with the possibility of support from other family members. The costs of residential and nursing home care are completely covered by the pensioner himself until his savings and income have declined to means-tested level.

These persons do not receive any means-tested benefits and the attendance allowance ceases after they have resided in publicly funded homes for more than four weeks.

17.2.8 Case studies 3c and 6c: fully disabled, low or average income, permanently resident in NHS hospitals or nursing homes Case study 3c represents 2 per cent of the short or critical-interval dependent elderly people. Case study 6c represents 2 per cent of the short or critical-interval dependent elderly people.

For hospital care, there are no differences according to income level. Hospital treatment is free at the point of provision but pensions are reduced to the level of personal allowances after six weeks in hospital.

Personal savings and income acquired from the sale of property, for example, are not used to fund hospital or NHS nursing home care.

The attendance allowance ceases after four weeks in hospital.

17.3   Overview

Within the UK, the welfare state provides a system of social protection which provides for universal health care within the framework of the National Health Service, means-tested personal social services into private households, means-tested support for long-term institutional care and income maintenance to ensure a minimum income for all members of the population with the exception of immigrants to the UK who have been given restricted 'leave' in terms of length of residence and the right to employment.

Income is a key regulator of social protection within the UK. Older people who are in receipt of income support receive health and personal services free at the point of delivery. Older people with higher incomes and assets are means-tested for a number of personal social services, although they receive them at below cost.

Unlike some other member states, such as Belgium, the UK does not have explicit criteria in terms of disability or social support for defining an individual's right to services. In the UK all services are rationed by health and social services professionals,[3] which inevitably means that there are no consistent criteria for determining eligibility to receive services. They use implicit criteria in making judgements. Thus the theoretical availability of social protection for all groups represented in the case studies is 100 per cent, but the actual utilisation will depend enormously on the availability of services within the local area, the professionals' perception of need and – for most personal social services and long-term care institutions – the ability of the older persons or their family to pay. There is evidence of substantial variations in service provision in different parts of the country.

18   Social Protection of Different Categories of Dependent Elderly People in Norway

18.1   The Definition of Case Studies (see Appendix 2)

All case studies refer to people with long-term and rather severe dependency in instrumental and/or personal activities of daily living. More or less all residents in institutional care answer to this definition, although variations in degree of dependency are resting. The great majority of elderly persons living in the community, on the other hand, are either independent or less severely incapacitated. According to the Norwegian level of living survey, 20–25 per cent of the 65+ living at home are dependent upon help for shopping and cleaning, while 2–4 per cent need help for dressing and to move around indoors. Only these latter two criteria imply a dependency level fairly close to a 'need for institutional care'.

It is estimated that about one-third of the severely dependent group are taken care of at home, while two-thirds live in institutions. In general, the more dependent, the higher the probability of being institutionalised.

The national old-age pension is the main source of income: it constitutes 64 per cent of the average income of old-age pensioners in 1993. The other major sources are income from occupational pensions (16 per cent) and savings (15 per cent). Average income for old-age pensioners was 13,426 ECU in 1993.

The low income category encompasses pensioners whose income is the minimum pension plus 10 per cent. This includes close to 20 per cent of the elderly population. The so-called 'minimum pension' is 7,689 ECU for single pensioners and 13,426 ECU for retired couples. The maximum national pension (including the supplementary pension) is approximately 2.5 times higher. The level is even higher for those covered also by an occupational supplementary pension. 41 per cent of old-age pensioners has a 'minimum pension'. The majority has also other income, mainly savings, although the amount is usually rather small. Besides, the spouses of the majority of female minimum pensioners have higher pensions. Quite a few, about 45,000 or 7 per cent of old-age pensioners, have the minimum pension as the sole source of income. About one quarter of them are single and the majority of them are female.

Some targeted cash transfers are available to compensate for high expenses for housing (housing allowances), disability (assistance allowance) and/or poor economy (social assistance). These transfers are modest compared to the pension, but may be substantial for the individual receiver. Approximately 6 per cent of old-age pensioners receive housing and assistance allowances, while only less than 1 per cent have social assistance.

The average income category encompasses pensioners whose income is about 14,646 ECU (single pensioner), which is about 80 per cent higher than the minimum pension.

Access to public services are equally available for singles and couples. However, several studies showed that – other things being equal – couples often receive less formal help than singles.

18.2   Social Protection of the Case Studies

18.2.1 Case studies 1, 4 and 7: fully disabled, low to average income, living in community with no or poor social network A high – and growing – proportion of the elderly live alone. While 17 per cent of the 65+ lived in single households in 1960, the proportion has increased to 37 per cent in 1990. Single households are in particular common among women, who normally outlive their husbands: in 1995, 23 per cent of men aged 65+ lived singly, compared to 49 per cent of women. Less than 10 per cent of people with children share household with them.

This case study concerns most often a woman aged 80 and above, never married or widowed, having no children and living in the city.

The person in this case study receives the minimum pension, which is 7,689 ECU for single pensioners. In case of a relatively high rent for the retirement flat, housing allowances are granted. Women of this generation will seldom have earned rights to a supplementary pension (based on earlier income). If widowed, she acquires right to 55 per cent of her late husband's supplement, implying that she may then have an average income.

Consultations of the general practitioner are given at a moderate fee. The bulk of expenses are paid by the municipality and the National Insurance Scheme. Fees are limited to a total of 146 ECU a year. Medicine which is considered to be vital is given on a 'blue prescription', implying that older people are only paying 10 per cent of the actual fee.

Considering the level of dependency, the person of this case study will have both home nursing and home help services. The majority of municipalities now provide home nursing on a 24 hour basis, but access is limited. Home help is normally provided on a regular basis, while home nursing varies more often according to need. Home nursing and home help services are charged with a moderate fee. Fees of persons with a low income, i.e. the minimum pension plus 20 per cent, are limited to 6 ECU a month. For other income groups, fees are income-related, but are in most cases rather moderate. While some municipalities deliver home nursing free of charge, practically all municipalities have fees for home help. Some may deliver home help free of charge for low income groups (i.e. minimum pension). Personal contributions account for 5 per cent of total costs. Local government (municipalities) and the state (since municipalities are receiving state transfers) cover the additional costs.

Meals-on-wheels are local arrangements and therefore payments vary. These services are usually subsidised through the municipality.

The connection to an alarm system, technical aids like a wheelchair and hospital bed are provided free of charge.

Other services available are: the local senior citizen centre, transport arrangements and a visitor of a voluntary organisation. Transport is provided for a low fee if disabled. The other services are free of charge.

18.2.2 Case studies 2 and 5: fully disabled, low to average income, living in community with spouse The minimum pension for couples, when both are aged 67 and above, was about 13,426 ECU in 1995. This is about 30 per cent less than two minimum pensions for singles. Very few couples have not the minimum pension as only source of income since the man, and in many cases also the woman, has a supplementary pension. Quite a few also have supplements from occupational pension schemes and other income, mainly from savings. Housing allowances are granted in case of high rent.

Income differences have little relevance for access to social and medical services, beyond the somewhat higher fees for higher income groups and the possibility of purchasing services, e.g. home maker services, privately. Hence, we refer to case study 1 for an overview of the different services.

The great majority of the dependent living at home receive (public, i.e. from the municipality) community services (home help and/or home nursing), but the very dependent normally also need extensive family care. Public services are then merely supplementing family care efforts. Access to public services are equally available for singles and couples. According to several studies, however, couples often receive less formal help than singles.

In some municipalities, a care plan or contract is worked out, which contains an agreement on the division of responsibility between the municipality and the family. Family members (beyond the spouse) have no formal obligation for care and economic support. However, children, in particular daughters, are important care providers.

Family members may be compensated economically for their care. In rural municipalities, where distances are often important, family members and/or neighbours have been engaged as (paid) home helpers. In 1988, an arrangement of 'care salary' was introduced obliging every municipality to offer payment for care to family members, provided the care obligations were long-term and extensive.

Respite care is available through short-term stays in nursing homes.

18.2.3 Case studies 3a and 3b/6a and 6b: fully disabled, low to average income, living in an old-age/a nursing home Nearly three-quarters of the institutions are (medical) nursing homes; one-quarter is of the residential (old-age) home type. Local nursing homes (as well as other institutional care such as service housing) are in general rather scarce and allocation is subject to needs assessment. In order to be admitted to an institution, a person has to show (normally) extensive disabilities. In 1993, average cost per year was 27,462 ECU in old-age homes and 40,155 ECU in nursing homes.

Personal contributions are based on income only and not on wealth. Residents in both types of institutions pay 75 per cent of their basic pension (minus a free amount) and 85 per cent of additional pension/income. A minimum pensioner pays about 5,856 ECU, i.e. about 72 per cent of his pension. On average, a pensioner pays about 6,347 ECU. Personal contributions amount to approximately 18–20 per cent of the gross expenditure in old-age homes. As costs of nursing homes are higher, the share of the elderly in total costs is lower i.e. approximately 12–14 per cent.

Personal contributions are usually drawn automatically from the pension, leaving the resident only with the remaining 'pocket money'.

The additional costs are covered by the municipalities and the state (since municipalities are receiving state transfers in terms of general block grants).

18.2.4 Case studies 3c and 6c: fully disabled, low to average income, staying in a hospital Average cost in general hospitals is approximately 427 ECU per treated day. Hospitalisation is free of charge. Counties, i.e. local governments, run hospitals. Hospitals are financed through the National Insurance Scheme. The share of the counties in total cost is 70 per cent, those of the state is 30 per cent.

Access depends upon how acute the need is.

18.2.5 Comments on other case studies

Case study 8: senile older person The number of demented elderly persons (of varying severity) is estimated to be about 50,000. The majority has dementia of the Alzheimer type.

Most of the severely demented people live in institutions or sheltered housing (collectivities). Quite a few – in particular the less severely demented – are taken care of at home. The primary care provider is the spouse and is supported by community services, such as home help and home nursing.

Respite care, either through day care centres (which are normally.connected to a nursing home) and/or short-term stay in nursing homes, is available.

In the last few years, attention is paid to care and support for demented patients and their carers. Carers of demented persons get psychosocial support from general practitioners and specialists in geriatrics and/or psychogerontology. Some of the larger hospitals have specialist teams or units who offer screening and support. Support groups for carers of demented persons have developed as joint efforts between professionals, voluntary organisations and informal carers. But services and support arrangements – as well as competent staff on various levels – are still too short and in need of improvements.

Case study 9: immigrant Norway has few immigrants in comparison with other countries.

Immigrants have access to the same services as any other resident in the country. Some projects are initiated in order to customise services to immigrants e.g. through senior citizen centres. Families are providing probably the main care work at present.

As full pension rights require 40 years residency in Norway, many immigrants have not acquired rights to a full pension. Some have pension rights from their home country, others have to apply for cash support through the need-tested social assistance program. Some may also get housing allowance. Otherwise, housing is provided to immigrants through special programmes.

18.3 Overview

The differences in protection between some of these cases are very small.

Differences that arise are mostly related to income.

For health services, hospitalisation is free of charge. Consultations of the general practitioner are given at a moderate fee and are limited to a ceiling.

Payments in (medical) nursing homes and residential (old-age) homes are based on income.

Home nursing and home help services are charged with a moderate fee, whereby fees of persons with a low income are limited to a ceiling. Fees for other income groups increase with higher income, but are in most cases rather moderate.

19   Cross-country Comparisons: Differences and Similarities in Social Protection

19.1   Differences and Similarities in Average Costs and Financing of Care

With the aid of graphs we have attempted to discuss the following issues for six services (old-age homes, nursing homes, general hospitals, district nursing, home help and meals-on-wheels):
- the average cost of the service;
- the financing of the service; who contributes and how much:
  * the state at the local, regional or national level, or social assistance (in the graphs shortly referred to as 'state');
  * the social security system;
  * the person himself, voluntary or compulsory private insurance, or dependency insurance;
  * relatives of the elderly person;
- the extent to which the services are income-related and/or means-tested.

19.1.1 Old-age homes and nursing homes The average cost of old-age homes varies between 700 and 2,980 ECU per month. Even within a single country, the range between which average costs of old-age homes vary is very large, as for example within Austria and France.

In most countries, the financing of old-age homes consists of a mix of state or social security involvement and personal or family contributions. In the UK, pensioners on average income, in contrast to low income pensioners, receive little or no public financing for support in homes. In France and Finland, pensioners on low income pay a lower share of the cost of accommodation than pensioners on average income.

The range between which average costs of nursing homes vary is even wider than for old-age homes, namely between 744 and 3,346 ECU per month. Again, there may exist wide differences within a given country (for instance in France, the UK and Austria).

When comparing old-age and nursing homes, the situation in Spain and Ireland is particularly striking. In contrast to public old-age homes, public nursing homes require no personal contributions at all from Spanish pensioners. In Ireland, pensioners on average income must completely rely on their private resources (including probably some family involvement) to pay for costs of a nursing home.

In Austria, France, Italy, Sweden, the UK and Norway, there are no differences in the level of social protection for an elderly person who lives in a nursing home or one who lives in an old-age home. In the Netherlands, on the other hand, until 1 January 1997 there was an important difference in the social protection of elderly persons staying in nursing homes and those in old-age homes. For a stay in an old-age home, people had to invest their own income and assets. People with a low income, however, might keep a certain amount as pocket money. Only when assets were no longer available and the individual was unable to cover the costs with his/her income (public and private pension), was social assistance granted.

For a stay in a nursing home, pensioners had to contribute a share of their income (maximum amount defined) and not of their assets.

In some countries, such as Belgium, Denmark, and France, pensioners (or those on private insurance or dependency insurance) have to pay for the hotel costs of a stay in a home. If income is insufficient, then in Belgium pensioners are granted pocket money by the social assistance agency. In France the low income pensioner can keep 10 per cent of his or her income. Except for the fact that the contributions of pensioners for care are higher in nursing homes than in old-age homes in France, there are no differences in the level of social protection of a pensioner in an old-age home and a pensioner in a nursing home.

In Austria, Ireland, Portugal, the United Kingdom and Norway, the pension of the older person is paid directly to the institution when a person is admitted to an old-age or nursing home. The older person receives pocket money from the institution, and the remainder of the pension is retained by the home. In Ireland, nursing home residents not only have 75 per cent of their income withheld, but they also pay any shortfalls between the public subvention (determined by a means-test) and the cost of stay and care.

Low income categories in Belgium, Luxembourg and Germany also have to use their total income when staying in a home and are left with pocket money. In Finland, as well, the pension of low income categories is reduced due to institutionalisation.

In Austria, Belgium, France, Italy and Luxembourg, relatives of pensioners on low incomes who live in old-age homes or nursing homes are required to cover the accommodation costs. This is also the case for relatives of pensioners living in nursing homes in Ireland. In the UK, relatives are able to top up the amount of income support which a low income pensioner receives for a stay in a nursing or residential home so as to secure better facilities (e.g. single room), but they are not obliged to do so.

19.1.2 General hospitals From Figure 4.5 it immediately becomes clear that general hospitals are a much more expensive care form than old-age homes and nursing homes: the average cost per month varies between 2,070 ECU (France) and 12,810 ECU (Norway) per month. State and social security financing is also much larger in general hospitals than in old-age and nursing homes. In Denmark, the United Kingdom, Portugal and Norway, no private contributions of pensioners are even required. France is the only country which mentions obligatory contributions of relatives.

19.1.3 District nursing, general practitioners and pharmaceuticals Norway is the only country where district nursing is income-related. In all the other countries district nursing is almost completely financed by the government or by social security.

In almost all countries, the cost of health care is, to a large extent, financed by social insurance or government subsidies. For pharmaceuticals, however, personal contributions are common. In Austria, Denmark, Belgium, Luxembourg, the Netherlands, Portugal and Sweden, the elderly have to cover a certain percentage of the cost, and this is frequently income-related. In Spain, Finland and the UK, on the other hand, all pensioners are given free prescriptions. Low income categories in Ireland and the Netherlands are also given free medicines.

Consultations by general practitioners are free in Austria, Denmark, Portugal and the United Kingdom. They are also free for low income categories in Ireland and the Netherlands.

19.1.4 Home help Denmark is the only country where home help does not require personal contributions from the pensioners. Only in Spain and France is there social security financing.

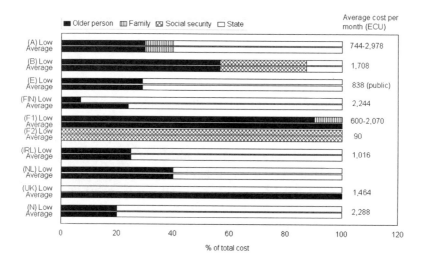

Notes

(E)   71% state and social security financing.
(F1) refers to hotel costs.
(F2) refers to costs of care.

Additional information about financing for countries not appearing in the graph:
(I)   health aspects of dependency are completely covered by the state; other costs have to be paid for by the older persons themselves or their relatives.
(L)   older person and his/her relatives have to pay for accommodation; social assistance intervenes in case of insufficient income and assets.
(P)   means-tested personal contributions for care and lodging.
(S)   pensioner pays 70% of total income for housing, care and services including cleaning, hairdressing and pedicure.

Figure 4.3   Average cost of old-age homes per month and estimated contribution of different partners to the financing of the old-age homes (according to income category: low or average income)

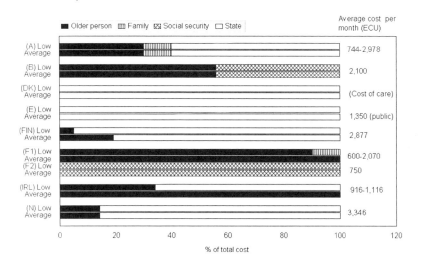

Notes

(E)   100% state and social security financing.
(F1) refers to hotel costs.
(F2) refers to costs of care.

Additional information about financing for countries not appearing in the graph:
(D)   financing of social security + social assistance (income-related and means-tested).
(I)   health aspects of dependency are completely covered by the state; other costs have to be paid for by the older persons themselves or their relatives.
(L)   older person and his/her relatives have to pay for accommodation; social assistance intervenes in case of insufficient income and assets.
(NL) pensioner pays 11% of income + social security financing.
(P)   means-tested personal contributions for care and lodging.
(S)   pensioner pays 70% of total income for housing, care and services including cleaning, hairdressing and pedicure.

Figure 4.4   Average cost of nursing homes per month and estimated contribution of different partners to the financing of nursing homes (according to income category: low or average income)

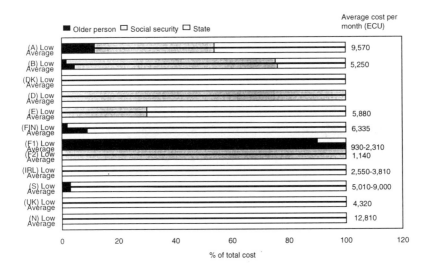

Figure 4.5 **Average cost of general hospitals per month and estimated contribution of different partners to the financing of general hospitals (according to income category: low or average income)**

Notes

(D)   pensioner pays during max. 14 days 6 ECU/day.

(F1)   refers to hotel costs.

(F2)   refers to costs of care.

(IRL) pensioner pays 25 ECU per day during max. 10 days in any year.

Additional information about financing for countries not appearing in the graph:

(L)   pensioner pays for accommodation after 3 to 6 months; social security pays for accommodation before 3 to 6 months; state pays if pensioner cannot pay.

(P)   no private contributions of pensioner.

19.1.5Meals-on-wheels Meals-on-wheels is mostly income-related, except in Denmark and Sweden. Neither family contributions nor social security financing (except for France) is mentioned for this service.

For social services that are more oriented towards aid in daily life activities (meals-on-wheels or home help), personal contributions are common. However, it is important to note that, especially for the care of the elderly, the trend is towards an integration of health and social care as, for example, in nursing homes. In various countries, such as Belgium and France, a large share of the accommodation costs in nursing homes is therefore paid by the pensioners themselves, while the costs for care are covered by social security or state budgets.

19.2 Differences and Similarities in the Organisation of Care

19.2.1 Formal versus informal care A preference for formal or for informal care can be detected in two ways: firstly, by analysing the differences between elderly persons either with or without a social network and, secondly, by the availability of additional allowances for the carer.[4]

In Belgium, the presence of a social network is taken into account when providing district nursing and home help. The availability of other social services for elderly persons living in the community does not differ according to the presence of a social network or spouse. In Denmark, when allocating home help, meals-on-wheels and the installation of an emergency alarm, the local authority considers the ability of the spouse. In Germany, home care can partly be provided in cash instead of in kind when a social network is available. In Finland the package of service is reduced when informal care can take over some duties. In France, one of the eligibility conditions for receiving home help is that the spouse must be incapable of providing informal care for his or her partner. In Spain, access to health and social services is in general dependent upon family circumstances. In Ireland, the presence of a spouse reduces the likelihood of some public services, particularly home help services. In Italy, no home help is provided when a social network is available. The spouse has an important task in taking care of the disabled. In Norway, couples often receive less formal help than singles. In Norway, family members (beyond the spouse) normally have no formal obligation for care and economic support. However, children, in particular daughters, are important care providers.

In several countries additional allowances for the carer are available: this is the case in Luxembourg, Finland, Ireland, Italy, Sweden and Norway. In

Luxembourg, costs of assistance and taking care of a dependent person can be deducted from taxes.

The differences between the social protection situation of pensioners with or without a social network are mostly minimal or nonexistent. However, it can influence the choice of the elderly persons themselves for institutional or community care, which places them in different situations. It can also influence the choice for in-cash or in-kind benefit, as is the case in the German *Pflegeversicherung*. In Germany, the older person can receive home nursing care in the form of in-cash help instead of in-kind, if he can count on relatives or friends to care for him or to help with household activities. In France, the newly created allowance is not only taking into account income and dependency, but also the informal care provided. In Austria, Luxembourg and Sweden, there are no formal differences in the protection of pensioners living either alone or with their spouse. In the UK, however, notwithstanding the fact that the eligibility for health and social services of pensioners does not differ according to whether they live alone or with a spouse, there is a special state retirement pension level for couples when only one of the two has made the necessary contributions and when the person who has made the contributions has not died. There are also special pensioner premiums and severe disability premiums for couples (both partner and spouse eligible for attendance allowance). In Denmark, when both marriage partners are pensioners, each partner has a lower public pension than a single pensioner, and the pension supplement is higher for pensioners living alone than for pensioners living with a spouse. However, with the exception of home help, there are no differences in the availability of services between single and married people. In Spain, the level of contributory pensions differs between couples and single persons. In Finland, couples each receive a smaller pension than does a pensioner living alone.

19.2.2 In-kind versus in-cash care The largest differences noted in the case studies relate to the degree to which the pensioner is charged for the use of the services. In some countries, such as the UK, many services are provided free of charge, while in the Netherlands, for example, most services are charged for (up to a maximum amount), though at differing rates according to the income level of the pensioner. The difference in personal contribution should not be interpreted as a lower level of social protection in the latter country, since it provides other kinds of support, such as benefits and additional income. The difference illustrates that the UK is more in-kind oriented, while the Netherlands is more in-cash oriented.

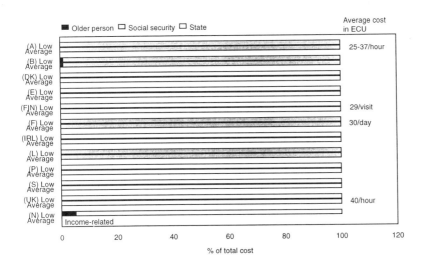

Notes

(E)   100% state and social security financing.

Additional information about financing for countries not appearing in the graph:
(D)   financing of social security (+ social assistance for low income categories).
(NL) financing of social security + contribution of the older person to the district nursing organisation.

Figure 4.6   Average cost of district nursing and estimated contribution of different partners to the financing of it (according to income category: low or average income)

A Belgian pensioner who enters an old-age home covers quite a large share of the costs (in particular, more of the accommodation costs, which are 53 per cent of the total costs), while British pensioners who receive income support lose their income when they enter an old-age home, but receive services completely free of charge. When making comparisons between countries which are oriented towards either in-cash or in-kind aid, it is thus important to consider the income of the pensioner, in addition to the degree to which he/she has to

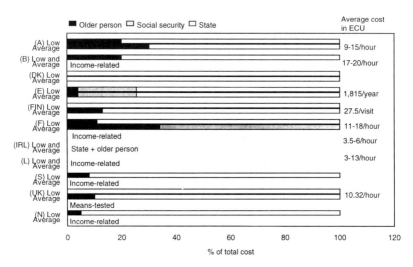

Figure 4.7   Average cost of home help and estimated contribution of different partners to the financing of it (according to income category: low or average income)

Notes

Additional information about financing for countries not appearing in the graph:
(D)   no means-testing.
(NL)   financing of social security + older person (income-related).
(P)   means-tested.

contribute to cover the costs of the use of health or social services. It has also become clear from the case studies that not only the pension should be considered, since in many countries this is topped up by additional benefits and income.

In Denmark, until 1995 both systems (in-kind and in-cash) could be used for the financing of the same service (the nursing homes). Either pensioners lost their general old-age pension when entering the nursing home to pay for housing, clothes, food and social services and received pocket money to cover additional expenses, or they continued to receive the general old-age pension

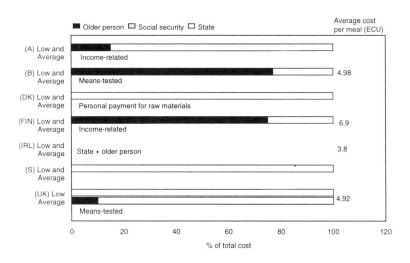

Notes

Additional information about financing for countries not appearing in the graph:
(D)   no means-testing.
(F)   financing of social security + state + older person (means-tested).
(NL) financing of state + older person (income-related).
(P)   income-related (25% of monthly income).
(N)   state + older person.

Figure 4.8   Average cost of meals-on-wheels and estimated contribution of different partners to the financing of them (according to income category: low or average income)

and paid a fee for housing and electricity. Services that they were free to choose (social services such as cleaning, meals, etc.), were charged for when utilised. From January 1995 on, the system of 'pocket-money' in Danish nursing homes has been abolished. All nursing home residents now keep their general old-age pension and pay about 15 per cent of their incomes in rent and a fee for housing and electricity. Services that they are free to choose (social services such as cleaning, meals, etc.), are now always charged for when utilised. Denmark has thus become more cash-oriented.

19.2.3 Universal systems versus selective systems Negative features of the welfare system that were identified are:

- the importance of means-testing or income-related contributions which, at first glance, seem to change universal systems into very selective ones;
- the fact that in Austria, Ireland, Portugal, the UK and Norway (and up until 1995 in Denmark) retirement benefits are withheld from pensioners who have been placed into the care of an institution. These pensioners are given only pocket money. This system does not contribute to their independence, nor is it indicative of real public responsibility. In fact, pension resources pay for the care and thus the resources of the pensioners themselves. This occurs in nursing homes as well as in old-age homes.

It is difficult to make a clear distinction between welfare systems of the Beveridge type and those of the Bismarck type, but one main feature of the Beveridge-based system is that, although universally defined, the services are to a large extent means-tested or income-related. In the Bismarck-based system, priority is given to applying new types of (universal) insurance, unrelated to income or means, so as to avoid what in these countries is described as a deterioration towards social assistance. Another characteristic in these countries is that when new proposals emerge, reference is made by preference to in-cash benefits. This is certainly clear in France, as well as in Belgium and, to a lesser degree, in Germany.

The cases are examined to see whether or not there is a universal system. There is no discrimination as far as entitlement is concerned, but the use of needs and income determines charges for a lot of the services. In most countries there is a tendency towards nondiscriminatory services. This should help to improve the older persons' freedom of choice, but it limits the scope for providing incentives to seek alternatives. Illustrative of this nondiscriminatory trend is the fact that new proposals talk about not channelling more resources into residential care than into community care. This conflicts with a cost-oriented subsidising system, and when different costs occur it may hamper neutrality. There is also less discrimination than before when alternating between formal and informal care. In the proposals in which a universal in-cash benefit is awarded, there is no discrimination; in other cases, a lower but significant amount of income is available where informal care is used instead of the professional variety.

19.3   Summary of the Micro-characteristics of the Care System

See Table 4.3.

19.4   *Synoptic Tables*

The most important social protection systems in the different countries are conveniently arranged in the synoptic tables. The tables aim at enabling cross-country comparisons of similar social protection arrangements from the viewpoint of the pensioner: the share of the population aged 65 and above using certain social protection services, the average cost and financing of these services, and the income and benefits received by the pensioners when using those services.

   Since it was impossible to include the complete set of available information from the case studies in one table, the synoptic tables are condensed and contain much less detailed information:
–   not all case studies, as defined in the original guidelines or discussed by the countries, have been separately integrated into the tables; only the distinction between low and average income has been taken into account;
–   from certain case studies, not all services for which pensioners are eligible have been mentioned.
For each service under consideration (old-age homes, nursing homes, general hospitals and community care (district nursing, home help and meals-on-wheels)), the following issues are discussed:
–   representativeness of the service;
–   the average cost of the service;
–   the financing of the service: who contributes and how much:
   *   the state at the local, regional or national level, or social assistance;
   *   the social security system;
   *   the person himself, voluntary or compulsory private insurance, or dependency insurance;
–   the income and other social benefits which are received by the pensioner in cash when using the service.

   The synoptic tables have been constructed in an attempt to provide a complete yet easily readable overview of social protection arrangements. It has to be remarked, however, that in some countries (e.g. Germany) the social protection systems seem to be so complex that it was very difficult to fit them into the tables.

Notes

1   In reality, nearly always 0 per cent (Debrabander, forthcoming; Hutten and Kerkstra, 1996).

2   Such a case illustrates well that pensions of low income groups have to be increased to cover the non-care costs if services remain universally eligible, without means- or income-test. Low income groups will be obliged to appeal on welfare (social assistance) if their incomes will not be increased.

3   Except for accidents and emergencies, where direct access to hospitals is available, all referrals to specialist medical care – including outpatient, day and respite care – are made through GPs. Community nursing, district nursing and health visiting is provided by community provider units and primary care organisations following referral by GPs.

4   The availability of these allocations naturally depends on the presence of a social network.

Table 4.3   Characteristics of the care system at micro level

	Service oriented		Cash oriented			Prioritising informal care	Indicators of underinsurance of long-term care		
	Residential care oriented	Community care oriented	Payment for care to		Rent subsidy	Formal care reduced when informal care available	Pocket money	Recall on family	Rationing
			carer	dependent person					
A				+			+	+	
B	+			+	+	+	+	+	
DK	+	+			+	+	+ ('95)		
D				+	+	+			
GR						+		+	
E									
FIN	+		+	+	+	+			
F	+	+	+	+	+	+		+	
IRL		+	+ +			+		+	
I								+	
L	+		+	+	+		+		home help: max. 2 hours/day extensive home care: max. 6 months insufficient care for demented persons
NL	+				+				
P				+	+		+		
S	+	+	+	+	+	+	+		
UK	+			+	+		+		
N			+	+					

Table 4.4   Synoptic table on old-age homes

Income height		Income	Share of the elderly	Average cost	State or public contributions	Social security contribution	Personal contributions	Family contributions
A	Low	Social Assistance (compensatory supplement) Pension and attendance allowance are withdrawn except pocket money Exemption from TV-, radio-, telephone and prescription fees Reductions for railway and other public transport, theatres, etc.	0.5–1%	744–2,978 ECU per month	30% regional; 30% local		20–30%	5–10%
	Average	Pension and attendance allowance are withdrawn except pocket money	0.5–1%	744–2,978 ECU per month	30% regional; 30% local		20–30%	5–10%
B	Low	Not different from person living in community. If income is completely used, Social Assistance must pay pocket money to pensioner	Categories B and C: 2.4% of 65+ Categories B and C: 46% of O, A, B and Cs in old-age homes	56.95 ECU per day (= total cost)	Social Assistance if neither person nor relatives can pay 30% of inhabitants are financially supported State contributions: 11.75%	20.9 to 30.6% of total expenditures	56.7% of total expenditures	Support duty if person cannot pay
	Average	Cf. person living in community		56.95 ECU per day (= total cost)	State contributions: 11.75%	20.9 to 30.6% of total expenditures	56.7% of total expenditures	
DK		Old-age homes do not exist						
D	Low and average	Cf. person living in community						
E	Low	Non contributory invalidity pension (332 ECU per month); the included increase because of dependency may be substituted for free lodging and care in an institution		Average cost in 1995 was 838 ECU per month in public old-age homes and 571 ECU per month in private old-age homes	71% (social security and central and regional state) (public old-age homes)		29% (public old-age homes)	

Table 4.4 cont'd

Income height	Income	Share of the elderly	Average cost	State or public contributions	Social security contribution	Personal contributions	Family contributions
E (cont'd) Average	Contributory invalidity pension (498 ECU per month); the included increase because of dependency may be substituted for free lodging and care in an institution		Average cost in 1995 was 838 ECU per month in public old-age homes and 571 ECU per month in private old-age homes	71% (social security and central and regional state) (public old-age homes)		29% (public old-age homes)	
FIN Low	National pension (222 ECU per month) (reduced due to institutionalisation)		2,244 per month	Local: 93% of costs		7% of costs	
Average	Employment pension (858 ECU per month)		2,244 per month	Local: 76% of costs		24% of costs	
F Low	Minimum guaranteed income Attendance allowance (343 to 687 ECU per month according to income and dependency)		Accommodation costs (20 to 69 ECU per day or more); costs of care (3 ECU per day)	For accommodation: Social Assistance if contributions of person and relatives are insufficient	100% cost of care	For accommodation: contribution of 90% of personal resources	Obligatory contributions of relatives
Average	Cf. person living in community 100%	0.62% 65+	Idem		100% cost of care	For accommodation: paid by person or possibly dependency insurance	Complements from family
IRL Low	75% of the pension is withdrawn; person receives pocket money	2.5% 65+	254 ECU per week (hotel + care)	75%		25% (in the form of withholding of pension)	
Average	75% of the pension is withdrawn; person receives pocket money		254 ECU per week (hotel + care)	75% (maximum)		25% (in the form of pension) + other charges arising from financial assessment of means	
I Low				100% for health aspects of dependency		100% for non-health aspects	Contributions of relatives
Average							

Table 4.4 cont'd

Income height	Income	Share of the elderly	Average cost	State or public contributions	Social security contribution	Personal contributions	Family contributions
L Low	Minimum pension (955 ECU/month), *Allocation de soins* (360 ECU/month) (private old-age homes), left with pocket money of 165 ECU per month			Social Assistance if income and assets of pensioner and relatives are insufficient State subsidises working and personnel costs in public old-age homes		For accommodation: 1,361 ECU per month	Obligatory contributions of relatives
Average	Pension of about 1,273 ECU per month, *Allocation de soins* (private old-age home)			Social Assistance if income and assets of pensioner and relatives are insufficient State subsidises working and personnel costs in public homes		For accommodation: 1,361 ECU per month	Obligatory contributions of relatives
NL Low and average	Not different from person living in the community, except for rent subsidies	6.4% of 65+ live in old-age homes		60% (regional)		40% private contributions	
P Low and average	75% of the per capita income is withdrawn; person receives pocket money					Means-tested contributions for care and lodging (75% of income is withdrawn)	
S Low and average	Cf. person living in the community					70% of total income for housing, care and services including cleaning, hairdressing, pedicure	

Table 4.4 cont'd

Income height	Income	Share of the elderly	Average cost	State or public contributions	Social security contribution	Personal contributions	Family contributions
UK Low	People receive only pocket money (16.8 ECU per week) and housing benefit. Attendance allowance (39.7 or 59.4 ECU per week) ceases after 4 weeks in publicly funded home		Average weekly cost is 366 ECU (Regional variation: 338–484 ECU)	Since April 1993 locally publicly financed 100%	Prior to April 1993, 100%		Not obligatory
Average	Little or no public finance for support in homes, not different from persons living in community. Attendance allowance (39.7 or 59.4 ECU per week) ceases after 4 weeks in publicly funded home		Idem			100% until income and savings declined to means-tested level	Not obligatory
N Low and average	Usually: pension is withdrawn; person receives pocket money	About 6% in old-age and nursing homes	27,462 ECU per year (1993)	National and local pay the remainder: i.e. approximately 80%		75% of basic pension + 85% of additional pension/income (not wealth) 18–20% of total costs	

Table 4.5 Synoptic table on nursing homes

	Income height	Income	Share of the elderly	Average cost	State or public contributions	Social security contribution	Personal contributions	Family contributions
A	Low and average	Cf. old-age homes	2–3%	744–2,978 ECU per month	30% regional; 30% local		20–30%	5–10%
B	Low	Cf. old-age homes	Categories B and C: 1.1% of 65+ 100% of inhabitants B and C category	70 ECU per day	Social Assistance if neither person nor relatives can pay 31% is financially supported	±50% (cost of care, depends upon level of disability)	55.9% of total costs	Support duty if person cannot pay
DK	Average Low and average	Cf. old-age homes Not different from person living in community except for rent subsidies. Personal allowances are granted if necessary	±4% of 65+	70 ECU per day	100% except rent	Idem	Idem Rent 15% of total income. Fee for electricity and heating. Other services charged	
D	Low	Cf. person living in community			Social Assistance for nursing costs and pocket money	Nursing aid: 1,467 ECU	Social Assistance is income-related and means-tested	
E	Average Low	Idem Cf. old-age homes		Average cost in 1995 was 1,350 ECU per month in public nursing homes and 980 ECU in private nursing homes	100% (State and social security system) (public nursing homes)	Idem		
	Average	Cf. old-age homes		Idem	100% (State and social security system) (public nursing homes)			
FIN	Low Average	Cf. old-age homes Cf. old-age homes		2,877 ECU per month 2,877 ECU per month	Local: 95% of costs Local: 81% of costs		5% of costs 19% of costs	
F	Low	Cf. old-age homes		Cost of care and cure 25 ECU per day; accommodation costs 20 to 69 ECU per day or more	For accommodation: Social Assistance if contributions of person and relatives are insufficient	100% cost of care and cure	Accommodation: contribution of 90% of personal resources	Obligatory contributions of relatives

Table 4.5 cont'd

	Income height	Income	Share of the elderly	Average cost	State or public contributions	Social security contribution	Personal contributions	Family contributions
F cont'd	Average	Cf. old-age homes	0.64% 65+	Idem		100% cost of care and cure	Accommodation: 100% paid by person or possibly dependency insurance	Complements from family
IRL	Low	Cf. old-age homes	2–3% of 65+ are residents in non-public nursing homes (2–5% of 65+ are residents in public long-stay homes)	229–279 ECU per week (hotel + care)	55–66% (maximum subvention)		25% (in the form of withholding of pension) + any shortfall between cost of care and subvention	Any shortfall between cost of care and subvention
	Average	Cf. old-age homes		229–279 ECU per week (hotel + care)			Private resources (approximately 254 ECU (= median est.) per week	(Probably some family involvement)
I	Low				100% for health aspects of dependency		100% for non-health aspects	Contributions of relatives
	Average							
L	Low	Minimum pension (955 ECU/month), left with pocket money of 165 ECU per month			Social Assistance if income and assets of pensioner and relatives are insufficient State subsidises working and personnel costs		For accommodation: 1,500 ECU per month	Obligatory contributions of relatives
	Average	Pension of about 1,273 ECU per month, left with pocket money of 165 ECU per month			Social Assistance if income and assets of pensioner and relatives are insufficient State subsidises working and personnel costs		For accommodation: 1,500 ECU per month	Obligatory contributions of relatives
NL	Low and average	Cf. person living in the community, except for rent subsidies	2.7% of 65+			AWBZ	11% of income (not of assets) (maximum monthly contribution = 1,028 ECU)	

Table 4.5 cont'd

	Income height	Income	Share of the elderly	Average cost	State or public contributions	Social security contribution	Personal contributions	Family contributions
P	Low and average	85% of the per capita income is withdrawn; person receives pocket money					Means-tested contributions for care and lodging (85% of income is withdrawn)	
S	Low and average	Cf. person living in the community					70% of total income for housing, care and services including cleaning, hairdressing, pedicure	
UK	Low and average	Cf. old-age homes		Average weekly cost is 521 ECU (Regional variation: 472–631 ECU)				
N	Low and average	Cf. old-age homes	About 6% in old-age and nursing homes	40,155 ECU per year (1993)	National and local pay the remainder: i.e. approximately 86% (not wealth)		75% of basic pension + 85% of additional pension/income 12–14% of total costs	

Table 4.6 Synoptic table on general hospitals

Income height	Income	Share of the elderly	Average cost	State or public contributions	Social security contribution	Personal contributions	Family contributions
A Low	Social Assistance (Compensatory supplement) + pension (total 587 ECU, 1996) Exemption from TV-, radio-, telephone- and prescription fees Reductions for railway and other public transport, theatres, etc. Attendance allowance is frozen	1%	Average hospital costs per day: 319 ECU, 1993	9.2% national; 13.8% regional; 20.7% local	39.8%	Elderly person: 2.2% (incl. hospital fees) Private insurance: 4.5% Others: ca. 5%	
Average	Pension (above 744 ECU, 1996)	1%	Idem	9.2% national; 13.8% regional; 20.7% local	39.8%	Idem	
B Low	Cf. person living in community	5.1% of 65+ in geriatric units	175 ECU per day	25% remaining accommodation costs	75% remaining accommodation costs	Days 1–8: 3.97 ECU per day, days 9–90: 2.62 ECU per day, >90 days: 5.75 ECU per day	
Average	Cf. person living in community		175 ECU per day	25% remaining accommodation costs	75% remaining accommodation costs	Day 1: 34.73 ECU, days 2–8: 9.31 ECU per day, day 9–90: 6.58 ECU per day, >90 days: 12.46 ECU per day	
DK Low and average				100%			
D Low and average	Cf. person living in community		Average cost is 5,880 ECU per month	Social Assistance for low income groups 70% (public hospitals)	100%	During max. 14 days: 6 ECU/day 0% (public hospitals)	
E Low and average	Cf. old-age homes			70% (public hospitals)	30% (public hospitals)	0% (public hospitals)	0% (public hospitals)

Table 4.6 cont'd

Income height	Income	Share of the elderly	Average cost	State or public contributions	Social security contribution	Personal contributions	Family contributions
FIN Low	Cf. old-age homes		6.335 ECU per month	Local: 98% of costs		2% of costs	
Average	Cf. old-age homes		6.335 ECU per month	Local: 91% of costs		9% of costs	
F Low	Cf. person living in community	0.1% 65+	Cost of care 38 ECU per day Accommodation cost 31 to 77 ECU per day	Accommodation: Social Assistance if contributions from person and relatives are insufficient	Cost of care: 100%	Accommodation: 90% of personal resources	Obligatory contributions of relatives
Average			Idem		Cost of care: 100%	For accommodation: 100% paid by person or possibly dependency insurance	Complements from family
IRL Low	Cf. person living in community	1.2% (approximately)	85–127 ECU per day (author estimate for public hospital services)	100% general taxation		20–30% (25 ECU per day; max. 10 days in any year) 0% (after 10 days) Compulsory private insurance (VHI)	
Average	Cf. person living in community		85–127 ECU per day (author estimate for public hospital services) Private hospital services	70–80% 100% if stay is greater than 10 days in any year Tax Breaks/ Sunk Capital Costs			
L Low	Minimum pension (955 ECU per month)			State if old-age pension of pensioner is insufficient (after 3 to 6 months) For accommodation: 2,288 ECU per month (first 3 to 6 months) (general hospital)	For accommodation: 2,288 ECU per month (first 3 to 6 months) (general hospital)	For accommodation: 2,288 ECU per month (after 3 to 6 months) (general hospital)	No (general hospital)

Table 4.6 cont'd

Income height	Income	Share of the elderly	Average cost	State or public contributions	Social security contribution	Personal contributions	Family contributions
L Average cont'd	Pension of about 1,273 ECU per month			State if old-age pension of pensioner is insufficient (after 3 to 6 months) (general hospital)	For accommodation: 2,288 ECU per month (first 3 to 6 months) (general hospital)	For accommodation: 2,288 ECU per month (after 3 to 6 months) (general hospital)	No (general hospital)
NL Low and average	Not applicable						
P Low and average	Not different from person living in the community, except for rent subsidy					0% (public hospitals)	
S Low	Basic pension (5,641 ECU/year) + pension supplement (2,315 ECU/year)		167–300 ECU per day	Ministry of Health: 10% Regional taxes: 87%		Daily fee of 5–9 ECU = 3% of total costs	
Average	Supplementary pension (ATP) (9,496 ECU/year)		Idem	Idem		Idem	
UK Low and average	Pensions are reduced to personal allowances after 6 weeks in NHS hospital Attendance allowance ceases after 4 weeks	2%	144 ECU per day	100%			
N Low and average			427 ECU per day	100% (30% state and 70% local)			

Table 4.7   Synoptic table on (dependent) elderly persons living in the community

Income height		Pension, social assistance, etc.	Income Housing allowance, rent subsidy, etc.	Payment for care
A	Low	Social Assistance (compensatory supplement) + pension (587 ECU for singles; 838 ECU for couples (1996); paid 14 times per year) Exemption from TV-, radio and telephone contributions as well as from medical prescription contributions		Attendance allowance (635 ECU (level 4, 1996))
	Average	Pension (1,335 ECU for male white collar worker (1994); paid 14 times per year)		
B	Low	Guaranteed minimum income for the elderly (6,382 ECU per year for singles; 8,509 ECU per year for couples (1.10.1997))	Rent subsidy	Attendance allowance Allowance for help for older persons (2,800 to 4,800 ECU per year (1.05.1996)) Allowance for help from a third person (13,216 ECU per year (1.12.1994))
	Average	Legal pension	Rent subsidy	Allowance for help from a third person (13,216 ECU per year (1.12.1994))
DK	Low	General old-age pension ('Folkepension': 12,329 ECU for singles; 8,911 ECU per person if couple (1996)) Employment-related pension (ATP: up to 1,847 ECU (1996)) Personal allowances	Rent subsidies (high)	
	Average	General old-age pension ('Folkepension': 10,732 ECU for singles; 16,302 ECU for couples (1994)) Employment-related pension (ATP: 272 ECU for singles; 543 ECU for couples (1994)) Income from savings (1,358 ECU (1994)) Personal allowances (lower)	Rent subsidies (lower)	
D	Low	Guaranteed minimum income	Allowances for suitable housing	'Hilfe zur Pflege' and 'Eingliederungshilfe für Behinderte'
	Average	Statutory pension		

Table 4.7 cont'd

Income height	Pension, social assistance, etc.	Income: Housing allowance, rent subsidy, etc.	Payment for care
E Low	Noncontributory invalidity pension (332 ECU per month (for singles and couples), i.e. including an increase because of dependency)		
Average	Contributory invalidity pension (498 ECU per month (586 ECU for couples), i.e. including an increase because of dependency)		
FIN Low	National pension (428 ECU per month (747 ECU for couples))	Pensioner's housing allowance (41 ECU in case of owning the house (71 ECU for couples); 261 ECU in case of renting the house (293 ECU for couples))	Pensioner's care allowance (239 ECU per month in case of severe disability) Home care allowance (445 ECU per month)
Average	Employment pension (858 ECU per month (1,232 ECU for couples))	Pensioner's housing allowance (153 ECU in case of renting the house (129 ECU for couples))	Pensioner's care allowance (239 ECU per month in case of severe disability) Home care allowance (445 ECU per month)
F Low	Minimum guaranteed income for the elderly (539 ECU per month for singles and 945 ECU per month for couples)	Social housing allocation (107 ECU per month)	Attendance allowance (if in need of third person to perform daily life activities, income-related) (343 to 687 ECU per month)
Average	Basic pension (>539 ECU per month for single; >945 ECU per month for couple)		Attendance allowance (if in need of third person to perform daily life activities, income-related) (343 to 687 ECU per month)
IRL Low	Noncontributory old-age pension (82.50 ECU per week for people under 80 years/89 ECU per week for people above 80)	Fuel allowance	Carer's allowance (82.5 ECU per week)
Average	Contributory old-age pension or retirement pension (95 ECU per week for people under 80 years/108 ECU per week for people above 80)		

Table 4.7 cont'd

	Income height	Pension, social assistance, etc.	Income Housing allowance, rent subsidy, etc.	Payment for care
I	Low	Minimum pension (363 ECU/month) if working career; social pension if no working career		Attendance allowance for the carer (389 ECU per month)
	Average	Average income of retired private sector wage earners + occupational pension + other private income		Attendance allowance for the carer (389 ECU per month)
L	Low	Minimum pension (<955 ECU per month)		Allocation de soins (360 ECU per month)
	Average	Average pension of about 1,273 ECU per month		Allocation de soins (360 ECU per month)
NL	Low	General Pension Act guarantees minimum income (703 ECU per month for singles; 975 ECU per month for couples) Social Assistance in case income insufficient for urgent need	Rent subsidy	
	Average	Average gross income for a single person with an additional pension was 16,686 ECU in 1994; for a couple it was 24,538 ECU Social Assistance in case income insufficient for urgent need		
P	Low	Income less than the Minimum Guaranteed Income, which was 280 ECU per month for a single person in 1997	Rent subsidy	Subsidy for the help of a third person (52 ECU per month (General Regime)) Complement of the pension for a conjoint at charge (23 ECU per month in 1997)
	Average	Income more than the Minimum Guaranteed Income, which was 280 ECU per month for a single person in 1997	Rent subsidy	Subsidy for the help of a third person (52 ECU per month (General Regime)) Complement of the pension for a conjoint at charge (23 ECU per month in 1997)
S	Low	Basic pension (5,641 ECU/year (1995)) + pension supplement (2,315 ECU/year at maximum (1996))	Means-tested rent subsidies (2,045 ECU/year on average (1995))	Attendance allowance (between 141 and 588 ECU per month) Carers allowance
	Average	Supplementary pension (ATP) (9,496 ECU/year for singles (1995))	Means-tested rent subsidies (2,045 ECU/year on average (1995))	

Table 4.7 cont'd

Income height		Pension, social assistance, etc.	Income Housing allowance, rent subsidy, etc.	Payment for care
UK	Low	Income support (personal allowance, including pensioner premium: 82.1 ECU/week max. for singles; 134.2 ECU/week max. for couples); State retirement and occupational pension	Benefits from the Regulated Social Fund (cold weather payments, etc.) Benefits from the Discretionary Social Fund (community care grants, etc.) Housing benefit Council tax benefit	Attendance allowance (39.7 or 59.4 ECU per week) Severe disability premium (44.6 ECU per week) Invalid care allowance
	Average	State retirement (74.9 or 44.9 ECU per week for singles; 119.8 ECU per week for couples) and occupational pension; Graduated retirement benefit		Attendance allowance (39.7 or 59.4 ECU per week) Severe disability premium (44.6 ECU per week)
N	Low	Minimum pension (7,689 ECU for singles; 13,426 ECU for couples)	Housing allowance	Care salary for relatives
	Average	Income of about 14,646 ECU		Care salary for relatives

Table 4.7a   Synoptic table on district nursing

	Income height	Share of the elderly	Average cost	State or public contributions	Social security contribution	Personal contributions	Family contributions
A	Low and average		'Medical' home nursing: between 25 and 37 ECU per hour		Health insurance	Pensioners pay health insurance contributions (3.5%)	
B	Low				±99% of total costs	±1% of total costs	
	Average				±75% of total costs	±25% of total costs (is in reality nearly always 0% (reinsurance))	
DK	Low and average			100%			
D	Low			Nursing help benefits from Social Assistance supplement health insurance under special conditions and if the need is not yet covered by social care insurance	If no social network: home care in kind (1.467 ECU/month) If social network: home care in cash (681 ECU/month) or combination in kind-in cash	Nursing help benefits from Social Assistance are income-related and means-tested	
E	Average				Idem		
	Low and average			100% (public district nursing)			
FIN	Low and average		4 visits a month: 117 ECU	Local: 100%			
F	Low and average		Fixed amount 30 ECU per day		100%		
IRL	Low and average	3.46 public health nurses per 1,000 old people >65 (1993)		100% general taxation			
L	Low and average			State subsidises part of personnel costs	100% (traditional nursing acts)	'Social' fee: 7.37 ECU at most per day (for personal hygiene) Contribution to district nursing organisation (22 ECU per year)	
NL	Low and average				Special social security scheme (AWBZ)		

Table 4.7a cont'd

	Income height	Share of the elderly	Average cost	State or public contributions	Social security contribution	Personal contributions	Family contributions
P	Low and average			National Health Service: 100%			
S	Low and average			100% (regional or local financing)			
UK	Low and average		40 ECU per hour	100%			
N	Low			National and local pay the remainder: i.e. approximately 95%		For elderly with minimum pension + 20%: max. 6 ECU/month Income-related 5% of total costs	
	Average	About 9% 65+		Idem			

Table 4.7b Synoptic table on home help

	Income height	Share of the elderly	Average cost	State or public contributions	Social security contribution	Personal contributions	Family contributions
A	Low and average		Between 9 and 15 ECU	Regional and local: about 70–80%		20–30% (income-related)	
B	Low and average	± 6% of 65+	20.34 ECU per hour in Flanders, 1996; 16.65 ECU per hour in private sector of Wallony, 1993	On the average 80% in Flanders; 86% in Wallony		Income-related (on the average 20% in Flanders; 14% in Wallony)	Yes (if living in same household as elderly person)
DK	Low and average			100%			
E	Low	0.93% of people 65+	Average annual cost was 1,815 ECU in 1995	74.6%	21.4%	4.0%	
	Average	0.16% of people 65+	Idem	74.6%	21.4%	4.0%	
FIN	Low		66 visits: 1,816 ECU	Local: 100%			
	Average		66 visits: 1,816 ECU	Local: 87% of costs			
F	Low		Varies according to social security situation and the department in which the pensioner lives, up to 90 hours per month, 11 to 18 ECU per hour	Social Assistance		13% of costs Vary from 0 to 2 ECU according to the department	
	Average		Idem		Varies from 1 to 12 ECU according to income	Personal contributions depend upon income	
IRL	Low	3.5% of 65+	3.49 to 6.12 ECU per hour	State + voluntary		Varies by region	Voluntary contributions possible Varies by region
	Average		Idem	State + voluntary State subsidises part of personnel costs		Contribution to cost	
L	Low and average					Contributions are income-related: 3.05 ECU to 12.71 ECU per hour	
NL	Low and average				Special Social Security Scheme (AWBZ)	Personal contributions related to income and limited to a certain amount per month	
P	Low and average					Means-tested	

Table 4.7b cont'd

Income height	Share of the elderly	Average cost	State or public contributions	Social security contribution	Personal contributions	Family contributions
S Low and average			92% (local financing)		Income-related personal contributions; 8% of total costs on average	
UK Low	About 15% 65+	10.32 ECU per hour	100%			
Average		Idem	Approx. 90%			
N Low			National and local pay the remainder: i.e. approximately 95%		Means-tested (approx. 10%) For elderly with minimum pension + 20%: max. 6 ECU/month Income-related	
Average			Idem		5% of total costs	

Table 4.7c   Synoptic table on meals-on-wheels

Income height	Share of the elderly	Average cost	State or public contributions	Social security contribution	Personal contributions	Family contributions
A Low and average			Regional and local: 80–90%		1.5–4 ECU per meal	
B Low and average		4.98 ECU per meal	±23% of total costs		Means-tested, ±77% of total costs	
DK Low and average			100% except raw materials		Payment for raw materials	
FIN Low and average		30 meals: 208 ECU	Local: 25% of costs		75% of costs	
F Low			Social Assistance (means-tested) and local state	CNAVTS contributions	Personal contributions small share of costs	
Average			Benefits from regional and local level	CNAVTS contributions	Individual contributions	
IRL Low	Share of the elderly receiving meals varies by health board region. Highest share receiving is just under 5% in the East (1992)	Approximately 3.8 ECU per meal	State + voluntary		Very nominal contribution	
NL Average		Idem	State + voluntary Local subsidy		Contribution to cost	
Low and average					Personal contributions related to income	
P Low and average					25% of the per capita monthly income	
S Low and average			100%			
UK Low		4.92 ECU per meal	100%			
Average		Idem	Approx. 90%			
N Low and average			100% + (local, i.e. municipalities)		Means-tested (approx. 10%) Payments vary since these are local arrangements	

5 Debate on Long-term Care Insurance

1 Introduction

In a number of countries there is a political discussion going on about how to adapt the social protection system, as described in the previous chapters, to the challenge of the increasing needs in the coming decades. This can be a discussion regarding the quantitative expansion of the services and systems, but most of the time the discussion revolves around the character of the intervention. The questions include: What is the role of the state? What elements have to be covered? In which organisational structure and under what conditions (income- or needs-related)? In the countries studied, the present discussion is different. Although the driving forces are universal in all those countries (demography, budgetary rationing, selectivity and so on), the starting point, the institutional (and to a lesser degree the cultural) context and the solutions are different. In what follows, we first give an overview of the present discussion in each country, concentrating on whatever concrete proposals for reform have been brought forward. Thereafter, we try to define some common aspects and draw conclusions.

2 Overview of the Situation in Each Country

2.1 Austria

In Austria, similarly to Germany, there is a pronounced attachment to the Bismarckian social insurance. Even the latest pension reform falls back on a 'conservative' 'insurance' principle for the public pension. The pension is not a basic entitlement but it is related to the years contributed and the calculation is even more dependent on past earnings since it refers not to the last 10 years but to the last 15 years. This implies a higher relation between contribution and benefits (here also with the intention to cut the expenditures since referring to a longer period probably includes years with a lower income). Reduction of the indexation, however, reduces the level of protection so that it risks evaluating to a basic level. The reduction of public subsidies, on the contrary, reinforces the insurance character.

The reform of thealth insurance aims at reducing hospital-based care, and aims to increase the development of community care. In reality the major part of the expenditures goes to the hospital sector and not to community services. For decades there existed partial systems of additional allowances for dependent persons to cover the extra costs of their dependency, for some categories, financed sometimes at regional level. Since 1 July 1993 the *Bundespflegegeldgesetz* created a tax-financed national system of an attendance allowance. This law aimed to harmonise and complete existing systems of allowances, and the new legislation was created without immediately changing constitutional divisions of competencies (an example for the debate in Belgium, where the new long-term insurance seems to be organised at a regional level in only one region). A state treaty was concluded between federal and regional authorities. The federal level guarantees the financing of the new scheme; the regional authorities adapt their regulation and engage themselves in the further expansion of residential, semi-residential and community care (see also Badelt et al., 1997). The administrative treatment of the new scheme was also attributed to existing administrations. For instance pensioners receiving an additional allowance, received it together with their pension, from the pension administration (no new pillar!). The scheme not only focused on the elderly, but on all dependent persons 'in need of care' above the age of three years. It is an in cash allowance meant to cover the additional costs of dependency for services, diets, housing and heating. It can be transformed into direct services if the person receiving the benefit is unable to organise the care himself but most of the time it is taken up as a cash benefit, and used to pay the informal care provided by the family. In that way it must be considered as an additional support of family income, and as a 'payment for care' it is a implicit 'acknowledgement of family care'. The entitlement of the allowance is not means tested, but dependent on a medical assessment of the care needed (from less than 50 hours a week to more than 180 hours a month). The amount varies in seven levels from 160 ECU per month to 1,600 ECU.

2.2 Belgium

2.2.1 Macro view on the present level of the care for the dependent older persons The legal (pay-as-you-go) pension scheme, residuary minimum income for the elderly, occupational pensions and additional private pension saving (from life insurance to individual retirement savings) is the most important pillar of the social protection of the elderly. Only a limited number of elderly are below the poverty line. The income of the elderly is supported by a high degree of home ownership (more than 70 per cent of the population) contrasted however with a relative low share of social housing.

Additional allowances exist for dependent older persons, for help from third persons, related to the degree of dependency and to income.

Health insurance is a compulsory national health insurance (social security) with almost complete coverage of the population and with a reasonable degree of public financing versus a limited co-insurance from the patient. Cost containment is realised in the sector by increase of this share and by control of the supply.

Social care is financed at regional level and with a more substantial own contribution. Also local authorities finance in a small way health and social services or provide additional income support (assistance). The health care and social care is provided by a substantial private non profit sector, a public sector (mostly local) and a commercial sector. For national and international standards, a broad scope of services is available, in reasonable quantity (waiting lists are not too long and there are not too many unmet needs, although some remain) and quality. Confronted with increasing numbers of elderly, increasing dependency, increasing costs, unmet demands for additional support, is there a need for an additional system of social protection, a long-term care insurance?

2.2.2 How far are we from a decent system on protection? What are the expenditures that should be covered by the long-term care insurance for the elderly in Belgium? Residential care and community care, especially district nursing and home help are the core services. The many new emerging needs and services and aspirations of the population are not covered in detail hereafter, but they will grow in importance, especially when new insurance schemes would emerge.

The adequacy of the pension scheme is a additional prerequisite for a good dependency insurance. It is not considered here. Neither is the health insurance covering acute health care mentioned. Again, it is supposed to be adequate, although problems are signalled.

What are these problems? There is the demographic pressure, requiring additional beds in future in old-age homes and nursing homes. There is the increased dependency in old-age homes and nursing homes requiring step-by-step increased staffing and financing, which has been undertaken. Already the real staffing is often higher than that reimbursed by health insurance. There is an expansion of the demand for better housing, a significant increase in district nursing (explosion of the budget, even after installing of lump sum financing) and signalled unmet needs in home help (20 per cent). There is the demand for a payment for care and increased demand for better wages in the care sector. Problems of a declining welfare state are the increased co-insurance; the rationing of some supply; the limitation of local communities in making new initiatives; and the withdrawing of regional authorities in financing housing of the elderly. Nevertheless a huge amount of social protection of the elderly remains. The health insurance expenditures for district nursing in Belgium evolved from 6.3 billion BEF (in 1987) to 13.6 (in 1994). The budget for old-age homes in that same period went from 3.0 to 10.5 billion BEF and for the rest and nursing homes from 1.7 to 9.6 billion. The total budget for health insurance increased from 240 billion BEF tot 384 billion BEF (see Pacolet, Lanoye and Bouten, 1998, p. 163). There are more and more indications that especially the cumulation of on-going expenditure for the elderly is becoming unbearable, and is pushing them towards social assistance, at least in residential care.

The people at dependency risk in Belgium who are eligible for dependency insurance were estimated in a recent proposal (1993) of the federal government at 234,000, of which 34,000 are in rest and nursing homes (ibid., p. 212). Sometimes even larger definitions of dependent elderly are used. Jegers et al. use a figure of 852,953 persons, increasing to 1,467,157 by the year 2035 (Jegers et al., 1996, p. 343). Other estimates arrive at 1,550,003 persons above 65, with 186,000 semi-dependent and 93,000 completely dependent (quoted in Pacolet, Lanoye and Bouten, 1998, p. 212) persons.

What are the main components of the long-term care insurance at the moment? What are the financing structure and the unmet needs? The majority of those expenditures are already included in health insurance. If this is sustained, then there is only a limited amount of additional money needed in Belgium.

Thanks to the until now reasonable coverage, a substantial improvement in coverage (perhaps even completion) could be estimated at 20 billion. Compared to the total expenditures in social security (1,200 billion in 1990) this is only 1.6 per cent of all social expenditures, or 0.3 per cent of GNP

(Pacolet, Lanoye and Bouten, 1998, p. 220). Even a doubling of the dependent elderly in 2035, as some expect, means then only 0.6 per cent of GNP, *ceteris paribus*. But who can tell us if everything else *will* stay the same (and the impact of greying of the population is not only to be looked for in this long-term care insurance but in the regular social protection (pensions and health)).

2.2.3 The proposed solutions Political interest in the impact of the greying of the population has been present in Belgium from the beginning of the 1980s. The then Minister of Social Affairs and now Prime Minister, J.L. Dehaene, launched studies to assess, and measures to accommodate, the impact on the social security system (especially pensions and health care). An important first step was the conversion of hospital beds to beds for nursing homes. This was not only a more rational use of hospitals (they are not meant for long-term care) but also a substantial reduction of public involvement. Since then it has been realised that this low involvement is not sustainable and public financing for those beds has increased again, becoming applicable also to beds in old-age homes, although at a lower level. Public funding for both these services is converging at a higher level. From the mid-1980, there was strong support for community care. The same Minister of Social Affairs proposed to study the feasibility of a financial allowance for the informal carer in the situation of community care.

The discussion of old-age insurance has been gaining momentum in Belgium in the 1990s. It was announced in the government declaration of 1992 and the 'State of the Union' of 1993, and it was included in the proposals for the 'Social Pact' and the 'General Plan', which were discussed at the political level in the autumn of 1993 (proposals for restoring financial equilibrium in social security and the government budget, and for improving the competitiveness of the economy through striving for higher levels of employment).

From that period on, long-term care insurance was also put on the political agenda in Flanders.

The federal proposals of the consecutive ministers of social affairs evolved from expanding the health insurance and social security to the long-term care (non-medical expenditures) to mixed systems where the public savings bank was invited to assess the feasibility of a funded semi-social long-term care insurance (1991) (see a description of earlier proposals in Pacolet, Versieck and Bouten, 1994).

Early proposals in 1985 refer to allowances in cash to compensate for the additional expenditures of (community) long-term care. On several occasions

Table 5.1   Calendar of the debate on present and future old-age protection in Belgium

Year	Summary of the proposals
1982	– Financing of care in nursing homes is based on the assessment of the degree of dependency (Katz scale).
1985	– Proposal of the federal Minister of Social Affairs: financial contribution towards the costs of community care.
1991	– Proposal of an insurance company- banking institution ('ASLK') (on the proposal of the Minister of Social Affairs): a semiprivate insurance for 'elderly' risks, in collaboration with health insurance organisations, funded.
	– Financing of care in old-age homes and financing of district nursing are based on the assessment of the degree of dependency (Katz scale).
1992	– Note of the federal Minister of Social Affairs on a dependency insurance: social insurance, in collaboration with health insurance organisations, funds obtained from health insurance, based on pay-as-you-go.
1993	– Proposal of the federal Minister of Social Affairs on a 'independency insurance': cover costs of dependent elderly persons in residential and community services, 'federal' social security, 'new' insurance.
1993	– Flemish Minister of Social Policy: the dependency insurance is a regional matter; the existing system (of public involvement) is the best to improve the autonomy of the elderly.
1994	– Proposals of the Flemish Christian-Democratic Members of Parliament: minimal social regime for the main carer.
	– Share of public financing of the infrastructure of residential services for the elderly is diminishing. Conditions and procedure for obtaining public financing are also changed.
1995	– The financing of the infrastructure of service flats is mobilising with less public subsidy more private capital.
1996	– Bill on the introduction of service vouchers. The proposal included in the Programme Act is withdrawn because the service voucher is seen as an area of Community competence and not as an area of federal competence.
1997	– Debate at community level between the Flemish Minister for Health Care and the Flemish Minister for Welfare concerning competence for the dependency insurance. Intention of the Flemish Minister for Health Care to start up a care insurance scheme for elderly people on 1 January 1999.
	– Additional beds in nursing homes (Protocol agreement on the policy on elderly people: 25,000 beds in old-age homes are converted into nursing home beds in Belgium spread across five years, from 1 January 1998).
	– Proposal for care insurance from G. Swennen (Socialist Party)
(1991–97)	– Convergence between the RIZIV fixed payments for nursing homes and those for old-age homes.
End of 1998	– The National Inter-Mutual College is still calling for a federal solution.
May–July 1998	– CVP (Flemish Christian Democrats) decision to develop a mixed capitalisation-redistribution system at the level of Flanders.
1997–98	– Proposals for improvement of the federal allowance for dependent older persons.
September 1998	– Socialist and Christian Democratic Party introduce in Flemish parliament a proposal for a long-term care insurance. This matches the proposal of the Flemish government to start with a (partly funded) long-term care insurance in Flanders from the year 2000 on. In the 1999 budget already 4 billion BEF is reserved for this insurance.

trade unions and sickness funds confirm their choice of an improved social security (enlarged health insurance) system for the long-term care. But the financial constraints on this system do not allow any substantial enlargement of the social protection at federal level. Nevertheless, step-by-step improvements have been realised (see above), but a remaining uncovered risk remains. In the mid-1990s a certain 'impasse' arose because of institutional conflicts between the federal and the regional level. Since 1993 the Flemish government has claimed that it is responsible for this policy strand, and in latter years their budgetary situation has allowed for new initiatives to be taken. After a period of standstill in new proposals, there has been, since 1998, a real upswing in new proposals from the Flemish parliament as well as from the Flemish government. It resulted in an enlargement for the years to come of more and new services for the elderly, as well as in the official announcement of the start of a Flemish long-term care insurance from January 2000 on. Already in the budget of the Flemish government of 1999 an amount of four billion BEF wass reserved to start the to a large extent funded (and not only pay-as-you-go financed) care insurance in which social sickness funds but also private insurers are allowed to participate. At the federal level, new proposals were formulated by the government to enlarge and improve the existing dependency allowance for older persons (increased amounts for more dependent persons, and make them less income-related). It could evolve to a real payment for care system, completing the other elements of improved social protection especially in health insurance (for instance, better support for chronically ill persons; better financing of old-age homes and nursing homes). Combined with the further development at regional level, Belgium could improve substantially the already well-developed (in level and scope) system of social protection of the elderly. Probably the opinion is sometimes formulated that all levels should be allowed to take some responsibility for financing of the long-term care risk: health insurance, federal allowances, regionally financed services for the elderly, an additional regional health insurance and private insurance. That is the last observable trend in Belgium: from an insurance sector that declared itself incapable of insuring this risk, and first hesitating when public authorities suggested or invited explicitly the insurance sector to enter this field, it is again invited/allowed to enter the market of the Flemish long-term care insurance to be launched in 2000. From being almost non-existent, we could identify in mid-1998 six clear private long-term care insurance products, and three months later, we could add two more products to that list. Nineteen ninety-nine and 2000 will be decisive years in answering the question of whether long-term care insurance in Belgium will be a major federal responsibility, or whether regionalisation or even privatisation will occur (see Pacolet, Lanoye and Bouten, 1998; Pacolet and Bouten, 1998; Pacolet, Versieck and Bouten, 1994).

2.3   Denmark

Within the Danish system of social protection up to the present time there has been no reason to initiate a general discussion on dependency insurance. However, the context is changing towards cutting back on health care expenditures, smaller rent subsidies and limits in social care (here, home care). This financing of long-term care is to a large extent a public responsibility and it is the general opinion that this should remain the case. The Danish system has to a large extent been a locally organised tax-based system of public organisation and financing. There has been no sharp institutional difference between health and dependency upon the provision of care, and for the Danish citizen the choice between institutional and community care has been rather neutral in terms of the economic aspects: there ought to be fairly complete public financing. This neutrality has even been installed at the organisational level: since hospitals and nursing homes are organised at two different levels (counties and municipalities), countries have been able to charge municipalities for extra stays in hospitals because of insufficient supply of places in nursing homes.

That the welfare state reached its maximum in this sector is illustrated by some forms of selectivity: home care is concentrated on personal (related with P-ADL) and less on I-ADL (cleaning, shopping). The welfare state reduces its role to personal care, and less to other (even vital) living conditions (contrary to the Netherlands).

The political debate and the measures taken were first of all in terms of the quality of the housing component in the care. A large-scale programme was launched in 1988 to improve the quality of housing for the elderly and at the same time to increase their autonomy. This reinforced attention given to housing comes up in the latest proposals: a new programme was launched in 1994 to develop housing and services for the elderly, and to continue to replace nursing homes by modern housing. Nursing housing should be possible, with more extensive and better staffed provision of care. This was a response to the observation that in the new housing for the elderly started in 1988 not enough attention was given to the fact that, after some years, these older people would certainly become dependent. Recent studies also confirm the need for better housing for the elderly and waiting lists for special housing for the elderly. For this reason, additional financial incentives will also be given to the municipalities for the construction of new housing. Nursing homes were replaced by special dwellings for elderly. The need for more care facilities within those dwellings is solved by more national funding, improving solidarity and equal access. On the other hand first but limited examples of privatisation are observed. Other incentives are to be given to the municipalities for the improvement of the services for the elderly. Hence, there are measures to stimulate the establishment of service areas in connection with housing for the elderly. For instance, the building and renting of special housing communities, organised by the private sector, will be subsidised by loan subsidies and rent subsidies. There is a discussion on the affordability and desirability of the higher rent benefits given to the elderly. The pension age is characterised as too low, but it is, in an international comparison, relatively high (real age on average 62).

Within the context of employment policies, the government has provided the possibility for municipalities to engage certain categories of unemployed persons in services for the elderly. Such persons would receive 80 per cent of their unemployment benefit as a subsidy from the state. From 1994 onward, this measure was redefined as a refunding system: 50 per cent of the increase in wage costs for services for the elderly is refunded by central government.

Those initiatives illustrate the broadening of an already mature system of social protection for the elderly which, to a large extent, is already oriented towards in-kind help. One remarkable characteristic of this system, which became clear in the case studies, is that as a matter of fact there is a significant creaming off of the income when these services are made available, due to the fact that the flat rate pension is retained when people are in institutions and are left with only a fixed amount of pocket money. By this means of financing the services, they become much less freely available and the choice for institutionalised care must be influenced by this fact. It is also an extreme form of 'in-kind' provision of help. An important new shift in this policy is to pay the pension to the residents and make them more responsible for their situation by giving them 'a voice' in their own affairs. This can indeed contribute to a feeling of increased autonomy. This paying of the pension, possibly together with an increased payment for the nursing home, will not substantially change the situation for those with only public pension. This experimental system was replaced by a permanent system in 1995. This remarkable high level of own contribution, leaving the elderly only 'pocket money', has come to an end. It still exists in several other countries.

Finally there are two legal aspects of the improvement of the protection for the elderly: namely, greater possibilities for appealing decisions on assignment of the allocation of home help and the installation of a board at the local level. This board can express its opinion on all matters concerning elderly people.

2.4   Germany: Installation of an Old-age Insurance System

In Germany, since July 1993 and after a discussion lasting several decades, a definitive proposal for a system of dependency insurance was put on the table and has been accepted. The proposal for a social insurance system was inspired by the pure facts of observed needs in the older population (25 per cent of people over 60 need ADL help, and more than half of these people are over 80) and the undercoverage of those needs (in West Germany, 70 per cent of older persons in residential services need social assistance, and in East Germany this figure is 100 per cent).

The old-age social insurance (*Pflegeversicherung*) went into force on 1 January 1995 for community care situations, and on 1 January 1996 for residential care. This difference in timing illustrates the incentive (or at least the priority) that the government wanted to give to community care. In some respects, priority is also being given to expenditure for rehabilitation, to prevent a further deterioration of the situation. From 1996 onward, the older person has been free to choose between residential and home care. It is noteworthy that the maximum amount is allowed be the same in both situations. Care insurance is a social insurance, part of the federal social security system, integrated under the umbrella of the healthinsurance system. This insurance covers 90 per cent of the population and is financed by an income contribution. This contribution is based on limited incomes and is equally split between employers and employees. Those in Germany who have private health insurance must be covered by a similar private old-age insurance scheme. The dependent groups are classified into three different groups and insurance is only applicable when there is an important degree of dependency. The lowest dependency category implies the need for daily help, the second implies the need for help three times a day, and the third category implies permanent dependency. The protection includes community care, as well as semi-residential (short-term or temporary) care and residential care. The allowance is higher if taken as assistance in kind rather than in cash. A combination of in-cash and in-kind allowances is also possible. This new insurance also takes care of the social contributions for pensions and work accidents for the informal carers up to a certain amount. The reimbursement of aid instruments is also provided for. Finally, financing of investment for residential services is catered for.

For those with private health insurance, the insurance companies have to guarantee similar protection.

Since the *Pflegeversicherung* is only a basic insurance, the possibility of taking on an additional private insurance is also provided for, for which a tax deduction of 360 DEM per person is made available.

The insured elements are summarised in the Table 5.2.

Table 5.2   Characteristics of the *Pflegeversicherung* in Germany

Elements (Date of start)	Type of help	
	In cash	In kind
Community care (from 1.1.1995)	Pflegegeld 400/800/ 1,200 DEM per month Relief help for 4 weeks (value up to 2,250 DEM per year) Social rights of carer	25/50/75 visits by professionals (= value of 750/1,800/2,800 DEM per month)
Residential care (from 1.1.1996)		Semi-residential day and night care temporary care Residential (housing and hotel cost for older person) investment cost Up to 2,800 DEM
	Coverage Budget	Financing modalities
Community	11.5 billion DEM	1 per cent of income
Social rights of carer	2.9 billion DEM	
Residential	11 billion DEM	1.7 per cent of income in 1996 (including community care)
Investment cost Administrative cost Financial Reserve	3.6 billion DEM	
Total gross cost in 1996	29 billion DEM	
Savings in social assistance ·	6 billion DEM	
Total net cost	23 billion DEM	

Financing was one of the discussion points: employers requested compensation for the cost increase, in particular through a reduction of income insurance for sickness and the cancellation of one holiday.

Two elements of this proposal are of additional importance. First of all, there is the voluntary aspect of the programme that old-age insurance could not be kept in the sphere of social assistance: by contributing to the social insurance system, people are *entitled* to a reasonable coverage of the risk. This coverage is not complete, however, since only the care costs are financed, and not the other living expenditures. There is no means-testing and no obligation for the family to pay back the costs. Coverage of the missing purchasing power (by the social assistance system) would probably remain only for the lowest income groups.

Another remarkable aspect is that the dependency insurance is situated within the health insurance ('under the umbrella'), yet not completely integrated into it.

2.5   Greece

The social protection institutions are characterised by 'administrative complexity and multiplicity of institutions', large differences in the level of protection and weak financial basis. Between 1980 and 1990 there was a substantial improvement in the average old-age pension, increasing from 48.5 to 78 per cent of the per capita GDP. Despite this kind of high replacement ratio and high level of expenditure on pensions, there is a high level of poverty amongst the elderly. For the health care sector, there is a decreasing public share in the expenditures. Despite free access to health care in theory, there is an increased (often illegal) share of own payments of the patient. Public financing for the health care system is only a limited part of the total cost, explaining the increasing need to recall on the patient to cover the expenditures. Also, services directly aimed at the elderly are less available. There is a low level of residential services (0.5 per cent of the elderly stay in an old-age home) and there is an emerging community care system. This is certainly related to the sociocultural preference for care within the community by the community and the family. Formal services – especially the residential services – are less developed, but there is an explicit programme to develop community care further. This is the KAPI-programme, which created some 257 'Open Care Centers for the Elderly', usually in urban areas. Those services provide a wide spectrum of community care services. The lack of information on these services is, however, the main reason that we cannot conclude how developed the social protection is. There seems to be a lack of (public) financial resources, combined with a low level of formal services. There is also no explicit public debate to change this situation by installing new systems of protection, perhaps also because of general budgetary considerations.

2.6   Spain

Up until 1999, there is not a clear cut consensus that dependency of the elderly is a major problem. Informal care by the family is the main source of support for the elderly, and there is currently a guarantee of pensions, cost-free health care and available social services. The creation of additional insurance for the elderly would disrupt the social security system. Private solutions are not viable since there is no market because of lack of interest of the population and lack of concern. The cost of long-term care is not identified as a universal risk, but an exceptional one (like work accident or handicap, but are those not universal risks?), not in the definition of the Dutch 'exceptional cost' insurance, referring to the exceptional high level of the costs. Dependency insurance is not included in the priorities of the reform of social security, which concentrates on the viability of the public pension scheme and the promotion of voluntary pension schemes. The debate that does take place on dependency is more related to the demographic challenge, the unequal distribution of resources over the territory, the ineffective use of resources, lack of fiscal expenditures for those needs and the emergence of a dual caring system.

The list of initiatives supporting the elderly in an additional way other than pure pensions and pure income support is impressive and well above a minimal level, at least in its variety: complementary benefits of 50 per cent for persons with a severe invalidity, in cash or in residential care; care allowance in the noncontributory pension (which is going to disappear), financial allowance according to dependency degree implying increase of pensions when third person support is required; support for families with low income caring for the own disabled elderly (in regions like Basque, Navarra, Catalonia) or (in some of the same regions) an allowance for those who take a non-related elderly person into the family.

One recent initiate of the public administration is proposing new steps in social protection against the cost of dependency, including support services for caring families, economic allowances (in cash, fiscal) for caring families, (new) services and additional financial support for those elderly living alone, improvement of community support and residential care. This programme is on the way to being realised, but the income allowances for elderly living alone and for the main carers remain problematic (underprovided).

The author concludes optimistically that better coordination and reordering existing resources can cover a lot of problems, with a 'small increase of cost'.

2.7   France

The financing of the new risk of care for older persons has been intensively discussed and studied in France during the last five years. From previous research it was already clear that for certain services for the elderly there was a lack of supply. The Schopflin Commission pointed out some of these problems. In the report for the Planning Bureau they observed an important shortage, especially of 'medicalised' places in the residential care system, and insufficient supply in the community care system. A second problem was the insufficient purchasing power of the older persons to pay for the needed services, so that they needed social assistance, with the negative impact that the family also could be charged for the costs (directly or via an inheritance). The Schopflin Commission and, in a rather similar manner, the Boulard Parliamentary Commission, arrived at the following proposals:

– increase the number of medicalised places and create a unified statute and financing system to avoid discrimination between care systems;
– improve the solvency of the older persons, especially for the middle income groups, who are at risk of becoming dependent on social assistance where the payment of the residential care is concerned. An allocation in cash (means-tested) has been proposed for these situations, replacing (or better generalising) the actual allowance. This allowance should be differentiated according to degree of dependency and can be attributed in institutional as well as home care situations;
– improve coordination in the sector.

In January 1993 the Social Affairs Administration (IGAS, *l'Inspection Générale des Affaires Sociales*) proposed an increase of medical places over the course of three years, an increase of the fixed rates for care by 20 per cent in the 'section de cure médicale', and an expansion of the district nursing programme to the level of 20 nurses per 1,000 inhabitants above the age of 75. They also propose the renovation of the *allocation compensatrice*, managed by COTOREP, into a generalised allocation for older persons, dependent on an age criterion of 60 years, the degree of dependency and the income situation.

Since 1992 several proposals have been made in parliament concerning some forms of allocation for dependency:

– in December 1992 a limited proposal was introduced and voted on at the *Assemblée Nationale* to change the *allocation compensatrice* into an *allocation autonomie dépendance*: a moderate amount of additional state financing would assure that a more equitable attribution of this allocation was realised, limiting the demand for social assistance. There were also

proposals for better coordination and multidisciplinary community services;
- in December 1992 another similar proposal was introduced in the Senate (but not voted on), concerning a dependency allocation, in cash or in kind, means-tested, with obligatory family support. The proposal intended to reinforce local coordination and family placement;
- in April 1993 a proposal was introduced to install a dependency fund that centralises several funds allocated to the care of older persons (federal, departmental, social security, pensions) and to install a dependency allocation based on the degree of dependency. The assessment of this dependency should be carried out by a medical commission;
- in April 1993 a proposition was again made to establish a dependency insurance system for persons 65 years of age and older, without means-testing and with a limited obligation for the family to help. The allocation would be granted on the basis of the degree of dependency, to be assessed by a medico-social team in terms of a nationally defined dependency scale. The allocation would be essentially in kind under the form of credits of home help, payment for informal care and equipment. A fund would be created in which the departmental funds are complemented with a contribution from the central government. Complementary to this proposal, initiatives have been announced concerning the regulation of dependency insurance contracts and the tarification of institutional care;

In 1995 (Gauthier, 1996) a PAPAD, 'prestation autonomie pour les personnes âgéés dépendantes' was tried out in 12 regions of France in the context of a national experiment for a kind of long-term care insurance. It is an example of how the debate in France is at the same time *lucides* but remains *temporiser et expérimenter* (Joël, 1995, p. 66).

The experiments comprise two allocations which can be combined:
- the already existing in-cash *allocation compensatrice* (between 2,027 and 4,054 FRF per month), allocated by the regions and for that reason also varying between regions;
- an additional dependency allowance, paid by the pension scheme of maximum 4,424.15 FRF per month. It is allocated according to the degree of dependency and an income test. It is recoverable from the family. The dependency is assessed by the ADL-scale AGGIR. The allowance is by preference in kind but can be in cash.

The first evaluations show that the amount is too low to compensate real dependent persons. On top of that the amounts risks to be taken up by the family as a compensation for their help, without any real additional creation of formal help (and jobs).

The results of the evaluation of this experiment are starting to become available:

- for 1997 a PSD, *prestation spécifiques dépendance*, was also announced;
- at the same time, new rules on the charges made by old-age homes were announced.

The debate remains stalled because of the economic situation, which does not allow increases in social contributions to create a real dependency insurance (why was it different in Germany?). At the same time there is a return to the role of the family, including the proposed systems elements of 'assistance' (recuperation on the family) and steps forward toward high standard new services are delayed because of strategies to create (low qualified) local jobs (*emplois de proximité*).

2.8   Finland

The highly developed welfare state is confronted with several forms of modernisation, without changing its nature. It remains a public and universal protection, with few incentives for additional private savings or insurance for those risks. The system is confronted with the results of a generous early exit system in active life that has to be turned round, by preference, by making it more attractive/possible to stay in the work place. There is some discussion about the fact that the present middle aged persons are the losing generation, and that the older and the future younger generations will benefit.

Despite the highly developed system there is a growing concern about quantitative undercoverage of community care provisions, especially because of unequal regional distribution of the services, among others in the regional variety.

The provision of services remains based on needs, with some indications of less eligibility for less dependent persons, introducing some form of means testing for less urgent services such as transportation. Policies are concentrated on reorienting institutional to community care, and improved selectivity or targeting for those services ('the right elderly on the right place'), creating, however, new forms of institutional care. The diminishing of institutional care (3,000 long-term beds disappeared) has not been completely compensated by increased community care. Even more, there is an increase level of charges in community care, and in institutional care too the charges allowed since 1993 are considered as high (80 per cent of income can be levied as a charge) leaving, in some instances, a very low level of, again, 'pocket money'. The result is a increased profile of this system of lower quality (too poorly qualified personnel), lower responsiveness to needs, lack of freedom to choose and unequal access. But even the affordability may be in some degree a problem: increased costs for community care may sometimes imply that not even a decent level of pocket money is available.

There is some debate on separating hotel, housing costs from medical and caring costs (opposite to the Netherlands), but no actions so far.

The financing of the system is organised by more funded systems, increased taxes and budgetary cuttings. There is no fundamental need for a new debate on the financing of care for the elderly and there is no debate on introducing any new dependency insurance systems in the country. What has been increased is the public discussion on the insufficient quality and quantity of elderly care, the former more regarding the institutional care, the latter regarding community care of the elderly.

2.9 *Ireland*

The Irish social protection system for older persons is based on three pillars: the pension system; the informal care system; and the existing formal care system. We give the major characteristics of the ongoing debate for them. A debate on the LTC-insurance emerges. Perhaps it can, as a fourth pillar bring the three first pillars into equilibrium.

The pension system, in general, provides, compared to other OECD countries, too low a replacement ratio on average but nevertheless revealing a picture of an older generation that is no longer a generation at risk. Public pensions are roughly only half of the income of pensions, but there is substantial additional private occupational pension income (one-quarter to one-fifth) and other social security income, so that there is little reliance on social assistance.

Most of the care is supported by the informal care system that is overburdened or at least providing a substantial share in the care for the elderly. Carers provide between four and seven hours each day, contributing substantially to the financing (not in cash but in kind, in time devoted to care) of the long-term care of the elderly. This seems, however, to be similar to other countries: in Flanders for instance care for a person in the community means, per week, an 'eight hour day' job for the professionals and a '40 hour a week' for the informal carer (Spinnewyn and Pacolet, 1986).

The professional caring system seems to be confronted with underprovision of community care: it is characterised by 'patchiness', with a shortage of basic (home care) and advanced (social and psychological needs) services. The core community care services are covered by general taxation sources.

The institutional care is financed in a similar way. Public long-stay beds are publicly financed, and for the private and voluntary nursing home sector, public subsidy schemes exist for those eligible on the basis of dependency and means (i.e. social assistance type). The free care system for public long-stay beds is, however, an illusion, since the institution retains almost all of their old-age pension: 'the institution receives the pension and then decides on the size of the allowance to be given to the elderly person'. On average this is 20 per cent of the gross income left for the elderly. It is a regressive financing system and certainly not very effective, since by those resources only 20 per cent of total cost of care is covered. The private places are even less subsidised by public sources, requiring higher contributions from the client (on average 10,720 ECU a year), which creates problems especially for the poorer elderly in regions where public long-term stay places are limited.

The substantial burden for the financing of long-term care is studied by the health insurance provider as well as by private insurance companies. Both are 'expressing *some* interest in offering *restricted* coverage for *some* client groups' (O'Shea, 1998, p. 31) (note the three limitations) by way of an additional insurance. A 1990 survey estimates that one in three people surveyed would welcome such a solution.

2.10 Italy

The Italian welfare state, as well as the state itself, is in an important period of transition. A reform of the welfare state was announced for the end of 1997, probably from a centralist, uncontrolled system to 'segmented solidarity', introducing aspects of decentralization, responsabilisation, privatization. The problems of a fragmented system, especially in health care, were, however, not overcome. They were, even before, linked to the high degree of decentralization.

The social security budgets are too much taken up with the fight against poverty, social assistance, unemployment problems and industrial change, so that the primary responsibility (pensions and health care) in view of the greying of the population, cannot be safeguarded. The system is permanently in financial distress, this within a context of huge budgetary problems (difficulties with meeting the convergence criteria of EMU), and will be confronted, however, after having the lowest birth rate from Europe for years, with this challenge. At the same time, the social security systems are not yet at the standards the population itself wants. What is the strategy for care of the dependent elderly?

Pension benefits will be improved, and become more of an insurance type (the longer you work, the higher your contribution, the higher the pension). Anomalies such as the 'baby-pensions' (very early retirement) will disappear gradually. The health care system has known changes in 1978, 1983, 1989 and 1992. An institutional and unsolved problem is the possible conflict between national policies and regional competencies. Another problem was from 1978 on, the conflict, or unclear distinction, between health (cure) and social (care) aspects. From 1983 on the local health boards (*unità sanitaria locale*) should provide health and social care (to the elderly also). In 1989 (dependent and chronically ill) elderly were supposed to enter institutions. They proved to be either unavailable or to have too little capacity (even in the family-oriented culture in Italy, a survey revealed that 6 to 8 per cent of the elderly above 65 wanted to have access to such an institution), or of bad quality.

The changes (a new decree) of that period also transferred health policy responsibilities to the social sector.

In 1992, as an answer to the problems of bad quality for the care of the elderly, the 'Progetto Obiettivo: Tutela della salute degli anziani' ('Project Objective: Protection of the health of the elderly') was launched, by both chambers of parliament (Senate and the *Camera*) to invite all (regional/local) authorities to improve the care system. This illustrates how several levels of competence can work together. The project proposes a global answer to the problem of chronically ill elderly, avoiding the elderly being pressed up against the health sector and inadequately equipped institutions or left completely to the family. The solution should also avoid falling back on charity or assistance. The proposed solutions were, however, of an experimental nature. It is not clear what the state of realization is. Some aspects are clearly expressed. There is a clear reference to medical aspects (strengthening of geriatric specialization, home hospitalization, creation of RSA (*Residenze Sanitarie Assistenziali*) a kind of nursing home the name of which illustrates the strategy of combining health (*sanitarie*) and social care (*assistenziali*) aspects.

The choice of community care is dominant however, due to family culture, but also because institutional care is too expensive (and of low quality). To support community care, an attendance allowance exists. Certain professional help is provided in an informal (black) way.

The state of social protection remains difficult to identify since part of the responsibilities are local (regional) and those authorities are not eager to provide the central level with adequate information. Part of the provision is also private, and less controlled, with an additional problem of data collection. Huge regional differences are obscured by this lack of data.

2.11   Luxembourg

After an in-depth preparatory study on dependency insurance in several other countries in 1992/93, the Luxembourg Christian-Democratic and Socialist government announced in 1994 the creation of te *assurance dépendance obligatoire*: a compulsory dependency insurance. The proposal was submitted to the parliament in October 1996 and was approved on 19 June 1998. An *assurance dépendance* started from 1 January 1999 on. The proposal is inspired by the German system. The public insurance scheme is based on the principle that this risk is both universal and substantial. It covers people of all ages. It will be organised within the social security system, without any means- or income-test.

The insurance scheme covers the costs created by increased dependency on third person help for the activities of daily life.

Four principles were the basis of this new law (similar to Germany): a) priority to reintegration and revalidation, also of the elderly (for instance by geriatric rehabilitation); b) priority to community care (implying equal benefits for institutional and community care and recognition of the informal carer); c) priority to in-kind benefits above in-cash benefits concretised by higher amounts for in-kind support; d) guarantee of continued care relations between provider and insurer and attention to coordinated care and quality control.

Dependency is based on four elements: a) physical and mental deficiencies '*causing*' need for help; b) the need for help is related to the activities of daily life (as well as with the personal as the instrumental activities); c) a minimal dependency is taken into account before becoming eligible; and d) a minimal period of need for regular support (irreversible need for help for six months). The dependency is assessed by a newly-created multidisciplinary 'evaluation and orientation team' whose the task is not only the assessment, but also some coordination in matching services with demand, coordination between providers, information of clients and providers and prevention. The assessment is done based on theADL-scale CTMSP developed in Canada and the team does not only assess the dependency but makes up a care plan that is 'indicative' (not obligatory) for the care providers and aims especially at prevention, community care and coordination of formal and informal care. We can wonder whether the criteria of irreversibility are not in contradiction with a strategy of prevention and readaptation.

The system is financed for 45 per cent of the expendi-tures by the state budget (equivalent to the already-used budget for the support of persons in need of help from third persons and the existing financing system for services for the elderly). These budgets are integrated in the new system. Further an additional (social) contribution of 1 per cent is levied on all incomes. It is a kind of social contribution because it is a flat rate one, but it has the characteristics of a tax because it is on all incomes. It is not deductible from taxable income and is very similar to the *contribution sociale généralisée* in France.

The new law defines the characteristics of the support system in residential and community care. Support is provided for in-kind help, in-cash help, for reimbursement of certain aid instruments and even for adaptation of the house and for the cost of moving on. The latter illustrates how housing enters the long-term care insurance.

The degree of dependency is based on an evaluation by an assessment service (*cellule d'évaluation et d'orientation*). This is a public service under the authority of the Minister of Social Affairs. Its role is not only to assess eligibility (degree of dependency and need of care), but also to advise on the care plan and eventual preventive measures of education and readaptation.

Dependency is related to the activities of daily life, as well the personal activities of daily life, as the instrumental activities. Besides personal care, the care plan indicates housekeeping activities, support and advice.

In case of community care for each of those activities of daily life, maxima are defined of the help that can be obtained:
- max. 24.5 hours help for personal activities of daily life;
- max. 4 hours help with housekeeping activities;
- max. 12 hours of support;
- on top of that, additional help for guiding and consulting is available and support for aid instruments, adaptation of the house and moving-on support.

The required help is weighted according to the kind of activities (for instance PADL-help is weighted with 1.0; support service with a weight of 0.25) (based on a detailed list of activities, needed time and needed qualifications of personnel). The budget available per hour (with a weight of 1.0) is 1,500 FLux or 38 ECU.[1] With this information, a total budget for needed support can be defined. This budget can be used according to the choice of the dependent person. Part of the budget (see hereafter) can be transformed into cash support (up to a maximum of 800 ECU/month); the rest can be used for the payment of services according to the discretion of the patient, but within the budget determined by the dependency.

When in-cash support is preferred, this is possible up to a time budget of seven hours plus 50 per cent of the hours between 7 and 14 hours professional help per week. In total this is a maximum of 10.5 hours per week. The payment

Table 5.3   Important characteristics of the new long-term care insurance in Luxembourg

	In cash	In kind	Combination
Community care			
Professional help	Support is determined on base of dependency and care plan	Support is determined on base of dependency and care plan related to dependency Maximum 40.5 hours per week weighted 0.24–1 amount per hour: 38 ECU Max. 24.5 hours PADL-help, 4 hours housekeeping, 12 hours support Budget: hours x 38 ECU x weights	
Informal help	Related to dependency Max. 7 + 50 per cent of 7 hours = 10.5 hours Remuneration: 50 per cent of 38 ECU/hour Max.: 800 ECU/month		In cash support can be combined with in kind support (budget less amount of in cash support)
Social insurance for main carer	Contributions paid by long-term care insurance, limited to minimum wage		
Guiding	Needed time		
Aid instruments		Fixed budgets	
Adaptation of the house		Fixed budgets for e.g.. alarm devices	
Moving on support			
Residential care		Fixed budget (maxima can be determined in the future) allocated to the residential services Amounts identical to community care Medical costs: for health insurance; hotels costs for elderly, family or assistance	

Source: Based on the law of Assurance Dépendance, Mémorial Journal officiel du Grand-Duché de Luxembourg (Recueil de législation, no. 48, 29 June 1998) and on gratefully acknowledged additional comments of N. Kerschen.

received for this support is 50 per cent of the hourly cost of 38 ECU of professional time. This gives a total maximum budget of 10.5 hours x 19 ECU x 4 weeks = 800 ECU/month (level from 1 January 1999). This amount is equivalent with the amount used for allowances for third persons providing help in the existing regulation (*allocation de soins* and *allocation pour personnes gravement handicapées).* For those receiving this support, they can choose between the old system, or the new long-term care insurance. When people already receive the old-age allowance and services, they have to choose the new long-term care insurance system that explicitly organises such mixed situations. The in-cash allowance is free from taxes and social security contributions. The long-term care insurance also pays the social security contribution for the minimum wage for those persons taking care of their family member at home.

In the case of residential care, the dependency is determined in a similar way as if the dependent person was at home. This budget becomes available for the residential service. The government *can* in the future determine a maximum amount paid for residential care, but in the first period the intention is to observe what the real needs and costs are. The payment of the nursing cost remains the responsibility of health insurance.

2.12 The Netherlands

The recent debate on the social protection of the elderly is situated within the traditional systems. Most of the discussion has concerned the pension system. In the spring of 1993, the Scientific Advice Council of the Dutch government began studying the problem of the pension system. Since a welfare-related pension system no longer seems to be a possibility for the future (which means that those who have contributed to this system will not receive what they hope to receive from it), the Council has advised either an increase of the social contributions by the active participants, or an increase of the premiums of those with a private pension from what they have saved in the past, or a raising of the pensionable age to 67. These and other choices remained to be made in 1994.

There have also been proposals for (private) pension savings, but the reaction of the government to such proposals has been rather negative: there is already a savings surplus in the economy.

The same undecided discussion is taking place on the relation between housing and care. The Netherlands has embarked on a strategy of de-institutionalisation because of the high level of institutionalisation. In 1990, 2.5 per cent of the aged lived in nursing homes, and 7.5 per cent in old-age homes. Forty per cent of the latter group of institutional care places have to be transformed into nursing homes; the rest should evolve in the direction of sheltered home facilities. This sector is meant to become an intermediate area between living independently and living in a nursing home. The living costs would be covered by the elderly themselves and the care costs by the Exceptional Medical Expenses Scheme.

In 1994 a Commission on 'Modernising the Care for the Elderly' studied especially the policy of maximal substitution and the relation between housing and care. Detailed studies discovered that there were too many people in institutions, implying sufficient nursing homes, an overcapacity of homes for the elderly, and about 112,000 elderly staying longer at home, requiring a rise of rent subsidies. A new borderline was drawn between elderly living in institutions, and belonging to the care sector, and elderly at home, belonging to the responsibility of public housing.

The division between old-age home (social sector) and nursing home (medical) therefore seems no longer relevant. With that long discussions came to an end. This change in regime was supported by changes in the Exceptional Medical Expenses Scheme. This scheme, introduced in 1962, was initially meant to cover long-term care for the whole population. The most recent changes in this system shift some medical expenditures to health insurance; but the scope is enlarged in institutional as well as community care; home help and district nursing too are financed by this scheme (facilitated, of course, by the merger of both types of providers) along the same principles of reimbursement. But in addition homes for the elderly and nursing homes are financed from 1 January 1997 (phasing in until 2002). This means a complete change for the homes, where before income and mean tests were applied and now the fee is only income-related.

In community care, finally, experiments with personal assistance budgets continue in an experimental way but have not been generalised. The growing to maturity of a system seems a long way away in health and elderly care.

A third issue that evolved in the 'Ouderen voor Ouderen' report is the financing of old-age care and the personnel needed for those services. Since increased needs, increased personnel requirements and increased wages imply higher financing costs, a larger share of GNP should be devoted to old-age care.

Remarkable, but is it to be attributed again to the author, is the recent interest in the Netherlands for integration, prevention of isolation, re-enforcement in decision-making (neither case-manager nor a third person budget-holder, but rather the elderly themselves can decide on their budget) participation. This policy was already proposed from 1990, but activated in a 1995–98 'Integrated Programme of Action'. This activation of the autonomy of the elderly is especially intended for the domain of care for the elderly.

2.13 Portugal

The country remains a younger country, even in the forthcoming decades. The relationship between active and inactive parts of the population remains the same (youngsters replaced by older persons, of course) but nevertheless there is a huge concern about the problem of the 'greying' of the population and the solidarity between generations. The general pension scheme does not provide a high level of social protection. For the majority of the population (general pension and agricultural workers) the pension income is below half of the minimum income. Only civil servants have a better pension (13 per cent of the elderly); the supplementary schemes are limited. Dichotomising according to low or high income does not make sense for the elderly: it is between the public sector and the rest, or between rural and urban areas. In theory, all services are available for the population, but the real use is limited. Health insurance is to a large extent free for the elderly. Social services are financed with some degree of co-insurance or out of pocket money, where the price setting or contribution is related to the (pension) income. The elderly are left with pocket money. The real take up of provisions of old-age homes or nursing homes are, however, limited. It is already difficult to assess if the system will stand higher levels of demand. This can occur because of changes in the socioeconomic environment. The previous generation of elderly took advantage of considerable solidarity of family and neighbours and income support in kind by means of their own produced goods. In the cities a substantial support of income might occur because there has been a rent stop for houses rented before 1990 or by the elderly, implying substantial support (especially after a period of inflation) for the income. In the last decade Portugal was confronted with migration to the cities, creating much less potential for solidarity both at home and in the cities. A very poignant contrast of solidarity is made by de Almeida describing the case of elderly in hospitals where it occurred that elderly were 'dropped in the urgency services of general hospitals by relatives, giving wrong addresses. They were abandoned' (de Almeida, Interim National Report, 1997, p. 30).

Institutional care for the elderly is underdeveloped: there are not enough places available (waiting lists), and indications of poor standards are that, for instance, in old-age homes there are still rooms of four to eight persons. Most of the formal care in communities or in institutions is provided by private institutions, on which limited statistical information is available. The figures provided in the country report refer mostly to the public sector (and is that a significant underestimation of the total sector?).

For the elderly at home there is an additional allowance for a third person's help (of 52 or 44 ECU), or an alternative taken up of in-kind services. It is augmented for the seriously dependent with an additional allowance. Also, the rent allowance is augmented for dependent persons. Community services, when provided, imply a significant part of the low pensions. They are said to be income-related, but it is not clear who pays for them.

The old-age homes and nursing homes (no distinction is warranted) are income related and 70 to 85 per cent of income can be paid to them, leaving the elderly only with pocket money. Special services for the demented hardly exist (with exception of mental hospitals).

Dependency, based on certain criteria of need for help, is defined by the local social worker.

2.14   Sweden

The Swedish welfare state system seems to have undergone a substantial qualitative and quantitative shock. The care system is said to be 'downsized to the level of the 1960s', implying, for instance, in the care system, cutbacks in services, increased fees and tightened eligibility. As a (late) response to increasing public complaints (the threat of an 'elderly party' was taken seriously), only in 1996 were new funds made available again for the local providers (municipalities), and the increased workforce of unemployed are re-channelled (active use of unemployment funds) to the care sector. Not only are there quantitative problems with the care system, but also the quality is not what is expected (again it is not clear if expectations are higher than in other countries). Especially because of the increase of own contributions, 'value for money' is expected. The Swedish system – as in Norway, based on public provision – is unregulated in terms of standards. A movement to determine the rights of the client is emerging, requiring this care system to change from performance-based on input, to performance-assessed on the basis of output and outcome.

Reform of the pension system will probably be delayed until after 2000. Insurance of the long-term care cost, for a long time not on the political agenda, has been introduced in this state-oriented Nordic country – contrary finally to Western Europe – essentially by the major insurance companies. A commission calculated the care gap for the year 2010 (two billion ECU by then) because of the greying of the population, keeping the same care level as in 1994. In 1997 these insurance companies started marketing private long-term care insurance. They assumed by that that there was a private market, and that public opinion (according to opinion polls) was prepared to consider private insurance. This seems the opposite to the public commitment to publicly financed systems in the other Nordic countries, but also Western Europe (but are opinion polls not answering what is asked?). Meanwhile the care gap is closed by proposals about increased taxes, increased cost-efficiency through intersectorial collaboration or a public/private or mixed long-term care insurance.

2.15 United Kingdom

The United Kingdom is characterised as being a typically need-based welfare system, where the priority is given to the in kind provision of needed services. Even the more recent far-reaching proposals for changing some aspects of the care go in this direction. The fact that private providers are subsidised for the creation and improvement of old-age homes may constitute a change in the ownership structure of the organisations, but there remains a significant public involvement (by means of supplementary benefits) in the financing. The same is expected for the health care system where free access is an even more fundamental achievement ('cornerstone of the welfare state' (Bond and Buck, 1998)). This is a universal free system, although private insurance is possible. It will, however, become more income-related, with charges for the users and possibilities of topping up have been introduced for those who can afford it. Social care is means-tested. The privatisation trend is especially to be noticed in the pension system, where there is an increasing number of private and occupational pension systems. This trend could already have emerged when in 1981 the de-indexing of the basic pension began, thus driving the state pension towards a minimal level. It is augmented with income maintenance benefits and state earnings-related pension schemes (SERPS). The former are means-tested, while for the latter there is a significant level of disinterest because people are 'opting out' of this system and moving into occupational and private pension schemes.

Although the ambition and actual policy of the UK leaves the social protection system intact, the reality – which is probably also due to the worsened economic situation – is an overall lower level of social protection than in other countries and a resulting need to pay additional attention to basic elements of living conditions that might not be problematic in other countries where the general income level is higher. Here we find a great interest in housing subsidies and other related expenditures such as heating costs. Just because home ownership increases slightly within the older groups of the population (in a country where the majority of people nevertheless remain tenants), does not mean that a magical majority of 'whoopies' has suddenly been created. This has remained a myth. In other aspects of the social protection system the pressure of budgetary constraints and a 'less state' policy is being felt. The lack of residential care that will, more and more, be only available for very frail elderly has been mentioned. Ethnic minorities can be special risk groups.

This leaves us with a reduced system of social security benefits and services, confronted with the increased needs of an increasingly disabled population of older persons. Although a majority of the population expect the state to provide the resources to finance the long-term care of frail older people, no public initiatives are being taken. There are, of course, the private initiatives, and these cover the complete range of private possibilities:

- personal pension plans (PPPs), including adaptation for long-term care needs;
- reversed mortgages to make use of housing wealth, or other systems for utilising personal capital for expenditures in later life;
- standard insurance policies, where disability is the risk insured.

Those solutions are relatively new so that their potential is unclear, but an assessment can be made based on foreign experience and theory. Private insurance will be available in the future for those who in the past have been able to afford the premiums. The use of personal wealth is an immediate solution but, once again, it is only available for those who have it. In a country where home ownership levels are among the lowest in Europe, it is remarkable that this wealth item is receiving so much attention within the context of the question of the financing of old-age care. In both systems the risk of ending up with 'two nations in old-age' remains (Titmuss, 1963, quoted by Bond and Buck, 1998).

2.16   Norway

There has been an intensive political debate on the implications of the ageing of the population, and its implications for general justice and equal distribution, also intergenerationally. The debate is concentrated on the pension system and services for the elderly.

In the pension scheme Norway also knows a 'cleavage' between policy makers, where left (because of less inequality) and right (because of less state) come to the same conclusion of a more flat-rate pension scheme (lower pensions, lower pension credit) while the citizen prefers the present scheme:

a continued statutory supplementary pension scheme. This scheme has been moderated and made more equal. A minor – but psychologically important for the dependency issue – improvement is the pension credit for informal care work since 1992. The pension age is high (67) but the real one is on average 61. To increase that age the 'revision of the welfare state' from 1996 stimulates the combination of work and pension. Tax deductions are installed for occupational pension schemes, allowing more inequality (and so a less ideological reaction towards non-mandatory solutions). The beneficial tax treatment for pensioners is proposed to be removed since the elderly seem wealthy enough, with the exception of some risk groups.

The debate on services has been as 'prominent', rising issues of volume, profile, quality, ownership, equality. By the definition of those services where 'medical an social services are ... integrated into a universal system, long-term care insurance is already included and not an issue for debate' (Daatland, 1998, p. 41), the complete scope of dependency insurance is covered and submitted to the same regime.

The expenditures are growing for those services, but certainly not only because of the demographic factor. Nevertheless there is the impression of 'volume and quality of care being too low'. Funds should be allocated to the more dependent, the frail elderly, concentrating on more curative, immediate care and personal ADL, leaving less room for prevention, rehabilitation, psychosocial support and I–ADL. Scarcity of public means lead to higher (but still limited) fees and especially in institutional care (old-age and nursing homes), three-quarters of the pension is used for the person's own contribution, however still covering only 10 to 20 per cent of total cost.

The shift towards informal care is illustrated by systems of payment for care, respite services. More efficiency is expected from the care system by creating an optimal supply mix and stimulation substitution. Deinstitution-alisation remains however low compared to Denmark, partly also because of moderate investment in home based services.

A 'White Paper on Quality of Care (1994)' aimed to promote the quality of the care system. This can be also promoted by installing an ombudsman for the elderly, which was proposed in 1990 but not accepted, and is further improved by the mandatory 'senior citizens councils' in each city from 1992 on. It could also be improved by a proposal of establishing national norms and standards to guarantee that basic needs are met and to guarantee equality among different regions. Government has recently promised single rooms for all clients in institutional care during a five year period (today one-third lives in double rooms) implying an investment which amounts to approximately an increase of 25 per cent of present costs for institutional care. Standards, implying more intensive care, have risen at the expense of less access, making eligibility more selective, based on proper assessment. Regulation was rather weak in this country, probably because government intervention was organised by own provision, previously leaving less room for norms and standards.

The growing scarcity of resources provokes the emergence of a private sector, but privatisation mostly occurs only by means of contracting out of services, especially for practical care (home help, meals), but to a growing extent also for medical care. Public opinion remains, however, in favour of public provision.

Following political and financing reforms between 1985 and 1990, services have increasingly been integrated at the local government (municipal) level. Earlier earmarked service by service state subsidies are replaced by general block grants and local decision within these limits. There were similar reforms in Denmark in the 1970s and in Sweden and Finland in the early 1990s. Total costs are then more closely monitored by the state. The integration of services has improved the service mix and profile. Municipalities do, however, have scarce resources and rationalisation in general hospitals (county responsibility) push patients on to municipalities. Municipalities are responding to scarcity by more selectivity in provision by a change in balance from institutional care to housing and community care and by increasing user fees. Also, private service provision (contracting out) is growing, and increasingly the public are concentrating responsibility to care, while housing (bed/breakfast) and practical help is taken as a personal/family responsibility.

Although there seems to be no need for a debate and an political initiative on financing long-term care for dependent elderly, the existing systems does not perform well: social and health services are integrated at local level, but are financed by general block grants instead of earmarked funds. By this global funding, substitution is improved, but the financing is 'too low and unfairly distributed'. And the included cost is not the total cost: clear distinction is made between housing and care, the first being financed privately, the latter publicly. This welfare system seems to fall back on the more primary aspects of social protection.

3 Main Characteristics of the Political Discussion on Present and Future Old-age Protection

3.1 Context of Changing Welfare States

See Table 5.4.

3.2 Changing Needs

In all of the countries taken into account in this overview, changes are evident in the care of the elderly. These changes are aimed mainly at diminishing the financing problems by substituting more expensive care with cheaper care models (home care), or by integrating informal care. Despite these efforts, the total costs have continued to increase due to the increasing need for care.

Table 5.5   Changing needs in the social protection system: summary

Income	Increasing importance of private pensions, though in many countries these are reminiscent of the old principles of social insurance
Housing	Quality standards are rising, but are prohibitively expensive for most private individuals
Hotel cost	Higher co-payment
Cost of care	Limitation to basic personal care needs
Cost of cure	Increasing medicalisation of services
Informal care	Reaching its limits; increasing requests for remuneration
Legal rights	First initiatives are emerging

In Tables 5.6–5.9 these changes are illustrated for each country separately and in general terms.

Most problematic is the increasing medicalisation of the services, which implies, for example, increases in the direct cost for nursing staff.[2] This trend can be observed in France; it is also the main reason that Germany has been considering establishing an old-age insurance system, and it is a distinct and rapidly developing trend in Belgium, where the cost of old-age services is one of the most rapidly increasing elements in the health insurance system. Some groups are even not fully covered by this care (the self-employed).

In some countries there is a clear strategy aimed at upgrading the quality of housing for older persons. In Denmark, this is to a large extent being financed collectively. In Flanders, programmes for better housing (service flats) have been initiated, but they have become unaffordable for most of the older population. In the Netherlands there is also renewed attention being given

Table 5.4   Political-socioeconomic context of the discussion on dependency insurance

	A	B	DK	D	F	GR	IRL	I	S	NL	P	UK	N
1 Purchasing power available (self insurance possible)											x	x[1]	
2 Decline of the welfare state							x	x	x		x		
3 Demographic pressure increasing and impact of dependency		x	x		x	x		x		x	x		
4 Privatisation in insurance									x		x	x	x
Privatisation in provision									x		x		
5 Macroeconomic perspectives getting worse													
6 Towards informal care					x					x			
7 Older persons have become relatively more affluent: higher degree of co-insurance possible													
8 Selective social protection or increased means-testing											x		
9 Others											x[2]		

Notes

1   At least this is the impression of the government.
2   The risk of rupture (bankruptcy) of the social security system.

(1993) to the relationship between housing and care.

The evolution towards community and informal care, and the means of supporting these forms of care, have become the objects of intense scientific and public scrutiny. There are legislative aspects to the issue of protecting certain rights of the main carer within the family. There are minimum support systems for the volunteers. On the basis of the principle of nondiscrimination between people who rely on formal care and those who rely on informal care, reimbursement for the informal care is being demanded. Such a system could be organised by giving the dependent elderly in-cash payments so that he/she can buy the care he/she wants. Such a scheme could take the form of a voucher system, as suggested in Belgium.

It is worth noting that the trend towards payment for informal care has developed most extensively in the Scandinavian countries, probably because in these societies the need for compensation for the opportunity cost has been clearest due to the high level of female labour market participation. But even here, although there is a tradition of paying informal carers, there are in fact very few of them relative to the numbers of professional care providers (and unpaid family care) (Daatland, 1998). The carers are mostly female, and therefore some people are against such payment for care because it might force women into this role. A point worth noting in the study of Evers et al. (1994) is that there is a similar trend in the USA towards giving priority to payment for care, so that here, for once, we find the public- (Europe) and privately-oriented (USA) systems moving in the same direction.

In most countries, discussions about the nature of care for the elderly and the best ways to organise it can be observed. Should it be social or health care? Should it be provided in-kind or in-cash? The *Report of the European Observatory* (Walker, Alber and Guillemard, 1993) gives a good summary of the discussion concerning whether social or health care should be provided. A clear (institutional) distinction has been made between the two. In the Netherlands, where there is a tendency towards more integration, it remains less clear. In Belgium the situation is ambiguous. Health and social services are separated and are financed at different levels. However, a lot of the care that is dispensed combines health and social services, so that there is a need for coordination of the organisation of health and social care, but the question as to whether this ought to be done at the national or regional level remains unanswered. In France the same distinction occurs, and it is called 'sterile'. In Ireland a comprehensive system is advocated. In Finland there is a strong trend towards integrated care systems, and special programmes at the regional and local levels have been launched to attain or promote this goal. There is a joint Ministry of Health and Social Affairs in that country and about 20 per cent of the Finnish municipalities have integrated even their welfare and health boards. In most municipalities, however, the integration takes the form of functional collaboration and coordination between the welfare and the health authorities in the planning and provision of care.

The above-mentioned discussion relates to shifts either from income support to services, or else back to more income support.

There are also shifts in the dimension of social insurance versus social assistance. When social protection becomes means-tested, there is a shift towards welfare assistance. In many countries, there has been a call for a dependency insurance to avoid the trap of social assistance. There is a shifting from social security towards (sometimes) more locally organised services. For several aspects, there is a trend towards more privatisation in a number of ways: private markets are discovering the possibility of insuring new risks; private initiatives are being taken to mobilise the capital of the elderly so that it can be used for reimbursing the care; and private initiatives are being taken to organise new services for the elderly. The commercial sector is discovering the potential of a growing group of older persons with (in some cases) growing purchasing power.

We describe below some of the common trends (or the lack of a common trend) more in detail.

In chapter 1 we schematised a matrix of income and care components, including the systems that provide them. The above-mentioned discussion relates to shifts in the vertical dimension: from income support to services, or back to more income support.

There are also shifts in the horizontal dimension of the first matrix. When social protection becomes means-tested, there is a shift towards welfare assistance. There is a shifting from social security towards (sometimes) more locally organised services. For several aspects, there is a trend towards more privatisation in a number of ways: private markets are discovering the possibility of insuring new risks, private initiatives are being taken to mobilise the equity of the elderly so that it can be used for reimbursing the care, and private initiatives are being taken to organise new services for the elderly. The commercial sector is discovering the potential of a growing group of older persons with (in some cases) a growing purchasing power.

Hereafter we describe some of the common trends (or the lack of a common trend) more in detail.

Table 5.6   Changes in the more Bismarck-oriented systems of social protection

	B	F	D	L	A
Income		'Solvabilisation' of large groups of older persons			Reform characterised by conservation of principles of social insurance
Housing	Rising standards (service flat) but unaffordable: 1/3 receives support for residential care from social assistance	Upgrading quality, especially private institutions; widespread rent subsidy exists (±450,000 elderly)			
Hotel cost	Increasing co-financing				
Cost of care		Underprovision of residential and community care	Limited group has coverage, for others social assistance was required before the *Pflegeversicherung* (70 per cent in old 'Länder', 100 per cent in new 'Länder')	Fragmented financing system, services oriented	
Cost of cure	Harmonisation of fixed medical rates intended for old-age homes and nursing homes	Increasing medicalisation of services, whose increasing costs are not being met			
Informal care	Requests for social scheme Propositions for payment for care New law on managing funds of the elderly	Several proposals for payments in cash and change of existing systems			
Legal rights					
Others	Increased attention for quality aspects	Dependency is recognised as a major social risk requiring a general solution			

Table 5.7   Changes in the more Beveridge oriented systems of social protection

	UK	NL	IRL
Income	Pension mix not sufficient to guarantee decent pensions Bad experience with private pension saving	Increasing importance of occupational or individual pensions	Need for comprehensive coverage of housing, income and care ('talk broadly, finance narrowly')
Housing	Privatisation (voluntary sector) of old-age homes or private old-age homes is subsidised Increasing ownership among pensioners, but houses of poor quality	Rising number of owners but still large amount of people receiving rent subsidy. Discussion on housing and care	
Hotel cost			
Cost of care	Included in 'topping up'		Need for coverage of home help, long-term residential care
Cost of cure	Increasing age rationing		Need to enlarge to paramedical care
Informal care	'Community care is care by the community' Regional, local differentiation growing; discretionary assessment	Attempt to substitute professional care by informal care	
Legal rights			Need for explicit financial support (recognition)
Others			Payments in cash could empower the elderly; now supply driven demand

Table 5.8   Changes in the Nordic systems of social protection

	S	DK	FIN	N
Income	Modernising pension system postponed	Increase of after-tax income from 1994 on High and continued early retirement, although intentions to change it	Current system is widely accepted	Proposal to return to more flat rate pensions, but without much support from public opinion Incentives to work until official pension age (67) Reduction of tax credits for pensions
Housing		Important programmes of upgrading housing standards Rent subsidies for elderly reduced from 1997 on (the proposal has not been implemented, but it is still the intention of the government)	Increasing new forms of service housing for the elderly. Advocating the idea that the general housing policy should dictate the design of housing and housing areas so that they better fit the needs of the elderly residents as well	Housing covered privately; services publicly; but: new subsidies for improvement of nursing homes and services housing Relatively expensive: 3/4 of income needed to pay 10 to 15 per cent of actual cost of residential care
Hotel cost			Some discussion about separating hotel costs from care costs in the residential care forms	
Cost of care	Emerging 'care-gap' around 2010 (all else equal) Sweden is dropping back to the level of the 1960s Municipalities are looking for new resources	Prioritising personal care instead of help with housework	There is a common objective to use the resources available as economically as possible to ensure sufficient care for the elderly	Medical and social aspects already integrated in existing LTC complaints about shortages, bad quality and regional inequalities
Cost of cure		Medicalisation of services in new housing for elderly is necessarily (but nursing home places have been substituted by special dwellings)	Same concerns of efficient use of the resources are mentioned Some discussion about prioritisation of cure expenditures according to the diseases Some claims for age discrimination, but no research evidence to back them up	
Informal care	Systems exist		Various efforts to support carer at home, such as home care allowance with support services and experiments with vouchers in organising support of informal carers	

Table 5.8 cont'd

	S	DK	FIN	N
Legal rights	Deteriorating quality of care	Better possibility of appeal. More influence for the elderly in nursing homes by means of the board of residents	The current framework legislation widely accepted; new legislation implemented on clients' rights	
Others	Concern about service inefficiency (no value for money – not doing the right things)	A general sense that there are shortages (of institutional places, of household help)	Quality of care: efforts and programmes to improve quality of care in health and social services	Selectivity: standards raised at the expense of access

Table 5.9   Changes in the systems of social protection in Mediterranean countries

	GR	P	E	I
Income	Low pensions despite high replacement ratio; high risk of poverty (80 per cent of private pensions are below the poverty line)	Average low income for the retired. The need to increase the importance of the 3rd pillar	Sustain viability of pension scheme Social pensions are being increased for dependency	Relatively high number of persons receiving pensions (including the so-called 'baby pensions'); high difference in replacement rates as well as declining value; shift towards a more earnings-related pension, topped up with a second pillar pension
Housing		To increase the quality and capacity of the elderly housing schemes		
Hotel cost Cost of care	Low level supply of residential and community care	Social services are means-tested	Dependency is considered as exceptional. Lack of coordination between health and social system	
Cost of cure	Increased user charges for health care (sometimes illegally), although in principle it is 'free of charge'	Low, but a long time lag to satisfy medical needs		
Informal care		Need to increase home help services	Is the main care system, far much more important than professional care, changing rapidly because of increased labour market participation of women	
Legal rights Others		Better protection for the elderly a) Need to increase family solidarity to support the elderly and to extend it to neighbours and the local community b) Need to avoid the social and cultural uprooting of the elderly (migration to urban regions has caused decline of solidarity network) c) Substantial regional differences in supply and take-up of services	Special situation of many older persons in urban areas Institutional debate about federal and regional competences	

3.3   Covered Costs

Both a narrow and a broader definition can be used when referring to dependency. The narrow definition is limited to functional, physical and mental criteria; the wider definition includes physical, mental, economic and social aspects. The evolution in the actual debate in the EU seems to be in favour of the wider definition. What are the basic needs to be covered? The systems of social protection for the elderly are not evolving in each country in the same direction, and certainly not always in a manner consistent with historical 'determinism'. We summarise this in Table 5.10.

In the countries where there has been some recent concern about the limits of the welfare state, there is a tendency to reduce coverage to the more primary needs (medical, P-ADL and not I-ADL), to the exclusion of housing and hotel costs and the reduction of quality of care while cutting on advanced services of integration and rehabilitation. This is also evident in the debate in the Nordic countries, for example about covering housing costs, despite the fact that they are coming from a high level. Some may wonder why the complaints about quantity and quality of care are present in so many reports in these countries. Perhaps this feeling is based on comparisons with how things were earlier and with the ideal situation, which implies that it is partly a crisis of expectations, and partly also a crisis of resources, as quantity (access) is reduced, albeit from a rather high level (comment by Daatland, 1998). The debate on what the welfare state should provide and the issue of affordability has been on the agenda for more than 15 years in the Netherlands (e.g. the debate on the 'Dutch disease'), but the new evidence gives the impression here that once again a wider (more generous, inclusive) definition of the needs to be covered by social protection is being used.

The debate in the much less developed Bismarckian-type welfare state (compared to the Nordic model) is pending, however, due to broad definitions of the cost of care (cure, personal care, housing and even paid informal care) and the public coverage of these elements.

3.4   Others

An isssue for further analysis is the direction of change between two periods – will there be a decrease or increase or an improvement in the coverage? Any answer could be related to the notion of a social Europe guaranteeing a point of no return to a lower level of (social) protection, at least as long as economies are growing richer.

Table 5.10   Components of the covered costs of dependency: recent trends

Member state	Costs included
A	Inclusion of all extra costs in additional allowance (services, diets, housing, heating)
B	Narrow definition: public responsibility especially for medicalised costs, but again enlarging its coverage.
DK	Trend to prioritise help for P-ADL over I-ADL
D	Relatively broad definition (medical, social, informal)
GR	
E	Additional support for informal care
FIN	A broad definition covering social and medical care, and housing, as well as economic risks and informal care to some degree, though there is an emerging debate about unbundling financing
F	Preference for a global approach, but in reality: housing/hotel for the elderly, social care at the local level, and medical care via health insurance
IRL	Preference for comprehensive system
I	Health and social care combined; attendance allowance (no special reference to housing)
L	Relatively broad definition
NL	Definition again growing broader (covering social care, housing and medical costs)
P	Attendance allowance, supplementary subsidies for housing (and rent control), free health care, social care with contributions by the person him/herself: broad scope but low level of provision.
S	
UK	Preference for free health and social services; growing fear on the part of the individual of depletion of his/her own resources
(N)	Despite global (local) funding and organisation, attempts to narrow the definition

4   Institutional Arrangements for Long-term (Old Age) Care Within (or Beyond?) the Existing Systems of Social Protection

In the Netherlands a great deal of attention is being paid to substituting more expensive care with cheaper care, but most of the needs are nonetheless being covered. This has become a reality since in 1980 the Exceptional Medical

Expenses Insurance Scheme (AWBZ) guaranteed the financing of most of the long-term care. As a consequence of this, there are no explicit new proposals for dependency insurance. The more general proposals for reform of the health care sector are intended to cover medical care, residential care, district nursing and home care. What is new, is that (similar to the UK reform) insurance companies and service providers are signing contracts for the delivery of care and they are having to compete. This should result in better quality and lower costs – or at least this is what is hoped for.[3]

In Denmark, which is already characterised by a high level of social provision of care for the elderly, there is also no discussion about additional protection in terms of long-term care for the elderly. Most of the long-term care is available to the population at a price that is highly subsidised by public funds, yet is organised at local level. The same is the case for Finland. In Denmark, additional attention is being given to the housing component.

Although there are countries where, at present, no explicit proposals for dependency insurance exist, this does not mean that there is no discussion taking place about the financing of long-term care or that there are no problems.

France and Germany have been – and continue to be – clearly confronted with underinsurance and have chosen to provide additional systems. The German system is oriented towards financing additional services, although with the *Pflegeversicherung* it has also become open for support of informal care and in-cash support. The French initiatives are often oriented towards providing additional income. This was the first choice, but after some new experiments, it has also resulted in some preference for services. The Austrian case could also be oriented to more care in-kind for the elderly, although it is a *Pflegegeld*.

The Belgian situation is far from clear. In the mid-1990s there were a number of insurance proposals, as well as some experimental forms of social insurance by the health insurance organisations ('sickness funds'), some private insurance initiatives, and some marginal support initiatives by local authorities. Later there were some proposals to create an insurance system either through a public insurance company or to organise it explicitly at the federal level. This has been announced in the present governmental declaration. Also at the regional level (Flemish region), proposals exist to improve the financing of services (the supply). However, other schemes have been proposed for more explicit long-term care insurance to be provided by the health insurance organisations (and possibly also by private insurers), with contributions subsidised by the government. There has also been some popular discussion or preference for in-cash (vouchers, *cheque de service*) systems of dependency insurance. The latest proposals of the federal and Flemish government are returning to better financing of regular services. The 'in-between' situation of Belgium is probably due to the reasonably well-developed social protection system already in place, which, if retained, will limit the need for additional insurance. Further improvements have been observed during recent years: 25,000 old-age home places have been converted into better (publicly) financed rest and nursing home places; in 1998 the health insurance enlarged its coverage of costs for chronically ill persons. Along these lines, Belgium could achieve an implicit long-term care insurance within the existing health insurance system.

In some countries (Ireland for instance), the point is being emphasised that giving money to the patient would 'empower' him or her, and therefore this system should be adopted. Others (such as in Belgium and the UK) recommend that means-testing should be avoided, since this results in using up the only wealth people have (and want to leave their heirs), because having a certain amount of wealth sometimes gives people a certain (sense of) empowerment.

In the other countries, the (expressed) need for additional insurance seems even more limited. In the UK, even in recent reforms, attention is being focused on the provision of required care in-kind. Additional support is being provided for housing aspects, and for the main carer a system of 'attendance allowance' is provided. However, in this same country a discrepancy between the cost of care and the available pension continues to exist. About 56 per cent in additional support is needed to pay for residential care (OECD, 1996). The reforms that have been proposed in the UK are oriented towards the organisation of the health sector: it remains nationally financed, but competition in the provision of services is being looked for at the local level. Contracts between the health insurers (who assess the need) and the care providers are being proposed. The UK system has retained a lot of in-kind aid, which makes it almost an example of a Beveridge-type system. However, in recent years there are indications of a growing 'care gap' (Walker, 1993, p. 48).

5   Summary of the Debate

5.1   Introduction

The European Year of the Elderly in 1993 created in the Member States of the EU a momentum of increased interest in the role of older citizens of the EU

Table 5.11   Explicit proposals (or existing systems) relating to dependency insurance systems

	B (proposals)	D (existing)	F (experiments?)
Initiative	Minister of Social Affairs Several proposals by social organisations New proposals in Flemish government	Minister of Labour	Several commissions, parliamentary initiatives Current experiments a) compensating allowance for help from third persons b) supplementary allowance c) specify dependency allowance (replaces partly a) from 1997)
Coverage	Most are new type of in cash allowance covering additional cost New proposals in Flanders refer back to services, but also a completely new, partly funded system	Nursing care at home and residential care Social rights of main carer in cash and in kind	First preference for 'In-cash aid 'prestation dependance'; now tendency to in-kind; can also be used for payment of informal care
Population (1995)	10,131,000	81,539,000	58,038,000 (1994)
Total +65 (in %)	1.550.003 (15.8 per cent)	9,677.709 (West) (15.4 per cent)	7,942,000 (14.7 per cent)
Eligible persons (in thousands)	90 to 220	1,650	271 to 321 For a) 210 elderly +65
Estimated budget (in billions of national currency)	10 to 20 BEF	25.8 DM	
Financing	0.15 to 0.3 per cent of GDP	1.7 per cent of income of active and retired persons	a) general budget b) social assistance should become social security
Private alternatives	Existing but limited until now, growing number of private long-term care insurance products	Are part of the scheme for those with private health insurance	Exists, but with limited success

Table 5.11 cont'd

	L (existing)	A (existing)	NL (existing)
Initiative	Government (Law of 19 June 1998 on 'assurance dépendance')	Federal government completing existing regional initiatives	Government (Exceptional Medical Expenses scheme)
Coverage	Regroups a number of existing, fragmented financing mechanisms. Covers from 1.1.1999 on institutional care, formal and informal care in the community; priority for in-kind (part of in kind support can be transformed to in cash help)	Cash allowance transferable (increased political support) to in-kind institutional and community care. Since installation, fees for services have increased substantially	
Population (1995)	385,000 (1991)	8,053,000	15,382,000 (1994)
Total +65 (in %)	14.3 (1991)	(13.1)	(13.1)
Eligible persons (in thousands)	Total dependent population	Dependent population above age of 2 years; (334) 7 categories based on care (number of hours) required	– Everyone resident in the Netherlands – Everyone subject to Dutch income tax legislation
Estimated budget (in billions of national currency) Financing	1) state budget: 45 per cent of total expenditures; 2) a 'special contribution' levied on the electricity sector (contribution of the firms) 3) additional (special) contribution of the individuals ('contribution dépendance') on total income (labour income, replacement income and revenues on assets); fixed yearly (for 1999 on 1 per cent)	Taxes; Increased (federal) allowance is compensated by increased fees or reduced local financing	Contributions paid by employers and the self-employed
Private alternatives		Are emerging as providers (since attendance allowance can be used to pay them)	

Table 5.12   Implicit solutions for dependency insurance

	UK	IRL (proposals)
Coverage	Included in NHS and National Assistance Act Underinsurance of residential and community care	Health insurance covers medical care and residential care Should be enlarged to a comprehensive insurance
Population (1995) Total +65 (in per cent)	57,808,000 (1991) (15.8)	3,571,000 (1994) (11.5)
Eligible persons (in thousands)		
Estimated budget		
Financing		
Private or public alternatives	Increasing supply to younger people (personal pension plan, reversed mortgages, dependency insurance) (Partial) Equity Release schemes National Care Insurance Scheme proposed by Joseph Rowntree Foundation (1.5 per cent of earnings)	

Table 5.13   Implicit solutions for dependency insurance in the Nordic countries

	DK	FIN	S	N
Initiative	Public Health Insurance Act Increasing financing of care facilities in dwellings	Included in Social Welfare Act, Primary Health Care Act, Act on Specialised Health Care and Act for Services and Assistance for Disabled Persons	Debate on LTC not started seriously	Long-term care included in existing protection, but pressure for additional funds (in 1990: +1 billion NOK) Medical and social is already integrated
Coverage			'Care gap' diagnosed in 1996 (all else equal) In January 1997, 10 billion SK for 'service, care and schools' and strategy to use employment schemes to support care system	
Population (1995)	5,251,027 (1996)	5,116,826 (1995)	8,816,000 (1994)	4,369,957 (1996)
Total +65 (in %)	(15.1)	(14.3)	(17.4)	(15.9)
Eligible persons (in thousands)		732,417		
Estimated budget (in billions of national currency)				
Financing	Taxes			
Private alternatives		There is potential interest Could be allowed in top segment Should be more important as providers, to improve competition	From 1997, private insurance started marketing LTC insurance Some contracting out	Some private proposals are emerging Contracting out for service provision

Table 5.14 Implicit solutions or no debate relating to dependency insurance systems in the Mediterranean countries

	GR	P	E	I
Initiative	Improvement of services under way, for instance, in Open Care Centres for the Elderly (KAPI) No explicit proposals for dependency insurance	No explicit proposals	Since dependency is not considered to be a major risk, no proposals have been put forward Political and scientific support for improvement of existing system and doubts that explicit new schemes are realistic Plans of INSERSO, 1996, for improving allowances for caring families, increased pensions for dependent elderly (exists for some), support for caring families, improvement of community and residential services	Improved pension system (preference for two 'pillars') Ambitious project (started in 1992) on 'Protection of the elderly', mobilising all policy levels No explicit proposals, but welfare state is evolving in the direction of more selectivity
Coverage Population (1995)	10,368,000 (1993)	9,927,000	38,662,000 (1994)	57,140,000
Total +65 (in %) (in thousands)	(14.8)	(14.8)	(14.8)	(16.5)
Eligible persons			Eligible for increased pensions: 825	
Estimated budget (in billions of national currency)				
Financing			Could be limited when restructuring existing resources	
Private alternatives			Almost nonexistent in insurance, but mentioned especially as providers	

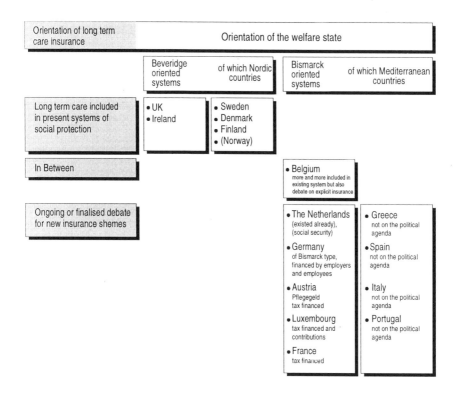

Scheme 5.1 Relation between type of the social protection and type of the long-term care insurance

and an awareness of the challenge that the greying of the population created for the existing systems of social protection. It created at the same time great expectations in the Member States to maintain or complete high standard systems of social protection for the elderly. The growing share of very dependent older persons in particular concerned many groups. It is in this context that in 1993 in six countries of the EU a research project was organised on the level of social protection for the needs of dependent elderly and that we now update this research for the first group and generalise it to the other Member States. The update shows that substantial changes can occur in the Member States. The enlargement of the study allows us to verify whether the observed changes are similar in the rest of the EU, since the first report was concentrated on the core region.

5.2   Present Situation of Social Protection of the Elderly and Discussion for Change: An Overview of the Main Characteristics of Each Country

Austria (A) Some form of long-term care insurance (in the form of *Pflegegeld*) has existed since 1 July 1993 at the federal level. This guarantees an additional income related to the degree of dependency; it is mostly paid for by the pension scheme and is defined as payment for care. It can also be used, however, to pay for additional services (community or even residential). The regions (*Länder*) have agreed to improve the supply side for these services.

Belgium (B) After a period of status quo in the debate on long-term care insurance because of budgetary and institutional considerations, recently (mid-1997, beginning 1998) new regional initiatives have been announced. In the meantime, several step-by-step adaptations of existing (federal) financing systems are taking place and can accommodate most of the financial problems: installation of 'social franchise' (limit on co-insurance for chronically ill); increased number of old-age homes converted to rest and nursing home beds with better financing conditions from health insurance; proposal for a better (legal) statute of the main informal carers; substantial enlargement of the staffing of health and elderly services after new action by the trade unions (asking more than 70,000 new jobs in the social and health sector of about 280,000 persons); improvement of protection of chronically ill persons in health insurance; and increased financing of services at regional level. The Flemish government is formulating explicit proposals on a long-term care insurance.

Germany (D) The introduction of long-term care insurance (*Pflegeversicherung*) on 1 January 1995 for community care and on 1 July 1996 for residential care as a fifth 'pillar' of social security, and structured according to the same principles of financing and universality. The financing is based on solidarity among the total population (including pensioners) and the principle that prevention and rehabilitation come before nursing care, and that home care comes before institutional/residential care. Support for the development of supply – and especially of infrastructure – remains the responsibility of the regions (*Länder*). (A large-scale programme for upgrading the quality in the new *Länder* has been launched). There is ongoing debate regarding the level of the benefits, still leading to recurrence of social assistance. There are also discussions on the borderline between long-term care insurance and health care insurance and insurance for the handicapped. The formula of in-cash help in the community care field has met with unexpected success. Substantial job creation (more than 70,000 jobs) has occurred. The financial situation due to large solidarity is under control (expenditures will only increase to 2.5 per cent of wages in 2030), but even from the start, additional financing is limited (due to the reduction of expenditures for social assistance, one paid holiday in exchange for employers contribution).

Denmark (DK) Discussion on the future financing of pensions and raising the retirement age; attempt to improve the quality of housing and home services for the elderly, including the introduction of rights to complain, a better national financing, and even privatisation.

Spain (E) The debate on the viability of the pension system, together with a debate on the health insurance resulted in the confirmation of the universalistic coverage. There are indications that the care system for dependent older persons, until recently relying on the informal carer, is insufficient. Up till now this has not led to a general demand for dependency insurance. The National *Plan Gerontológico* seems to propose a selective dependency insurance system covering most of the traditional care services, though with an optimistic view of the overall cost (by regrouping resources).

France (F) Several propositions for long-term care insurance are under consideration, though no final and substantial choice has yet been made. These propositions are a response to long-term discussion and to increased social expectations. Sector reorganisation and job creation are expected from voucher-like systems of long-term care insurance.

Meanwhile, the quantitative and qualitative deficiencies remain clear. These include the lack of professional help available, without limiting the autonomy of the elderly. Proposals exist involving several systems of social security, as well as involving the reform/creation of existing and new systems of dependency allowances at national or regional level. Discussion continues as to whether this support should be recoverable from the family, and whether the support should by preference be in-kind.

On 18 December 1996 new (but transitory?) legislation was adopted on a long- term care insurance system (*Prestation spécifique dépendance*) organised at the regional (*Département*) level. It is income-tested, dependency and care-plan related (with a proper assessment), recoverable from inheritance, oriented to community and residential care, though without any clear additional financing. One of the advantages will probably also be the stimulation of more coordination in the sector.

Italy (I) Debate has concentrated on reforming the pension system and moving it more in the direction of a funded, income-related, mixed system. Health care is mixed responsibility of national and regional authorities causing some problems. The reform of care for the dependent elderly should be a combination of health care and social aspects.

Ireland (IRL) The reform proposals under discussion are based on the principles of a holistic and comprehensive approach, with priority given to community care, public financing and private competitive services. The public financing, however, is of a front-end character (long-term care limited to one year), to be supplemented with private insurance.

Greece (GR) Despite the high replacement ratio and the high level of expenditure on pensions, there is high level of poverty amongst the elderly. Despite the free access to health care, there is an increasing incidence of (often illegal) additional patient payments. There is a low level of residential services, and an emerging system of community care.

Luxembourg (L) Concrete plan for introducing a public long-term care insurance system structured along the lines of the German scheme (law accepted on 19 June 1998).

Netherlands (NL) After several reforms of the health insurance system, new definition and task divisions have been drawn up for health insurance and the system for exceptional medical expenses. The latter was originally meant to be long-term care insurance. It includes both health and care components, as well as housing aspects. Organisational reforms are bringing together social and medical disciplines in a common provider, under a common system of regulation, thus illustrating that the borderline is becoming less and less clear.

Portugal (P) The (to a large extent private) sector of elderly care, especially residential, is underdeveloped and, if available, it is very costly to the elderly. For the majority, pensions for the elderly are low (with exception of civil servants). Some income support comes from rent subsidies and even rent control. The dependent elderly can obtain additional rent subsidies, attendance allowances or in-kind help.

United Kingdom (UK) There is ongoing debate on the reform of the state pensions and additional private or occupational pensions; this is resulting in a convergence of both political opinions to create a mixed system. There is conflict between the universal NHS solution and the income-/means-tested personal social services solution for long-term care. The first seems to have the support of public opinion and this may result in a final choice for a continuation of the existing systems of free (health) care. A Royal Commission on Long Term Care was installed in 1998.

Finland (FIN) There is debate both on the quantitative and on the qualitative levels of the care system. There is emerging support for more rehabilitation and freedom of choice, but also for more co-payment. Special attention is being given to housing for the elderly. There is a general need to reshuffle the supply in the care system towards more community based services; (for instance, there are still long-term beds in hospitals and the residential care is expensive for the elderly because their income is reduced to pocket money).

Sweden (S) The care system has undergone a substantial qualitative and quantitative shock having been 'downsized to the level of the 1960s' (which can also be seen in health expenditures, see above), and this has created widespread discontent with the availability and quality of services (no good quality standards), and the fear of an even larger care gap by the year 2010. The threats of a newly emerging party of the elderly changed the policy in 1996. In the meantime, 'privatisation by default' has occurred in the long-term care insurance: this failing public system has resulted in the emergence of a market for private long-term care insurance, offered by the major insurance companies from 1997 onward and welcomed by public opinion. In contrast to many other Member States of the EU, this state-oriented system most clearly welcomed a private insurance solution.

Norway (N) There has been debate on the pension scheme (ambitions to raise pension age) and on the quantity and quality of health and social services. The complete scope of dependency is insured, but limited resources, which are causing the welfare state to become more selective (for instance, less housing costs covered, basic care first), is challenging all aspects.

5.3ʾ   Common Tendencies in the European Project

The exceptional German solution of traditional social insurance has spread to several countries which are either close to realising a long-term care insurance system (Luxembourg, Austria) or have at least initiated the debate that went on for more than 20 years in Germany (France, Belgium). This finalisation of the social protection system is concentrated in the Bismarck-oriented welfare states of the core regions. In the Nordic countries and the Netherlands, an all-inclusive protection system seems to exist already. In the southern part of Europe this is not the case. Some parts of the care system, especially those related to social services (institutional and community care), are provided to a lesser extent, even in relation to the demand in those countries. More or less the same picture is evident in Portugal, Greece, Italy and Spain. There is a low level of provision for residential and community care. This is probably influenced by cultural factors such as the priority being given to staying at home and the preference for care by the family. This factor explains why the topic of expansion of these services came late on the agenda. The explicit choice of the population is not clear because there are complaints about availability, quality, accessibility and affordability. Confronted with the problem of budgetary deficits, it is not clear if new systems of social protection can be introduced in the years to come. Spain has a more explicit interest in this problem, already starting with the debate on the gerontological plan. It has long gone unrecognised as an explicit new risk, so that no explicit new plan was estimated as being realistic. It has only recently been accepted that pensions and health care should be covered universally, but it is considered too early to create a new scheme for long-term care. It should be possible within the existing resources, concentrating on even more support for informal care.

We also do not have a conclusive picture for the Scandinavian countries. However, again the first information confirms a trend towards further upgrading of the social protection, at the local as well as the federal level. The reference to rehabilitation and activation announces an even further improvement. In Germany also, the reference to rehabilitation is strongly present. In this reading of what is happening in each country, we are far from the threat of trading-off care for the elderly with other social expenditures. Nonetheless, the image of a highly developed, advanced and generous welfare state is not always confirmed.

There are some other aspects worth noting which indicate the substainability of these systems: broad definitions of needs are used to define dependency and long-term care. The real nature of this risk is not purely medical, but also includes other kinds of care and housing. For this reason, the distinction between social and health aspects is becoming less and less clear and there is a tendency to include other aspects. Of course this is not a general rule. In some countries there is a reduction of public money available for housing aspects. In other, the continued support for rent subsidy and (social) housing exists, (once again sometimes because policy-makers realise that substantial problems remain or can be caused by measures in other fields).

After years of hesitation, previous institutional, regulatory and professional barriers are being abandoned. The real nature of long-term care needs is broader than the purely medical, and this fact is eroding the barriers between previously existing operators. The need is both for medical and social care. But the risk is the same: in total high and continued expenditures. The potential for efficiency gains in this 'multi-product setting' on the supply side has to be further promoted, because at the same time there is a gain in quality (e.g. the need for a coordinated service) from the demand side. The dichotomies between housing and care and between medical and social services that have been made for years is being replaced by combined supply and organisational structures; this leads to the same rules of financing being applied to all services.

In several systems, both ongoing and new support of formal care are supplemented by the recognition of informal care. In principle, this is accomplished by improving the legal rights of the informal carer, and even by installing systems of payment for care. There is also more focus on aiming for better quality care, implying that there is dissatisfaction with the present level of quality. A certain empowerment of the elderly can contribute to improving quality. However, this optimistic view is hampered by the possible fear that there is a strategy behind it of substituting more expensive formal care by less expensive informal care. The contradiction for this is that in the German and Luxembourg care insurance systems, the government is prepared to pay twice as much for in-kind aid as for in-cash help. Nevertheless, in Germany there has been a substantial preference for in-cash support. In Austria, the introduction of *Pflegegeld* (more purchasing power) created higher prices for the services. In Flanders, for example, there is a discussion as to whether the government should stimulate supply or demand. In France, (and this is similar to the debate on *services de proximité*), there is the belief that creating purchasing power at the level of the client creates its own supply. In Germany, there was a substantial increase in the number of providers after the creation of the *Pflegeversicherung*. This created an additional 70,000 jobs. In France, the new allocation promises coverage of new services without additional funding. But even the German case shows that a new insurance scheme is not a guarantee for new money (or additional costs), since a large part was recovered from other expenditures.

The stagnation in the development of the welfare state seems not to be confirmed by the first conclusions of this debate 'on the social protection of the dependent elderly', because it is indeed one of the rare fields in which expansion is taking place. However, this does not mean that the welfare state is not shrinking in other fields. A further confirmation of this reassuring observation is that in many countries the situation of the elderly during the past decade has been improving relatively more than for the population as a whole. But in many other countries – and this needs to be either confirmed or refuted – the creation of new care insurance systems for dependent elderly people has been delayed because of budgetary constraints, or is not even on the agenda. The fact that the development of such systems in other countries has sometimes required an 'incubation' period of decades can provide us with some comfort.

Notes

1   A probably maximalistic example: a person might receive: a) 24.5 hours PADL-help x 1 x 38 ECU = 931 ECU; b) four hours housekeeping x 0.4 x 38 ECU = 61 ECU; c) 12 hours support x 0.25 x 38 ECU = 114 ECU; total = 1,106 ECU/week or 4,424 ECU/month.
2   Problematic, for instance, in the UK and Germany (mentioned in reports of the Observatory).
3   The problems in the American health care system constitute a good example of the opposite result.

6 Some Theoretical and Policy Conclusions

1 The Place of Social Insurance

Our study has been focused on social protection, which at the current time is mostly of a public nature. Alternative proposals have been made, however, and some private initiatives are either already in existence or are emerging. The explicit solutions in Germany, France, Belgium, Luxembourg and Austria are of a public character. Certain theoretical arguments are required to justify this public solution in a period of privatisation. Some of these trends can be interpreted by comparing them with the conclusions of a study on financing long-term care in the USA. There, the same theoretical arguments are used to contend that a larger public involvement is needed in health and old-age care. This is, in fact, the direction of the present health care reform movement in the USA. Although aspects of privatisation are visible in most countries, the question is being raised as to how widespread the phenomenon is. As is suggested by our picture of the level of public involvement in this social sector, the *private* level is so low that 'there is no place to go but up', as was suggested in a study on care for the elderly in the USA (Rivlin and Wiener, 1988). As far as the formal sector of care for the elderly is concerned, it is not clear whether there is an increasing amount of private organisation nowadays, since the government is also involved in many new initiatives. The private informal sector (and we should not forget that even this sector is inspired by the same kind of altruism that also inspires the public initiatives), is being stimulated everywhere, but there is an increasing awareness that this sector is complementary to and supported by a significant formal sector. The limits of this support are becoming clear, and there is even emerging doubt as to whether we should go any further in this direction.

There are obvious limits to the trend towards personal responsibility. In countries such as Germany, Belgium and France, the fact is already being stressed that the cost of certain services is too high for some pensioners and that they risk having to fall back on a system of public assistance (with the danger of losing all their private resources before they can call upon public help). This can also occur when services become too selective, so that the criteria for admission are too strict or there is means testing. Depending on the income situation, greater co-insurance could be a way of making the services more selective and 'skimming' the purchasing power (as an alternative to progressive taxes). The consequence of making those services too selective, however, will be that the higher income groups – which are often also more assertive users (both as consumers and as an influence group at the political level) – will leave the public system of services and choose the private system (Barr, Glennerster and Le Grand, 1989, p. 6).[1] The public sector would thus lose possible public interest, both as a policy forum and in terms of individual consumers. The risk is of a further degeneration of the public sector, which could lead to the development of a dual care system of high quality but expensive private care and lower quality – though not necessarily lower cost – public care. (In macroeconomic terms this is the case, for example, with health care in the USA, where a larger proportion of the GNP is required for a lower degree of protection for the total population, in comparison with systems where there is a higher level of public provision of services (see Rivlin and Wiener, 1988; Barr, 1987).) Public services and social security become public assistance and welfare services. In the USA this has been called the great contradiction in the current health insurance system, where a large part of the population is underinsured. When such a risk exists, Rivlin and Wiener conclude that there is room for a general, compulsory insurance, preferably included in the social security system.

Another risk associated with less state involvement in this sector is under-consumption by certain groups. Some form of co-insurance can to a certain extent, prevent over-consumption, which is conceivable in view of the increasing overall growth of welfare. But the risk of under-provision also exists. The impossibility of paying a decent living wage to employees in the sector, or of compensating for the often difficult working conditions, or of preventing people from leaving the sector, results in labour shortages.

How large will the relative shares of private and public provision of services be? This depends of course on the type of sector and on the definition of the services. One can again quote the American study in which the future share of the private/public provision of care for the disabled elderly is estimated. The public alternatives studied range from an enlarged welfare system, on the one hand, to public insurance, on the other. It is interesting that the authors support the latter strategy.

This approach would provide near-universal coverage for the elderly and would explicitly recognise that using long-term care is a normal, insurable risk associated with growing old. Everyone should contribute to public long-term care insurance and earn the right to needed benefits without having to prove impoverishment (Rivlin and Wiener, 1988, p. 26). It is this broadest definition of solidarity that is used in the German *Pflegeversicheringe*, to which the total population is contributing (active employees and pensioners).

Another private solution could involve a private insurance scheme to cover the cost of old age care. In several countries, systems of individual retirement accounts have been introduced following the example of the USA. Individual insurance for care of the elderly is also currently being considered. In the USA, the Individual Medical Account and Long-Term Care Insurance have been studied, but for a number of reasons have not remained viable options (ibid., pp. 109–22). Interest in the issue is limited (due to the short-sightedness of the future elderly population), except when it is stimulated by fiscal instruments. Furthermore, it is not possible to insure against inflation and future technical progress when considering the higher care opportunities. Another problem is that not everybody has the purchasing power to buy this insurance (high premiums only payable with higher income). Thus for some groups it is conceivable, but the present lack of interest on the part of the insurance companies for this product proves that it is technically difficult to organise. Even private insurers are not interested because they cannot secure the cost of increasing demand in the future. Other risks, from the viewpoint of the elderly, are that private insurance will either restrict costs and thus diminish quality, or else it will move in the direction of adverse selection.

The conclusion was that even in a much less government-oriented system such as the American one, the private share of long-term care for the elderly can only increase to something like 10 per cent to 15 per cent of total expenditures, even assuming there would be tax subsidies for it. The overall macroeconomic cost of this public provision of long-term care for the elderly is also limited, since it is concentrated on a limited part of the total population.

Rivlin and Wiener calculated that this cost is bearable; the present burden should increase from 1.6 per cent to 2.94 per cent of GNP, assuming all the anticipated increases in care. Similar figures in the European countries have been the subject of discussion. Again, the first evaluative report on the German long-term care insurance system concludes that the costs of the system are under control and will only rise from 1.7 per cent (and this is already not at all completely new money) of income to 2.4 per cent in 2030 (Bundesministeriums für Arbeit, 12.1997).

Table 6.1   Trend towards private solutions

	Situation of the care system		Trend towards private solutions		
	Health	**Social**	**Private funded**	**Private insurance**	**Private provision**
A	Pflege				Growing
B	Mixed	Mixed		Now proposed	Important
DK	Public health act				
D	Pflege			Exists	Growing
GR					
E					
FIN	Primary health care			Emerging	Mentioned
F	Mixed			Limited	
IRL	Health insurance			Limited	
I					
L					
NL	Exceptional medical expenses				Important
P					
S				Starting	
UK	in NHS			Proposed	
N					

Note: see also chapter 4, Table 4.3 – Characteristics of the care system at micro level.

2   The Social Protection Systems Have Reached Maturity

The social protection systems are sometimes contested in several countries; at the moment they are coming to maturity and have to prove their superiority. They might not even have the chance to prove they are a superior efficiency device (Barr, 1987). 'Superiority' for us has to be defined in terms of outcome. The domestic objectives of economic welfare policy are growth of income, equity, full employment and price stability. This needs to be translated into the objectives of social protection. This objective can be the avoidance and solving the problem of poverty, but it is also aimed at health and pension systems of a high level.

These are normative systems. The motives behind them, the history and the present organisation can all be different, but they all have reached the point of compulsory collective insurance and financing. The risks are becoming clearer only now, in this ageing 'process'. The risks of health care, long-term care and pensions are the major part (two-thirds) of social expenditure and are largely determined by age. In a recent publication on the 'social quality of Europe', several contributors came to the conclusion that economic growth is compatible with social protection (Beck, van der Maesen and Walker, 1997). This was in line with the conclusions of the European conference in early 1997 in the Netherlands on 'Social Policy and Economic Performance' (Dutch Ministry of Social Affairs and Employment, 1997). The social protection of the elderly in many countries has also continued to follow this pattern of evolution. The standards and quality levels are determined not only by economic factors but also by political choices: these systems can be developed either to meet a basic, minimal standard or else to measure up to the standards of the evolution of economic welfare. There are indications that they are continuing to follow the latter path.

This continued support for the development of the social protection of existing and new needs (here the needs of dependent older persons) is probably explained by the implicit knowledge of the policy makers about the compatibility of the welfare state with economic development. This point was made more explicitly at the European level in the Dutch Presidency Conference 'Social Policy and Economic Performance: employment, activating the welfare state and economic competitiveness'.

There should be an even more explicit realisation that developed welfare states with high levels of formal services and caring personnel have created jobs in these health and social services, and, by definition, have created added value in these sectors, as well as economic growth in general. This explains once again why there need not be any incompatibility between economic development and social protection. This has been the case explicitly in the Nordic countries; it offers a huge opportunity for creating new services in the Mediterranean countries.

There is a convergence between Bismarck-oriented and Beveridge-oriented systems of social protection. This is probably due in part to the fact that the terms themselves are becoming less clear. When we refer to Beveridge-oriented systems we think of tax financed, flat-rate, basic (though not always), universal (total population), and sometimes also income or means-tested, state managed, and with some preference for in-kind help. When we refer to Bismarck-oriented systems we think of contributions-financed, with explicit social insurance, universal but limited to those contributing, social partners governed, with some preference for in-cash support, and related to previous income (insurance). With so many dimensions it is easy to understand that no clear classification of the countries is possible. For this reason we use the term 'oriented'. These systems can differ in scope, financing and coverage, but the differences are not essential in economic terms, although they might be in political or institutional terms. The link to wages is not only a financing aspect, but is essential for identifying social insurance schemes and distinguishing them from tax financed assistance schemes. Whenever tax financed universal schemes refer to basic protection, they risk letting the various levels of protection be reduced to a minimal level, thus creating room for supplementary private solutions (in pensions and health care). The financing scheme cannot substantially change the burden of financing as long as new resources are not tapped, and national income is to a large extent only composed of capital and labour income. The financing cannot change the so-called 'burden' on added value. Sometimes health and family allowances or even basic pensions are discarded from labour. But in practice they, and other subsystems, remain interchangeable. Housing benefits, rent subsidies and so on are traded off against pension entitlements. Also for this reason, financing or even formula (in-cash or in-kind) does not matter, and universal treatment should be favoured. Not only new, but also traditional care systems have resisted the need for savings in public spending, but they have also continued to be developed, especially for the elderly. The same can be said for the pension and health care systems.

3   Conclusions for the EU Project

Social protection for the elderly is less uniform than might have been expected at first sight. Income support and services for the elderly include a wide spectrum of protection systems that can change the relative circumstances of dependent elderly people in each country. The relevant points in this context include not only the perennial protection systems, such as pensions, health insurance and traditional services, but also additional income support, housing benefits and tax spending.

Only scattered, fragmented information about this protection and the budgets involved are available. And the exact amount of resources that society spends to sustain this solidarity with older people is not known. At the same time, this means that there is no clear evidence that indicates whether the system is being driven towards more or less social protection.

Information concerning the needs of older people is also sparse. No standardised intelligence-gathering system, such as the one utilised for the labour market, is available for investigating the dependency and needs of older people.

In this survey we have tried to throw some more light on the services that are available. As case studies show, there are sharp differences between the social protection systems in the countries under consideration. Most of the systems are now being improved. However, the changes that are being made tend to focus more on diversification, innovation and experimentation with new forms of care, rather than on the provision of extra public resources and the quantitative spread of the available systems. This tendency can be observed in all countries, but especially in those countries where there used to be universal coverage. The trend towards diversification is indicative of the highly developed welfare state systems we have been examining, though the opposite tendency – towards cutting public spending – is illustrative of the overall trend towards 'less state'. When it comes to services for the elderly and long-term care needs, the trend runs counter to the demographic trend and the purchasing power of (at least) the oldest generations (whose needs for care are the greatest). For this reason, in a lot of countries there is at the same time a trend towards quantitative enlargement, better paid systems (e.g. in Germany and Belgium), more care with medical help provided (for instance France), and better housing and care for the elderly (Denmark, the Netherlands). Increased demand for social assistance to cover these needs has been noted in several countries. New proposals are being floated in many countries with a view to introducing a system of social insurance for long-term care. There is clearly a need for these sorts of proposals, even though they are being given political expression at an awkward time. It is in countries with Bismarck-type social protection where explicit proposals are more frequently being introduced. In welfare states where the Beveridge model is applied, no need seems to be felt for explicit supplementary insurance schemes. The policies in the latter countries tend to favour even more selectivity and conditionally. In the country where this model emerged – the UK – there is a general feeling of unacceptable rationing, so there is sure to be a debate on wider social protection systems to cover the risk of old age.

Under the terms of the subsidiarity principle adopted by the EU, social security matters are generally the responsibility of the Member States. This EU survey proposes not only harmonising the public social security systems, but evening out the various public support systems for the elderly as well. Retirement benefits, free in-kind services, or repayments of costs and additional incomes – are many variations on the same established theme of public protection or social security coverage. The fact that the needs of the elderly and the circumstances in which they find themselves vary to such an extent, is indicative of an urgent need for a more routine examination of the institutional factors and the real-life implications at the European level. This multiplicity will probably continue as the group becomes larger, the duality within it more open and the selectivity or conditionality of services more general. There is no doubt a willingness to achieve clear-cut, universal and nondiscriminatory systems, but the lack of clear information in all areas, the trend towards innovation and the creation of new institutions will produce further complexity and a risk of discrimination.

This report on social protection for dependent elderly persons proves that, to a large extent, the policy for elderly care returns the discussion of the problems to where it belongs: within the context of the debate over the established social security systems.

There will always be new needs and new care systems, but the vast majority of all these dependency needs can be reduced to the normal social security needs: the need for income and the need for health and other (social) services, which to a large extent are triggered by medical aspects and in many countries assessed by a medical or a multi-disciplinary team. The best way to develop a dependency insurance for these old age risks is not to create a new system, but rather to consolidate and/or upgrade the existing systems.

In a lot of EU countries, as well as in other OECD countries, there is an ongoing debate concerning the financing of the long-term care of dependent elderly persons. This debate is in fact a debate on the sustainability of the social security system. 'La prise en charge des personnes âgées dépendantes', 'Die Soziale Sicherung bei Pflegebedürftigkeit': these are all concerned with the increasing cost of these services due to increasing dependency and the nonexistence of a separate insurance system, or even the trend to exclude some of these costs, (which exists in countries such as the UK and Belgium).

For example, upon examining the Belgian discussion in more detail, the conclusion could be drawn that there is no substantial need for a dependency insurance when the existing social security system continues to provide this care. This system will have the difficult task of covering the existing risks with a reasonable level of quality. Given the budgetary problems, the creation of new systems would be even more difficult. This is illustrated by the fact that the new system would have to take over important budgets from the existing system, thus creating no additional protection.

In several other countries, similar trends can be observed. When examining the German proposal in more detail, we see that to a large extent it is aimed at covering medical help, which in other countries is better covered by social security. It also tries to utilise parts of the existing systems. In France, the Schopflin Commission concluded in any case that the *prise en charge* should consolidate the present system of financing mechanisms and organisations involved. The new allowance (the *prestation spécifique dépendance*) can be criticised because it wants to guarantee additional protection without generating additional money, and in some cases social protection is even reduced (Joël, 1998). The official Belgian proposal utilises significant parts of existing systems and there is limited space for new protection.

It is clear that when discussions are taking place in several different countries about old-age insurance, the context in each case may be completely different. In some countries the discussion brings to light a partial under-development of the social protection system and in other countries it relates to a further expansion of the system, while in still other countries it may reveal a trend towards substituting existing forms of social protection by private insurance. This implies that the solutions can also differ from country to country, being oriented either towards more in-cash or more in-kind aid, and towards more private or more public structures.

In the discussion concerning old-age care insurance, it might not surprise us that we are looking for solutions within the existing systems. We must not forget that this debate is certainly intermingled with the debate on private versus social solutions, on systems based on repartition versus funded systems, and on protection in-cash versus protection in-kind. The proposals also involve the all-important discussion of how to pay for informal care, (in fact, the financing of home labour). Do we make the systems universal (related only to dependency), or do we also take the elderly person's resources into account? In other words, do these systems become means-tested or not? Almost none of the new emerging systems refers to means or even income, except in France, where eligibility is conditional on income and benefits are recovered from inheritance. In all the other cases it is not used. Which care model we want to promote is also one of the decisions that must be made. These elements are important in terms of putting the previous observations into perspective. They are essential for the social protection of the elderly, a burden that is probably destined to consume a significant share of our national wealth. The choice we make regarding the social protection of the dependent elderly must lie in the same direction as the choice we make regarding health and old age.

The social protection of the elderly, sometimes envisioned in the new systems, aims at dealing with the same risks that were initially targeted in the traditional subsystems of, for example, health insurance. These 'new' risks are the result of the traditional risks maturing over time. However, other rules are suddenly being used. The planned systems are excluding the risks of the older persons, although it was precisely for these risks that they were initially created. Aspects that were unthinkable in the social security system, (such as means-testing and first using the person's own resources), are now sometimes being proposed, especially when the care of the elderly is under discussion. There is no reason why social protection for the elderly should be organised differently than social protection for the rest of the population. The creation of new insurance based on age involves the risk of creating new forms of discrimination based on age. The way in which the nature of social protection runs the risk of being changed is an example of implicit or explicit age discrimination of a very structural and far-reaching kind. This also is an argument – and politically speaking, perhaps even the best argument – for keeping old-age insurance within the existing universal systems of social security. This equal treatment is the best guarantee for the social integration and re-emancipation of the elderly. It is a solid foundation for autonomy instead of dependency.

Until now, the evolution towards privatisation (in many definitions) of social protection of care for the elderly has been limited, demonstrating a common sense of maintaining the present form of social protection. The European debate on the competitive power of this system supports these observations. This result is not universal or generic. In more market-oriented systems of social protection, such as the USA and Australia, the emergence of funded and private systems has been larger (Institute of Actuaries of Australia, 1997). Solutions such as reversed mortgages and using wealth (why not pension capital?) to buy insurance against the risk of dependency is, for some, an attractive financial innovation. The use of these new financial products is being stimulated by financial institutions looking for new markets. The 'baby-boomers' still have 15 years before they retire, and another 15 years before they become severely dependent (Holland, 1997). This is, by definition, a huge market (three decades for the largest cohorts) for the banking and insurance industry. Previously, the lack of competition in these industries ensured that they did not enter this market. The increasing competition, stimulated by the internal market of the EU and globalisation, and the overcapacity in these industries will speed up this process. The solution of overcapacity in one business might be the privatisation of social protection. However, this situation does not emerge from our comparison of the systems of social protection of the elderly in the European Union.

The political debate is still focused on the traditional principles of the social protection systems that until now have proved their viability. These principles are:

- long-term care is included in social expenditures, or, more precisely health insurance, organised in the same way as the rest of social protection system;
- especially in the Bismarck-oriented system, a certain willingness (though not absolute commitment) is present to define a new 'pillar' for long-term care;
- broad definitions of the risk to be covered are maintained, since there is an increasingly unclear borderline between social services and health;
- prioritising in-kind provision, or at least not rendering it unaffordable; (for example, Germany has double the amount of resources available for in-kind help as are available for the in-cash insurance scheme);
- very often (though to a varying degree) including housing costs in the covered risk;
- enlargement of the welfare state by (supplementary) systems of payment for care or support for informal care;
- resistance to including income testing in social assistance systems or to placing too much emphasis on it, and retaining a preference for social security schemes. There is less willingness to apply the rules of calling on the family to help with financial costs, the depletion of the person's own resources, and the recovery of costs from the inheritance;
- almost no presence of funded systems. Most of the solutions are pay-as-you-go publicly financed (or social security) systems. Some countries have chosen funded pension systems, but the 'funded' solution is almost totally absent in the practical European debate on long-term care;
- after a period of rationalisation in health care expenditures there is again an expansionary trend in expenditure, while services for the elderly continue to grow in variety and availability. This happened during a period when the European Union began a process of budgetary discipline in the context of Monetary Union. A further development of the social Europe seems to be compatible with this.

This generally positive conclusion does not prevent us from paying attention to problems of under-protection, deteriorating quality and uncovered needs, or to the fact that the social protection system is falling behind the rest of the economy. Although the positive picture is based on facts and figures at this moment in time, it can also change, as illustrated above. For this reason, these phenomena will have to be closely monitored.

Note

1   Their conclusion is: 'All tax relief for private medical insurance, including that which currently exists, should be dropped' (ibid., p. 7). This argument resembles the position of a large mutual health insurance organisation in Belgium (Christelijke Mutualiteiten) which was not in favour of great selectivity and any private re-insurance of the existing personal contributions of the patient.

ANNEXES

Annex 1 List of Institutions of National Correspondents

Austria
Kai Leichsenring
Europäisches Zentrum für Wohlfahrtspolitik und
Sozialforschung

Belgium
Jozef Pacolet, Hilde Lanoye, Ria Bouten
HIVA-Higher Institute of Labour Studies
Katholieke Universiteit Leuven

Denmark
Eigil Boll Hansen
AKF, Institute of Local Government Studies

Finland
Vappu Taipale/Marja Vaarama/Mikko Kautto
STAKES
National Research and Development Centre for Welfare
and Health

France
Marie-Eve Joël
LEGOS Université Paris-Dauphine

Germany
Bernd Schulte
Max-Planck-Institut für Ausländisches und
Internationales Sozialrecht

Greece
John Yfantopoulos
Athens University of Economics and Business
Department of International and European Economic
Studies

Ireland	Eamon O'Shea University College Galway Department of Economics
Italy	Francesco Belletti/Harmke Keen CISF – International Center for Family Studies
Luxembourg	Nicole Kerschen Ministère de la Sécurité Sociale
The Netherlands	Norma Schuijt-Lucassen/Kees Knipscheer Free University Amsterdam Faculteit SCW Vakgroep Sociologie
Norway	Svein Olav Daatland NOVA – Norwegian Social Research
Portugal	Manuel de Almeida/J. Manuel Nazareth Universidade Nova de Lisboa Faculdade de Ciências Sociais e Humanas
Spain	Gregorio Rodriguez Cabrero Professor Sociology Universidad Alcala Universidad de Alcalá Facultad de Ciencias Económicas y empresariales Departamento de Fundamentos de Económia e Historia Económica
Sweden	Lennarth Johansson Socialstyrelsen (The National Board of Health and Welfare)
United Kingdom	John Bond University of Newcastle Upon Tyne Centre for Health Services Research

Annex 2 List of Invited Experts for Consultation on the Project

Austria

Christoph Badelt
Vienna University of Economics and Business
Administration
Social Policy Unit

Belgium

Xavier Leroy
Service d'études socio-économiques de la Santé
Université Catholique de Louvain

Denmark

Georg Gottschalk
Statens Byggeforskningsinstitut (SBI)
Danish Building Research Institute

Finland

Simo Koskinen
Associate Professor
University of Lapland

France

Hannelore Jani-Le Bris
Director of Research
CLEIRPPA – Centre de Liaison, d'Etude, d'Information
et de Recherche sur les Problèmes des Personnes Agées

Germany

Roland Eisen
Johann Wolfgang Goethe-Universität Frankfurt am
Main
Institut für Konjunktur, Wachstum und Verteilung

Greece	Panos Tsakloglou Athens University of Economics and Business Department of International and European Economic Studies
Ireland	Freda Donoghue Policy Research Centre National College of Industrial Relations
Italy	M. Ferrera University of Pavia Department of Political Studies
Luxembourg	Andrée Kerger Centre d'Etudes de Population, de Pauvreté et de Politiques Socio-Economiques (CEPS)
The Netherlands	Theo Miltenburg Instituut voor Toegepaste Sociale Wetenschappen ITS
Norway	Kari Wærness University of Bergen Institute of Sociology
Portugal	A. Bruto Da Costa Universidade Catolica Portuguesa Faculdade de Ciencias Humanas
Spain	–
Sweden	Mats Thorslund Stockholm University Department of Social Work
United Kingdom	A. Walker University of Sheffield Department of Sociological Studies

Annex 3 Exchange Rates used in the Report

	ECU
BEF	39.3307
NLG	2.1395
DEM	1.9089
GBP	0.8162
DKK	7.3612
FRF	6.5196
ITL	1,926.6899
IEP	0.7877
GRD	304.0009
ESP	160.9559
PTE	195.3670
ATS	13.4331
NOK	8.1932
SEK	8,5089
FIM	5.7771

Source: 'Geld- en valutamarkt', *De Financieel-Economische Tijd*, 11 September 1996.

Bibliography[1]

Alber, J. (1993), *Social and Economic Policies and Older People in Germany*, Konstanz.

Badelt, C., Holzmann, A., Matul, C. and Österle, A. (1995), *Kosten der Pflegesicherung*, Bohlau, Wien.

Badelt, C., Holzmann, A., Matul, C., Österle, A. and Czegka, B. (1997), *Analyse der Auswirkungen des Pflegevorsorgesystems, Bündesministeriums für Arbeit, Gesundheit und Soziales*, Wien.

Barr, N. (1987), 'The Welfare State as an Efficiency Device', *Welfare State Programme*, No. 22 (October), STICERD, London.

Barr, N. (1996), 'The Economics of the Welfare State', *Welfare State Programme 'Alternatives to Fundholding'*, No. 123.

Barr, N., Glennester, H. and Le Grand, J. (1989), 'Working for Patients? The Right Approach?', *Welfare State Programme*, No. 40 (February), STICERD, London.

Beck, W., van der Maesen, L. and Walker, A. (eds) (1997), *The Social Quality of Europe*, Kluwer Law International, Den Haag.

Besseling, P.J. and Zeeuw, R.F. (November 1993), *The Financing of Pensions in Europe: Challenges and Opportunities*, Onderzoeksmemorandum, No. 111, Centraal Planbureau, 's-Gravenhage.

Bogaert, G. and De Prins, P. (1996), *Dagprijsverschillen in de rustoordsector*, HIVA, Leuven.

Bouchet, M., De Doncker, H. and Timmermans, T. (1997), 'Het belang van de pensioenfondsen en levensverzekeringen in het spaarwezen en het pensioenstelsel in België', *Bank- en Financiewezen*, No. 8, Vol. 61 (October), pp. 548–55.

Bouten, R. and Pacolet, J. (forthcoming), *Pensioenen en pensioenfondsen*, HIVA, Leuven.

Bundesministeriums für Arbeit und Sozialordnung (1997), *Erster Bericht des Bundesministeriums für Arbeit und Sozialordnung gemäss § 10 Abs*, 4 SGB XI, 9 December 1997.

Commission of the European Communities (1998), *Social Protection in Europe 1997*, Report from the Commission, Brussels.

Council of Europe (1995), *Ageing and social protection*, Council of Europe, Strasbourg.

Council of Europe (1995), *6th Conference of European Ministers responsible for social security. Dependence and social security. Memorandum submitted by ILO*, Council of Europe, Strasbourg.

Council of Europe (1995a), *6th Conference of European Ministers responsible for social security. Dependence and social security. Memorandum submitted by OECD*, Council of Europe, Strasbourg.

Council of Europe (1995b), *6th Conference of European Ministers responsible for social security. Dependence and social security. Memorandum submitted by the European Trade Union Confederation (ETUC)*, Council of Europe, Strasbourg.

Council of Europe (1995c), *6th Conference of European Ministers responsible for social security. Dependence and social security. Memorandum submitted by the Parliamentary Assembly of the Council of Europe*, Council of Europe, Strasbourg.

Council of Europe (1995d), *6th Conference of European Ministers responsible for social security. Dependence and social security. Memorandum submitted by UNICE*, Council of Europe, Strasbourg.

Council of Europe (1995e), *6th Conference of European Ministers responsible for social security. The situation of dependence in relation to the protection afforded by social security,* Council of Europe, Strasbourg.

Council of Europe (199f5), *6th Conference of European Ministers responsible for social security. The situation of dependence in relation to the protection afforded by social security: summary, proposals and questions for discussion,* Council of Europe, Strasbourg.

Council of Europe (1995g), *6th Conference of European Ministers responsible for social security. The special needs of dependent persons, costs and financing,* Council of Europe, Strasbourg.

Council of Europe (1995h), *6th Conference of European Ministers responsible for social security. The special needs of dependent persons, costs and financing: summary proposals and questions for discussion,* Council of Europe, Strasbourg.

Council of Europe (1995i), *6th Conference of European Ministers responsible for social security. Work undertaken at international level on dependence,* Council of Europe, Strasbourg.

Debrabander, K. (1998), *Financieringswijze van de welzijnszorg in Vlaanderen*, HIVA, Leuven.

De Ryck, K. (1997), 'Het pensioenprobleem in België en buitenlandse oplossingen', *Bank- en Financiewezen*, 61, 8 (8 October), p. 566.

Diels (1996), 'Sociale en fiscale franchise. Een evaluatie', April–May, *CM-informatie*.

Dutch Ministry of Social Affairs and Employment (1997), *Dutch Presidency Conference on 'Social Policy and Economic Performance'*, Amsterdam.

Edvartsen, T.O., *Possibilities and Problems in a Cross-National Comparative Analysis of Long-Term Care Systems*, PflEG-PROJECT. Pflegesicherung in der EG. Forschungsprojekt gefördert von der Volkswagen-Stiftung, No. 6, Johann Wolfgang Goethe-Universität Frankfurt am Main, Frankfurt am Main.

Eisen, R. (1995), *An International Comparison of Securing Long-Term Care Systems*, PflEG-PROJECT. Pflegesicherung in der EG. Forschungsprojekt gefördert von der Volkswagen-Stiftung, No. 5, Johann Wolfgang Goethe-Universität Frankfurt am Main.

Eisen, R. and Mager, H.-C. (1995), *Family Decisions Regarding Long-Term Care. A Model And Some Preliminary Results*, PflEG-PROJECT. Pflegesicherung in der EG. Forschungsprojekt gefördert von der Volkswagen-Stiftung, No. 5, Johann Wolfgang Goethe-Universität Frankfurt am Main.

Eisen, R. and Sloan, F.A. (1996), *Long-Term Care: Economic Issues and Policy Solutions*, PflEG-PROJECT, Kluwer Academic Publishers, Boston/Dordrecht/London.

European Commission (1997a), *Modernising and Improving Social Protection in the European Union. Communication from the Commission*, European Commission, Brussels.

European Commission (1997b), *Supplementary Pensions in the Single Market. A Green Paper.*

European Commission DGV for Employment, Industrial Relations and Social Affairs (1994), *Social Europe. Supplementary Pensions in the European Union, Supplement 3*, Office for Official Publications of the European Communities, Luxembourg.

European Commission DGV for Employment, Industrial Relations and Social Affairs (1996), *MISSOC Social Protection in the Member States of the European Union. Situation on July 1 1994 and evolution*, Office for Official Publications of the European Communities, Luxembourg.

Eurostat (1996), *Digest of Statistics on Social Protection in Europe. Old age and survivors: an update*, Office for Official Publications of the European Communities, Luxembourg.

Eurostat (1996), *Eurostat Jaarboek '96: een statistische blik op Europa 1985–1995*, Bureau voor officiële publicaties van de Europese Gemeenschappen, Luxemburg.

Eurostat (1996), *Social Portrait of Europe*, Office for Official Publications of the European Communities, Luxembourg.

Eurostat (1996), *Social Protection Expenditures and Receipts 1980–1994*, Office for Official Publications of the European Communities, Luxembourg.

Evers, A., Pijl, M. and Ungerson, C. (eds) (1994), *Payments for Care. A comparative Overview*, Euopean Centre Vienna, Avebury.

Gerste, B. and Rehbein, I. (1998), *Der Pflegemarkt in Deutschland*, Ein statistischen Überblick, Wissenschaftliches Institüt der AOK, Bonn.

Gottschalk, G. (1991), 'Denmark', in Nijkamp, P., Pacolet, J., Spinnewyn, H. et al., *Proceedings of a Seminar on National Diversity and European Trends in Services for the Elderly*, HIVA-K.U.Leuven and Vrije Universiteit Amsterdam, Leuven/Amsterdam, pp. 23–28.

Grindheim, J.E. and Selle, P. (1990), 'The Role of Voluntary Social Welfare Organisations in Norway: A Democratic Alternative to a Bureacratic Welfare State?', *Voluntas*, Vol. 1, No. 1, pp. 62–76.

Joël, M.-E. (1995), *Besoins, coûts et financement de la dépendance. Rapport d'information.*, LEGOS, Université Paris-Dauphine, Paris.

Joël, M.-E. (1998), *La prestation spécifique dépendance: quelle réforme?*, LEGOS, Université Paris-Dauphine, Paris.

Holland, D.M. (1997), 'International Long Term Care Insurance and Reinsurance', in Institute of Actuaries of Australia, *Financing of Long Term Health and Community Care*, a one day seminar, 25 August, Sydney.

Hutten, F.B.F. and Kerkstra, A. (1996), *Home Care in Europe*, Arena Ashgate Publishing Limited, Hants/Vermont.

Institute of Actuaries of Australia (1997), *Financing of Long Term Health and Community Care*, a one day seminar, 25 August, Sydney.

Köstler, U. (1995), *Wohlfahrtstheoretische Überlegungen zur Sicherung bei Pflegebedürftigkeit*, PflEG-PROJECT. Pflegesicherung in der EG. Forschungsprojekt gefördert von der Volkswagen-Stiftung, No. 3, Johann Wolfgang Goethe-Universität, Frankfurt am Main.

Leroy, X. (September 1995), 'De afhankelijkheid van de oudere persoon. Moet de sociale zekerheid dit risico dekken?', *Belgisch tijdschrift voor de sociale zekerheid*, 3–4, pp. 805–29.

Loi du 19 juin 1998 portant introduction d'une assurance dépendance, Mémorial Journal Officiel du Grand-Duché de Luxembourg, A-n°48, 29 June 1998.

Mager, H.-C. (1995), *Instrumente zur Steuerung der Nachfrage in der gezetzlichen Pflegeversicherung*, PflEG-PROJECT. Pflegesicherung in der EG. Forschungsprojekt gefördert von der Volkswagen-Stiftung, No. 4, Johann Wolfgang Goethe-Universität, Frankfurt am Main.

Neyt, P. (1995), *De pensioenmarkt in ontwikkeling: de plaats en de toekomst van aanvullende pensioenen*, 17 May, UFSIA/Rijksuniversiteit Limburg (Maastricht).

Nijkamp, P., Pacolet, J., Spinnewyn, H. et al. (1991), *Services for the Elderly in Europe. A Cross-National Comparative Study*, HIVA and Vrije Universiteit Amsterdam, Leuven.

OECD (1996), 'Caring for Frail Elderly People. Policies in Evolution', *Social Policy Studies*, 19, Paris.

OECD Health Data 1996 and 1997.

Pacolet, J. (1990), 'Financiering van de welzijnszorg', in *De welzijnszorg in de Vlaamse Gemeenschap*, Garant, Leuven/Apeldoorn, pp. 351–74.

Pacolet, J. (ed.) (1996), *Social Protection and the European Economic and Monetary Union*, Aldershot, Avebury.

Pacolet, J., (1997), 'Conclusions of the Rapporteur', in Bosso, A. and Hutsebaut, M. (eds), *Social Protection in Europe. Facing up to Changes and Challenges*, European Trade Union Institute, Brussel, pp. 371–8.

Pacolet, J. and Bouten, R. (december 1998), 'Een zorgverzekering voor afhankelijke bejaarden in Vlaanderen en België', *De Gids op Maatschappelijk Gebied*, No. 12, jrg. 89 December), pp. 945–65.

Pacolet, J., Gos, E. and O'Shea, E. (1993), *EMU, Social Protection, Social Charter and Regional Social Cohesion*, HIVA, Leuven.

Pacolet, J., Lanoye, H., Van Dender, K. and Spinnewyn, H. (1994), *De financiering van de bejaardenzorg: nood aan een afhankelijkheidsverzekering?*, HIVA, Leuven.

Pacolet, J. and Versieck, K. (eds) (1998), *The State of the Welfare State Anno 1992. Volume 1: Comparative Report*, HIVA, Leuven.

Pacolet, J. and Versieck, K. (eds) (1998), *The State of the Welfare State Anno 1992. Volume 2: Report on the Member States, EU 12 B, D, DK, E, F, G, I*, HIVA, Leuven.

Pacolet, J. and Versieck, K. (eds) (1998), *The State of the Welfare State Anno 1992. Volume 3: Report on the Member States, EU 12 IRL, L, NL, P, UK; EU 15 A, FIN, SWE*, HIVA, Leuven.

Pacolet, J., Versieck, K. and Bouten, R. (1994), *Social Protection for Dependency in Old Age*, HIVA, Leuven.

Pflegegeld in Europa (1993), *Soziales Europa*, 1, Bundesministerium für Arbeit und Soziales.

Rivlin, A.M., Wiener, J.M., Hanley, R.J. and Spence, D.A. (1988), *Caring for the Disabled Elderly. Who Will Pay?*, The Brookings Institution, Washington DC.

RIZIV (1996), RIZIV-statistieken: Dienst Geneeskundige Verzorging – Sectie Rustoorden (30 September).

Schieber, G.J. and Poullier, J.-P. (1989), 'International health care expenditure trends: 1987', *Health affairs*, Vol. 8, No. 3, pp. 169–77.

S.N. (1996), 'Werken wanneer je ouder bent dan 55', *M-Informatie*, June–July, p. 15.

Sonn, U. and Åsberg, K.H. (1991), 'Assessment of Activities of Daily Living in the Elderly. A Study of a Population of 76-year-Olds in Gothenburg, Sweden', *Scandinavian Journal of Rehabilitation Medicine*, No. 23, pp. 193–202.

Spinnewyn, H. (1991), 'Typology of services in care of the elderly', in Nijkamp, P., Pacolet, J., Spinnewyn H. et al., *Proceedings of a Seminar on National Diversity and European Trends in Services for the Elderly*, HIVA, Leuven, pp. 91–103.

Turner, J. and Noriyasu, W. (1995), *Private Pension Policies in Industrialized Countries. A Comparative Analysis*, W.E. Upjohn Institute for Employment Research, Kalamazoo, Michigan.

Van Camp and Van Rensbergen (1995), *Jaarverslag erkenningsdossiers RO-RVT 1993/ Populatiegegevens*, Ministerie van de Vlaamse Gemeenschap, administratie Gezondheidszorg, Brussels.

van der Maesen, L.J.G. (ed.) (November 1995), *Social Policy and the Public-Private Mix of Welfare Provisions for Older People in Western and Eastern Europe. Papers on behalf of the third European congress of Gerontology in August 1995*, SISWO/ Instituut voor Maatschappijwetenschappen, Amsterdam.

Van Velthoven, J. and Boeckxstaens, J. (1993), *Is de ene bejaarde gelijker dan de andere?*, Garant, Leuven/Apeldoorn.

VVI-Informatie (November 1995).

Walker, A., Alber, J., Guillemard, A.-M. et al. (1993), *Older People in Europe: Social and Economic Policies. The 1993 Report of the European Observatory*,

Commission of the European Communities.

Weekers, S. and Pijl, M. (1998), *Home care and care allowances in the European Union*, NIZW, Utrecht.

X (1996), 'Werken wanneer je ouder bent dan 55', *CM informatie* (June–July), No. 172.

Wijkström, F. (1996), 'Review of Adalbert Evers, Maarja Pijl and Clare Ungerson (eds), Payments for Care: A Comparative Overview', *Voluntas*, Vol. 7, No. 1, pp. 87–91.

Wilkin, D. (1987), 'Conceptual Problems in Dependency Research', *Social Science Medicine*, No. 10, pp. 867–73.

Wilkin, D. and Thompson, C. (1987), 'Users' Guide to Dependency Measures for Elderly People', *Social Services Monographs: Research in Practice*, University of Sheffield, Joint Unit for Social Services Research.

Winters, S. (1991), 'Typology of services in care of the elderly', in Nijkamp, P., Pacolet, J., Spinnewyn, H. et al., *Proceedings of a Seminar on National Diversity and European Trends in Services for the Elderly*, HIVA, Leuven, pp. 129–41.

Note

1   See also 'List of Publications – Social Protection for Dependency in Old Age in the EU and Norway'.

List of Publications – Social Protection for Dependency in Old Age in the EU and Norway

I   National Reports

Belletti, F. and Keen, H. (1998), 'Social Protection for Dependency in Old Age in Italy', *National Reports Series of the Social Protection for Dependency in Old Age in the 15 EU Member States and Norway Project*, edited by Pacolet, J. and Bouten, R., HIVA-K.U.Leuven, Leuven (Belgium).

Bond, J. and Buck, D. (1998), 'Social Protection for Dependency in Old Age in the United Kingdom', *National Reports Series of the Social Protection for Dependency in Old Age in the 15 EU Member States and Norway Project*, edited by Pacolet, J. and Bouten, R., HIVA-K.U.Leuven, Leuven (Belgium).

Daatland, S.O. (1998), 'Social Protection for Dependency in Old Age in Norway', *National Reports Series of the Social Protection for Dependency in Old Age in the 15 EU Member States and Norway Project*, edited by Pacolet, J. and Bouten, R., HIVA-K.U.Leuven, Leuven (Belgium).

de Almeida, M. (1998), 'Social Protection for Dependency in Old Age in Portugal', *National Reports Series of the Social Protection for Dependency in Old Age in the 15 EU Member States and Norway Project*, edited by Pacolet, J. and Bouten, R., HIVA-K.U.Leuven, Leuven (Belgium).

Hansen E.B., 'Social Protection for Dependency in Old Age in Denmark', *National Reports Series of the Social Protection for Dependency in Old Age in the 15 EU Member States and Norway Project*, edited by Pacolet, J. and Bouten, R., HIVA-K.U.Leuven, Leuven (Belgium), 1998.

Joël, M.-E. (1998), 'La Protection Sociale des Personnes Agées en France', *National Reports Series of the Social Protection for Dependency in Old Age in the 15 EU Member States and Norway Project*, edited by Pacolet, J. and Bouten, R., HIVA-K.U.Leuven, Leuven (Belgium).

Johansson, L. (1998), 'Social Protection for Dependency in Old Age in Sweden', *National Reports Series of the Social Protection for Dependency in Old Age in the 15 EU Member States and Norway Project*, edited by Pacolet, J. and Bouten, R., HIVA-K.U.Leuven, Leuven (Belgium).

Kerschen, N. (1998), 'La Protection Sociale de la Dépendance des Personnes Agées au Luxembourg', *National Reports Series of the Social Protection for Dependency in Old Age in the 15 EU Member States and Norway Project*, edited by Pacolet, J. and Bouten, R., HIVA-K.U.Leuven, Leuven (Belgium).

Leichsenring, K. (1998), 'Social Protection for Dependency in Old Age in Austria', *National Reports Series of the Social Protection for Dependency in Old Age in the 15 EU Member States and Norway Project*, edited by Pacolet, J. and Bouten, R., HIVA-K.U.Leuven, Leuven (Belgium).

O'Shea, E., 'Social Protection for Dependency in Old Age in Ireland', *National Reports Series of the Social Protection for Dependency in Old Age in the 15 EU Member States and Norway Project*, edited by Pacolet, J. and Bouten, R., HIVA-K.U.Leuven, Leuven (Belgium).

Pacolet, J., Lanoye, H. and Bouten, R. (1998), *La protection sociale des personnes âgées dépendantes en Belgique: vers une assurance dépendance*, HIVA-K.U.Leuven, Leuven.

Pacolet, J., Lanoye, H. and Bouten, R. (1998), 'Social Protection for Dependency in Old Age in Belgium', *National Reports Series of the Social Protection for Dependency in Old Age in the 15 EU Member States and Norway Project*, edited by Pacolet, J. and Bouten, R., HIVA-K.U.Leuven, Leuven (Belgium).

Pacolet, J., Lanoye, H. and Bouten, R. (1998), *Sociale bescherming van zorgbehoevende bejaarden in België: op weg naar een zorgverzekering*, HIVA-K.U.Leuven, Leuven.

Rodriguez Cabrero, G. (1998), 'Social Protection for Dependency in Old Age in Spain', *National Reports Series of the Social Protection for Dependency in Old Age in the 15 EU Member States and Norway Project*, edited by Pacolet, J. and Bouten, R., HIVA-K.U.Leuven, Leuven (Belgium).

Schuijt-Lucassen, N. and Knipscheer, C. (1998), 'Social Protection for Dependency in Old Age in the Netherlands', *National Reports Series of the Social Protection for Dependency in Old Age in the 15 EU Member States and Norway Project*, edited by Pacolet, J. and Bouten, R., HIVA-K.U.Leuven, Leuven (Belgium).

Schulte, B. (1998), 'Die Soziale Absicherung bei Pflegebedürftigkeit in Deutschland', *National Reports Series of the Social Protection for Dependency in Old Age in the 15 EU Member States and Norway Project*, edited by Pacolet, J. and Bouten, R., HIVA-K.U.Leuven, Leuven (Belgium).

Vaarama, M. and Kautto, M. (1998), 'Social Protection for Dependency in Old Age in Finland', *National Reports Series of the Social Protection for Dependency in Old Age in the 15 EU Member States and Norway Project*, edited by Pacolet, J. and Bouten, R., HIVA-K.U.Leuven, Leuven (Belgium).

Yfantopoulos, Y. and Georgakopoulos, T. (1998), 'Social Protection for Dependency in Old Age in Greece', *National Reports Series of the Social Protection for Dependency in Old Age in the 15 EU Member States and Norway Project*, edited by Pacolet, J. and Bouten, R., HIVA-K.U.Leuven, Leuven (Belgium).

II   European Comparative Reports

Pacolet, J., Bouten, R., Lanoye, H. and Versieck, K. (1999), *Social Protection for Dependency in Old Age in the 15 EU Member states and Norway. Volume 2. Statistical and Institutional Annexes*, HIVA-K.U.Leuven, Leuven.

Pacolet, J., Bouten, R., Lanoye, H. and Versieck, K. (2000), *Social Protection for Dependency in Old Age in the 15 EU Member States and Norway. Volume 1. Basic Report*, Ashgate, Aldershot.

III   European Synthesis Reports

Pacolet, J., Bouten, R., Lanoye, H. and Versieck, K. (1998), 'La Proteccion Social de las Personas Mayores Dependientes en Europa', in Rodriguez Cabrero, G. (ed.), *Research on Social Protection in Spain (Preliminary Title)*, Universidad de Alcala, Alcala.

Pacolet, J., Bouten, R., Lanoye, H. and Versieck, K. (1999), *Protection Sociale des personnes âgées dépendantes dans les 15 pays de l'UE et Norvége. Rapport de synthèse*, Commission des Communautés européennes, Brussels.

Pacolet, J., Bouten, R., Lanoye, H. and Versieck, K. (1999), *Social Protection for Dependency in Old Age in the 15 EU Member states and Norway. Synthesis Report*, Commission of the European Communities, Brussels.

Pacolet, J., Bouten, R., Lanoye, H. and Versieck, K. (1999), *Sociale bescherming van zorgbehoevende bejaarden in de 15 lidstaten van de EU en Noorwegen. Syntheserapport*, HIVA-K.U.Leuven, Leuven.

Pacolet, J., Bouten, R., Lanoye, H. and Versieck, K. (1999), *Sozialschutz bei Pflegebedürftigkeit im Alter in der EU und in Norwegen*, Kommission der Europäischen Gemeinschaften, Brussels.

For information and to order:

HIVA-K.U.Leuven
E. Van Evenstraat 2e
B-3000 Leuven
Belgium

Tel. +32 16 323332
Fax +32 16 323344
Email Liesbeth.Villa@hiva.kuleuven.ac.be